SUCCEEDING
AGAINST
GREAT ODDS

SUCCEEDING
AGAINST
GREAT ODDS

Alcorn State University in Its Second Century

JOSEPHINE MCCANN POSEY

University Press of Mississippi | Jackson

www.upress.state.ms.us

The University Press of Mississippi is a member
of the Association of American University Presses.

First printing 2017

∞

All images, unless otherwise noted, are courtesy of Alcorn State University.

Library of Congress Cataloging-in-Publication Data

Names: Posey, Josephine McCann.
Title: Succeeding against great odds : Alcorn State University in its second
century / Josephine McCann Posey.
Description: Jackson : University Press of Mississippi, 2017. | Includes
index.
Identifiers: LCCN 2017005533 (print) | LCCN 2017006992 (ebook) | ISBN
9781496810205 (hardback) | ISBN 9781496810212 (epub single) | ISBN
9781496810229 (epub institutional) | ISBN 9781496810236 (pdf single) |
ISBN 9781496810243 (pdf institutional)
Subjects: LCSH: Alcorn State University—History. | BISAC: EDUCATION /
Organizations & Institutions. | EDUCATION / Higher. | HISTORY / United
States / State & Local / South (AL, AR, FL, GA, KY, LA, MS, NC, SC, TN,
VA, WV). | SOCIAL SCIENCE / Ethnic Studies / African American Studies.
Classification: LCC LD131.A24 P67 2017 (print) | LCC LD131.A24 (ebook) | DDC
378.762/283—dc23
LC record available at https://lccn.loc.gov/2017005533

British Library Cataloging-in-Publication Data available

Special Dedication

This book on the history of Alcorn State University is especially dedicated to the nineteenth president of Alcorn State University, Dr. Alfred Rankins Jr., who is the fifth Alcornite to serve in the position as well as the youngest alumnus to serve, and the presidents who took over the helm of the institution as interim and/or acting president, with one serving twice. These men took on huge responsibilities that enabled the institution to continue to prosper, working together with faculty, staff, students, and alumni, striving for excellence. They carried out the major duties expected of a president with the same commitment and sincerity of a person in the position permanently. They demonstrated that great leadership was key to succeeding against great odds. These five courageous interim and/or acting presidents were:

- Andrew Howard (Acting), 1894 (completed the unfinished term of President Wilson H. Reynolds)
- Isiah S. Sanders (Acting), June 29–August 24, 1934
- Rudolph E. Waters Sr. (Interim), 1994–1995
- Malvin A. Williams Sr. (Interim), 2006–2008
- Norris Allen Edney (Interim), 2010–2011; (Acting), December 20, 2013– March 9, 2014

Special recognition is given to previous presidents, for they, too, were key to Alcorn's continuous success, with President Walter Washington serving the longest term not only in Alcorn's history but of any other institution in American history. Alcorn inherited $4.2 million from his legacy.

Alcorn Ode

Beneath the shade of giant trees,
Fanned by a balmy southern breeze
Thy classic walls have dared to stand
A giant thou art in learning's band;
O, Alcorn dear, our mother, hear
Thy name, we praise, thy name we sing.

Thy name thy sons have honored far;
A crown of gems thy daughters are;
When country called her flag to bear,
The Gold and Purple answered, "Here"
O, Alcorn dear, our mother, hear
Thy name, we praise, thy name we sing.

Far as our race thy clan shall need—
So far to progress they shalt lead
Thy sons with clashing arms of trade;
In useful arts full garbed thy maids;
O, Alcorn dear, we proudly bear
Thy standard on to victory.

—Mrs. J. S. Himes (Estelle Charlotte Bomar)

CONTENTS

PREFACE XI

ACKNOWLEDGMENTS XIII

Introduction 3

1   *Alcorn . . . Born to Succeed with Excellence* 9

2   *Possessing the Wisdom for Excellence* 22

3   *Carrying the Torch for Excellence* 25

4   *Continuing the Thrust for Excellence* 33

5   *Addressing Challenges toward Excellence* 41

6   *Demonstrating Family and Religious Values toward Excellence* 50

7   *Pursuing Excellence without Excuse* 55

8   *Advancing to a New Height of Excellence* 67

9   *Students: Succeeding with Excellence* 82

10 *Alumni: Succeeding with Excellence* 91

    Additional Noteworthy Historical Facts and Photos 105

    Afterword 113

APPENDIXES 115

LIST OF SOURCES 245

ABOUT THE AUTHOR 247

INDEX 251

PREFACE

Dr. Josephine M. Posey authored the last history of Alcorn State University, *Against Great Odds: The History of Alcorn State University*, in 1994. Prior to this, two histories had been published: one by Milan Davis in 1938, entitled *Pushing Forward*, and one by Melerson Guy Dunham, in 1971, entitled *The Centennial History of Alcorn A&M College*.

Against Great Odds: The History of Alcorn State University summarized the years from Alcorn's founding to the publication of the centennial edition in 1971 and focused specifically on Alcorn State University from 1971 to 1994. It detailed Alcorn's struggle to survive during turbulent times; how Alcorn ventured into a new era serving the people more efficiently through a grow-ing variety of academic choices; how students were taught to make a living and how to live balancing work and play; the updating of university facilities toward modern structures; preparing to win on and off the field in athletics; and sharing the Alcorn spirit all in an effort to remain in coherence with the determined mission of the great institution.

This history, entitled *Succeeding against Great Odds: Alcorn State Univer-sity in Its Second Century*, briefly summarizes the history from the founding to 1994 but focuses specifically on the tenure of three interim and/or acting presidents (Drs. Rudolph E. Waters Sr., Malvin A. Williams Sr., and Norris A. Edney Sr., with Edney serving twice) and four permanent presidents (Drs. Clinton Bristow Jr., George E. Ross, M. Christopher Brown II, and Alfred Rankins Jr.), who all served since the last history was published in 1994. This history culminates as of June 30, 2015, with the first year and almost four months of the fourth permanent president to serve in the position since 1994, Alfred Rankins Jr., who has made many accomplishments since his appointment.

This history can be viewed very much as a second edition to *Against Great Odds: The History of Alcorn State University*, showing a transition to a level of progress as the university succeeds against great odds. This history is intentionally designed to include more entries in the appendixes than usual in a book and less narrative in the text in order for the reader to view more synthetically the documentation of historical facts encompassing Alcorn's rich and illustrious history.

Acknowledgments

Researching and updating the history of Alcorn State University have presented great challenges and enriching learning experiences. I am again grateful to the late President Walter Washington for the faith and confidence he placed in me to undertake the authorship of my first Alcorn history publication, *Against Great Odds: The History of Alcorn State University*, in 1994. Today, in 2015, I am grateful to Interim President Norris Allen Edney Sr., President M. Christopher Brown II, and President Alfred Rankins Jr. for the faith and confidence placed in me to update this history summarizing 1871–1994 and specifically focusing on 1994 to the present.

I extend appreciation to the individuals, deans, department chairpersons, unit heads, and other university employees, alumni, and those internal and external to the campus who responded to my various requests for historical data. I am convinced, however, that there is still more information that never surfaced in spite of the continuous requests. I also believe that some information was just not available or had gotten lost in the shuffle somewhere through the years.

My thanks go to Belinda Benjamin, Lekita Carr, and Patrician Keys for letting their work-study students and/or graduate assistants assist me whenever they were available. Throughout the entire process, I had two regular assistants for a short period of time: Raneisha Smith and Jacqueline Ford. I thank them for their assistance, which enabled more continuity in the process. Once they transitioned to regular employment positions, I again had the assistance of work-study students and/or graduate assistants, and I thank them for their help.

My appreciation goes to university employees, alumni, and friends who took time to talk with me as I sought to obtain additional information or to validate some existing information. Special thanks go to alumna Calola Williams, who sent me information on a continuous basis that was very helpful, and to alumna Gertrude Payton, who gave me very valuable tips for

Tanya Carr.

publication consideration. I am appreciative to those individuals who would just stop me along the way and wish me well as the research progressed, and to alumnus Robert Smith, retired chairperson of the Department of Health, Physical Education and Recreation, who has been one of my greatest supporters in my professional research initiatives.

During the last year and a half working on the publication, I was fortunate enough to be assigned a special assistant from Marketing and Communication, Office Manager Tanya Carr, who assisted with the finalities of the publication. I thank Vice President Clara Ross Stamps for allowing her to assist me although she was a full-time employee in Marketing and Communication. It was when Tanya started assisting after hours and on weekends that all of the pieces began to come back together after my office was flooded, damaging most of my historical data. She exemplified all of the necessary skills and was knowledgeable of expectations of the University Press of Mississippi in getting a book published. Tanya was my guardian angel as we worked through the mechanics involved, and her input and know-how were highly valued. I thank Tanya for her dedication and commitment to doing the tasks right the first time. The success for the completion of this manuscript and all publication mechanics involved leading up to the publication of this book are attributed to God and Tanya Carr.

Special appreciation goes to my sorority sister and college classmate Annette Guyton Raper, who always had sisterly words of wisdom and support regarding several obstacles that I personally encountered during this research process. I am forever grateful to her for being the Christian woman that she is and for the long enduring friendship that we have shared since we met at Alcorn our first year in 1966.

My family members were my greatest supporters throughout this writing. I especially thank my eighty-four-year-old mother for her continuous interest and questions about the Alcorn book that I was writing, my husband, and all of my other family members.

I thank my granddaughter Carleigh for trying to help "Big Mama" keep her papers straight, which were often scattered all over the desk, the table, the floor, and sometimes the bed! Additionally, my appreciation goes to my grandsons, Carson, Courtland, and Cartez, for their interest in the book.

And lastly, I thank and praise Leila Salisbury and her staff at the University Press of Mississippi for the untiring advice and directions given throughout this entire process. My visits to the press for meetings were always meaningful, and I always left with a renewed motivation to return and continue enthusiastically on the writing. Additionally, appreciation goes to the members of the Institutions of Higher Learning (IHL) governing board for their significant role in the publication process.

To God, I give all the glory and honor for enabling my second written publication to become reality. Throughout unexpected health challenges, he allowed me to get it done!

SUCCEEDING
AGAINST
GREAT ODDS

INTRODUCTION

Alcorn State University, the oldest public historically black land-grant institution in the United States and the second-oldest state-supported institution
of higher learning in the state of Mississippi, was founded in 1871 as a result
of the people of Mississippi's efforts to educate the descendants of formerly
enslaved Africans. Named in honor of then governor of Mississippi James
L. Alcorn, it was founded on the site originally occupied by Oakland College, a school established by Presbyterians in 1828. Early on, the issue of race
intruded on the quiet, isolated campus. Oakland College's first president,
Jeremiah Chamberlain, was assassinated at the gate of the president's home
located next to Oakland Memorial Chapel as the result of a dispute over slav-
ery. Today, he and members of his family lie buried in the cemetery located
on the campus of Alcorn.

The Civil War closed Oakland College, and in 1871 the state of Mississippi
purchased the abandoned campus for $40,000, named it after the governor,
and designated it for the education of blacks. John R. Lynch, a leading black
politician and Speaker of the Mississippi House of Representatives, signed
the bill that created the new school. Only the University of Mississippi in
Oxford predates Alcorn. To serve the land-grant mission, Alcorn received
three-fifths of the allocations from the state, with two-fifths going to the
University of Mississippi. Alcorn's first president was Hiram R. Revels, who
resigned his seat as the first black senator in American history to assume
the post. The state legislature provided $50,000 in cash for ten successive
years for the school's establishment and overall operations. The state also
granted Alcorn three-fifths of the proceeds earned from the sale of 30 acres
of land scrip. The land was sold for $188,928; Alcorn's share was $113,400.
This money, to be used only for the agricultural and mechanical components
of the college, was invested, and the 8 percent interest went toward expanding the college's income.

In 1878, Alcorn University became Alcorn Agricultural and Mechanical College and was named a land-grant college on the basis of the federal government's 1862 Morrill Act. (The state's original purchase of 225 acres of land has grown to become a more than 1,700-acre campus.) The departments of study were English, Latin, mathematics, and the industrial department, which included agriculture, carpentry, blacksmithing, shoemaking, printing, painting, nurse training, sewing, domestic science, and laundering. In 1974, Alcorn Agricultural and Mechanical College became Alcorn State University. Governor William L. Waller signed House Bill 298, granting university status to Alcorn and to the other state-supported colleges.

The goals for the institution set by the Mississippi legislature clearly emphasized training rather than education. (For the original goals of the institution, see the preface of *Against Great Odds: The History of Alcorn State University*.) University goals and core values in 2015 are quite varied. (For university goals and core values, see Appendix 1.) At first the school was exclusively for black males, but in 1895 women were admitted. A women's dormitory, however, was not built until 1902. Today, in 2015, women outnumber men at the university.

Alcorn continually adopted expanding goals and objectives. Emphasis was put on preparing youth for service in both general and applied knowledge areas. These included agriculture, home economics, mechanical industries, general education and sciences, and teacher education. Emphasis was also put on developing generic leadership skills in addition to those that were specific to various areas, functions, and services of land-grant colleges. This included incorporating adult programs necessary to provide citizens basic education on a short-term basis. All of these goals were accomplished despite lukewarm support from state officials. In 2009, the mission and vision statements for the university were revised and approved by the Mississippi Institutions of Higher Learning (IHL) Board of Trustees. (For the university mission and vision statements, see Appendix 2.)

By the early 1990s, however, Alcorn had grown from this limited emphasis to become a more diversified university. It had branched out in its educational services to meet the varied needs of the community at large. It provided an undergraduate education that enabled students to continue their work in graduate and professional schools, and to engage in teaching and other professions. Graduate programs equipped students for further training in specialized fields while they contributed to the advancement of knowledge through scholarly research and inquiry. There were more opportunities for students to develop as responsible citizens and scholars in a democratic society. In the post–civil rights world, as Mississippi has come to recognize the importance of educating all its citizens, Alcorn has grown in status.

Alcorn's location in rural southwest Mississippi has also been an important determinant of its character, and, at Alcorn, knowledge and character
matter. Situated in Claiborne County, it is 7 miles west of Lorman, Mississippi,
80 miles south of the capital city of Jackson, 45 miles south of Vicksburg, and
40 miles north of historic Natchez. The school is set apart from heavily popu-
lated areas, and its geography symbolically expresses its separation for most
of its history from the rest of the state. Although the isolation has helped
the college survive, unfortunately at times it also means a distance from the
crucial nurture of the outside world. Minutes were kept on significant occurrences to document happenings on the isolated campus. (For sample minutes
from Sunday school assemblies in 1959 and 1960, see Appendix 3. For sample
minutes from meetings with the president in 1921 and 1922, see Appendix 4.)

Alcorn began with eight faculty members in 1871. Today, in 2015, there are
more than 800 faculty and staff. The student body has grown from 179 mostly
local male students to almost 4,000 students from all over the world. While
early graduates of Alcorn had limited horizons, more recent alumni are
successful doctors, lawyers, dentists, teachers, principals, ministers, administrators, managers, and business owners.

Over the decades, the school that was a struggling institution has become
one of the leading historically black universities in the nation and is experiencing success against great odds. Alcorn State University is now fully
accredited with five schools and degree programs in more than fifty areas.
(For accreditations, see Appendix 5.) The first graduating class consisted of
three members, Lafayette Murphy, A. J. Gossin, and A. D. Snodgrass. Today, in
2015, the total is more than 600. Alumni throughout the world have, because
of their successes, heightened the school's reputation, demonstrating that
graduates leave the university qualified to perform responsibly as citizens
nationally and internationally.

Alcorn has a history so special that even non-Alcornites through the
years have made themselves a part of its tradition. Listening to graduates
tell of their days at Alcorn, especially in the early years, is to realize how far
Alcorn has come since 1871. Alumni often talk about the crooked roads from
Highway 61 to the campus and how they thought they would never get to
Alcorn. The school was at times in its history almost inaccessible, especially
if it rained, because there was only a dirt road leading to the campus. At one
time individuals on the way to the campus had to pass through a cattle gap, a
crossing that kept cattle from escaping. That was an Alcorn landmark. Crossing it, people felt they had really made the journey.

Alcorn has been described as a home away from home. Many parents
have viewed Alcorn as a place where their children will be removed from the
contaminating influences of city life. Alumni who moved away to big cities

talk about the advantage of getting youth into an environment conducive to good behavior and concentrated study. In 2011, "Why We Love Alcorn: Top 100 Reasons" was compiled, depicting many of the great attributes associated with the university. (For "Why We Love Alcorn: Top 100 Reasons," see Appendix 6.)

Through the years Alcorn has been called a place where dreams come true. The administration, faculty, staff, and students appear to share a common belief that the American dream is not dead, that an individual can make it even though life is not easy and getting a college education may not be either. Alcorn has taken strong and positive actions to ensure that black people have a chance at survival. Alumni express immense pride in Alcorn, pride in their degrees, and pride in Alcorn's reputation for excellence. They voice that whatever they are today, Alcorn is responsible. Alumni throughout history have agreed with former president Levi Rowan when he said that "the state might easily build another college elsewhere and name it Alcorn, but nothing would ever carry away and wipe out the triumphant history of the institution."

Throughout the university's history, Alcorn has followed a carefully structured plan to retain and enhance the image and potential of students, a plan that was designed to attract young people whose intent was to receive a quality education. The student body not only includes blacks but also now includes Caucasians, Asians, Africans, and West Indians; the current faculty is a culturally diverse group of men and women; the student population is now representative of most counties in Mississippi and most states, and at least eighteen foreign countries. The college has grown to a multifaceted state university with numerous degree offerings. The facilities have increased from three historic buildings to more than eighty modern structures. (For a list of university buildings, see Appendix 7.) The athletics program, once composed of football, basketball, and baseball, now includes track and field, cross country, golf, tennis, soccer, volleyball, and softball. (For a list of current athletics coaches, see Appendix 8.) The alumni membership has grown from three to more than 25,000.

The Schools of Nursing and Business are located in Natchez, Mississippi, where selected course offerings from other degree areas are taught as well. The Alcorn Vicksburg Expansion Program is located in Vicksburg, Mississippi, where several course offerings are available. In 2015, it is located in the Pemberton Square Mall and directed by Dr. Ivan Banks, who succeeded Dr. Cheryl Kariuki. Previous directors of the office were Drs. Barbara Raegan and John Gill. Each director implemented significant initiatives for the Vicksburg office.

The "new Alcorn," as President Washington labeled the university during his tenure, will continue to serve the generations to come. Its distinct heritage must never be lost, and the preservation of that heritage is the responsibility of all concerned Alcornites and friends. It is my hope that this history of the university will help inspire the determination to preserve all that is good from the past and to continue improvements into the future as we continue to succeed against great odds.

1

ALCORN... BORN TO SUCCEED WITH EXCELLENCE

Governor James L. Alcorn.

In 1871, Alcorn was named in honor of then governor of Mississippi James L. Alcorn, a wealthy plantation owner. Alcorn State University has had nineteen permanent presidents and six interim and/or acting presidents, with one serving twice. They are as follows in order of service:

- Hiram R. Revels—1871–1882
- John H. Burrus—1882–1893
- Wilson H. Reynolds—1893–1894
- Andrew Howard (Acting)—1894 (completed unfinished term of Wilson H. Reynolds)

- Thomas J. Callaway—1894–1896
- Edward H. Triplett—1896–1899
- William H. Lanier—1899–1905
- Levi J. Rowan—1905–1911
- John Adams Martin—1911–1915
- Levi J. Rowan—1915–1934
- Isiah S. Sanders (Acting)—June 29–August 24, 1934
- William H. Bell—1934–1944
- Preston S. Bowles—1944–1945
- William H. Pipes—1945–1949
- Jesse R. Otis—1949–1957
- John D. Boyd—1957–1969
- Walter Washington—1969–1994
- Rudolph E. Waters (Interim)—1994–1995
- Clinton Bristow Jr.—1995–2006
- Malvin A. Williams Sr. (Interim)—2006–2008
- George E. Ross—2008–2010
- Norris A. Edney Sr. (Interim)—2010–2011
- M. Christopher Brown II—2011–2013
- Norris A. Edney Sr. (Acting)—December 20, 2013–March 9, 2014
- Alfred Rankins Jr.—2014–present

(For excerpts from the inaugural programs of the last five permanent presidents, see Appendix 9. For the Mississippi Institutions of Higher Learning [IHL] Board of Trustees at the time of inauguration of the last five permanent presidents, see Appendix 10.)

Prior to becoming the first president of Alcorn University, Hiram R. Revels worked with the Freedman's Bureau in Vicksburg, Mississippi, and settled in Natchez, Mississippi, in 1866, where he served as pastor of Zion A.M.E. Church on Pine Street. In 1868, he became a city alderman and, in 1869, state senator from Adams County. During Hiram Revels's tenure, he served as a professor of philosophy. It was also possible to study Latin for five years and Greek for four years. Four-year scholarships were awarded to one student from each district on a competitive basis. Each student also received a $100 stipend from a school fund; however, this was discontinued in 1878. Room and board, including laundry, was $5, payable in advance.

Revels resigned from the position of president the first time when Governor Alcorn abandoned the Republicans to become a Democrat and was defeated in his bid for reelection as governor by Adelbert Ames. The new governor offered the position of president to Frederick Douglass, but Douglass declined, citing a lack of formal education. Revels was later reinstated when the Democrats took control of the state government. It was under his leadership that, in 1878, the state legislature reorganized the institution and changed the name to Alcorn Agricultural and Mechanical College. Revels envisioned greatness for Alcorn. This reorganization enabled Alcorn to officially become the first college for blacks established under the Morrill Act of 1862.

In 1882, Revels resigned as president because of failing health. He died in 1901 of a stroke. Although the first decade of Alcorn's existence was full of struggles, Alcorn would overcome the barriers and serve the race. The university operated under certain policies that addressed areas of the university. Among these today are policies on staff transfer, refunds and dropping classes, overtime compensation, conflict of interest, and others. From Revels's term until today, many modifications have been made to university policies.

Upon the resignation of Revels in 1882, John Burrus became the second president of Alcorn Agricultural and Mechanical College and was professor of mental and moral science and constitutional law. He struggled with a state board in which half of the members were opposed to higher education for blacks; however, he refused to bend to pressure. Enrollment was better than ever, showing an average of 216 students in 1885. In 1890, the enrollment was 248 students, and by 1900, the enrollment had increased to 339 students.

Burrus had a constant concern about Alcorn fulfilling the mandate of a land-grant institution because it was evident to him that the agricultural and mechanical programs were in need of much improvement and the curriculum had not changed much. The Morrill Act of 1890 was passed during his administration. He wanted Alcorn to receive its proper share of the benefits from the new Morrill Act. By this time, enrollment had increased to the point that students were being denied admission because the existing dormitories could not accommodate them. He was successful in acquiring a special appropriation for buildings and repairs that resulted in a hospital and a combination classroom/dormitory.

It was during Burrus's administration that a college brass band and a literary society were established. The Young Men's Christian Association (YMCA) was organized in 1885. He was instrumental in establishing the first trade department, and from 1883 to 1887 all maintenance was done by students. The Departments of Blacksmithing and Carpentry were initiated in 1893. Alcorn graduates were succeeding in the marketplace, taking over leadership roles in various capacities all over the state, especially in elementary and secondary schools. In 1893, Burrus established the first professional organization for black teachers in Mississippi. In spite of Burrus's success, he resigned in 1893 citing health problems as the reason after being charged with violations

Hiram R. Revels, first president.

John H. Burrus, second president.

relating to the financial affairs of the college. An investigation revealed that the allegations were false. It was due to personality conflicts with the Board of Trustees rather than to any lack of efficiency. The faculty and students supported him as president, but he did not return. After his resignation, he spent a year practicing law in Vicksburg, Mississippi, and later returned to Nashville, Tennessee, where he died March 27, 1917.

Wilson H. Reynolds was selected by the Board of Trustees to become the third president of Alcorn in 1893. One of his first priorities as president was to make the college a graded school in order to catch up with modern education. He was concerned with uniformity in studies so that student classification could be determined. He believed that the college needed better publicity and that a college newspaper would help the local public admire and appreciate Alcorn's activities. Although he had great plans for the college, after only four months of service, he suffered an influenza attack and died suddenly in 1894. Andrew Howard, a mathematics teacher, was asked by the Board of Trustees to complete the school term until a replacement was selected.

In 1894, the board chose Thomas J. Callaway as the fourth president of Alcorn. He was recommended by Booker T. Washington, who described him as having great executive ability and the talent of getting to the heart of all issues. Callaway was chiefly concerned with the college's statewide reputation. The Morrill Act of 1890 aided in the development of industrial education at the college, and it became a reality in 1895. Callaway strongly wanted and

Wilson H. Reynolds, third president.   Thomas J. Callaway, fourth president.

instituted the Department of Industrial Education, and the department grew. Twenty-seven young men were trained, and 107 pairs of shoes were made in the first year. Iron beds were purchased from the department, a two-horse wagon made in the blacksmith shop was awarded a medal, a dozen shoes received honorable mention at an international exposition, and most of the Alcorn community's printing was done by the department's printing office. He challenged students to sell subscriptions to the college paper carrying the story of Alcorn and its benefits to every corner of the state.

Callaway wanted to admit women to the college, but the all-male Board of Trustees did not act on his suggestion. He cited this as being strange since other states favored coeducation. He appealed to the legislature to act favorably; however, this desire was not accommodated. His tenure lasted only two years, after a misunderstanding with the local secretary-treasurer over the financial management of the college. Existing records do not indicate the exact nature of the problem.

Edward H. Triplett replaced Callaway and became Alcorn's fifth president in 1896. Triplett was a renowned Baptist minister. He was not college trained, and his administrative style did not gain faculty support. He was not viewed as being of presidential quality, and the faculty felt that he had become president through favoritism rather than qualification. Faculty unrest resulted in the Board of Trustees releasing the entire faculty, charging the president to hire completely new personnel. Despite the president's popularity with the board, friction increased between him and other school personnel. In 1897, during the Christmas holidays, he was shot; the suspect was the secretary-treasurer of the college. Triplett lived, but the board dropped him as president in 1899. He remained at Alcorn as a history professor. He never got an opportunity to make major contributions to the college; however, during his administration, the board began to think highly of Alcorn's industrial education program and put more funds into it. His administration was a difficult time for Alcorn, full of internal struggles and changes in leadership. The president appeared to be completely out of step with his faculty members.

In 1899, William H. Lanier of Jackson, Mississippi, became the sixth president of Alcorn. He also started his administration by focusing on industrial education. He felt that the current offerings in agriculture, carpentry, dairying, and stock raising were insufficient, so he added harnessing and tailoring. He believed that industrial training was the special mission of black colleges. In 1899, Lanier was given a report by the Board of Trustees that the college was enjoying the most prosperous year in its history and was a well-organized and efficient institution of higher learning. In 1900, the governor of Mississippi, Anselm McLaurin, commented on the improved harmonious tone at Alcorn. It was reported that all the departments were working harmoniously and satisfactorily and that the friction and inharmoniousness that had been ongoing for several years had been removed.

Women were finally admitted in 1895, and a dormitory for women was constructed in 1902. The mechanical and industrial areas of the college were expanding, new teachers were hired, the enrollment was continuing to increase, and the Board of Trustees began to take notice. Alcorn was now being seen as a college that produced useful graduates in the state and the nation. Lanier served as president until 1905.

Alcorn now had enough talented alumni so that one of its own was chosen as its leader. In 1905, Levi J. Rowan, who was born in Rodney, Mississippi, in 1871, the year Alcorn was founded, became the seventh president of Alcorn. He served two separate terms that totaled twenty-five years and was labeled as doing well each term. In 1907, during his first term as president from 1905 to 1911, Mississippi Hall, a dormitory for males, was built. In 1910, there were 170 females and 445 males enrolled, and the faculty had increased to twenty-one. Enrollment continued to expand to other geographical areas. Although he was experiencing many successes, harmony on the campus did not last. In 1911, he recommended the reappointment of some faculty members that the board was displeased with for reasons unknown, and the board fired him. The faculty and staff protested the board's actions, but Rowan remained at Alcorn only as chairman of the English department, not president.

Edward H. Triplett, fifth president.

William H. Lanier, sixth president.

Another Alcorn alumnus, John Adams Martin, became the eighth president of Alcorn in 1911. Martin Elementary School in Jackson, Mississippi, where he once served as principal, was named after him. He gained recognition for reorganizing the Association for Black Educators that had been initiated by Burrus, and it became the Mississippi Association of Teachers in Colored Schools. He served as president of the association from 1906 to 1912, the first Alcornite to do so. During his second year as president, his health began to fail, and he was forced to give up his duties. After his health improved, he returned and served two more years until 1915. Martin's tenure saw the establishment of the manual training department in which students of any grade could study. Physical education became a major focus, and a professor was chosen to work with the students in athletics; however, the Bachelor of Science degree was not offered in health and physical education until 1946. During his administration, specific requirements for graduation were mandated, which was one of his most significant contributions. Martin died suddenly in December 1915 during his fourth year as president, and Levi Rowan was named president for a second time.

During Rowan's second term, he had several major goals, including increasing the length of the school year, selecting better prepared teachers, and increasing faculty salaries. Each year as president, he made sure that some type of improvement took place. He put Alcorn in communication with the outside world through a telephone line to Port Gibson, Mississippi. He established an

Levi J. Rowan, seventh and ninth president.   John Adams Martin, eighth president.

engineering department that had little success because of low funding. In 1928, the legislature appropriated $200,000 to match $100,000 given by the General Education Board. These funds ensured a building program for Alcorn, which resulted in the Rowan Administration Building, Bowles Industrial Hall, the expansion of the library, and other needed improvements.

By now, the fiftieth anniversary of the college was observed. The most significant event of the day, however, was the homecoming of graduates who shared life stories and how Alcorn had prepared them for what they were doing. By the mid-1920s, 98 percent of all black county extension agents in Mississippi were Alcorn graduates. A 1932 statute consolidated the separate boards of trustees at state colleges and universities into one board that would govern all of the state institutions. In 1934, Alcorn was given the authority to add new programs and expand those that were ongoing. President Rowan served Alcorn well both on and off campus. He died in June 1934. Isiah S. Sanders served as acting president from June to August 1934 until a president was selected to replace Rowan.

In 1934, William H. Bell was chosen by the Board of Trustees to become Alcorn's tenth president. Under his leadership, he pushed through an improvement in academic standards, and the enrollment became the largest in Alcorn's history. The college also qualified for a "B" rating from the Southern Association of Colleges and Schools (SACS), the first time in the history of Alcorn that the college was rated by a regional accrediting team. Business courses became a part of the curriculum. There was an effort to improve instruction in black rural schools and to cooperate with the State

Bust of Levi J. Rowan.

Isiah S. Sanders, acting president.

Board of Health in ensuring health consciousness in the schools. The demand for physical education teachers and coaches became even greater. The first baseball team was fielded in 1875, was discontinued in 1937, and then returned seventeen years later; however, football came on the scene in 1922, and Alcorn became a charter member of the South Central Athletic Conference in 1923 during Rowan's term.

Bell's first priority was to make the college more accessible to the people whom it served and to maintain contact with them. He felt that one way to do this was by improving the road from the campus to Highway 61. The Mississippi legislature authorized and empowered the highway commission to construct and pave a road, but no appropriation was made to put the law into effect. He protested the common complaint that the college was too far down in the woods to serve blacks efficiently. He also stressed that Mississippi was one of the few remaining states that did not give black youth the opportunity to be trained in a first-class "A" grade college.

Bell believed that, under his leadership, the work of the college had been successful and that faculty and students had accomplished a lot, but the Board of Trustees thought the college was in shambles and needed a new president. His administration had taken place in the midst of World War II, when the college had to adjust activities to support the war effort in keeping with the pattern of participation set by state and federal authorities. War industry courses were organized, students bought war stamps, teachers participated in the 10 percent plan for purchasing war bonds, civilian defense training was conducted, and

William H. Bell, tenth president.

Preston S. Bowles, eleventh president.

many students joined some branch of the armed services. Bell's tenure ended in 1944, one year before the war ended. He resigned under pressure.

Another Alcorn graduate, Preston Sewell Bowles, became the eleventh president of Alcorn and served only one year. Bowles was instrumental in adding literature to the curriculum. He made an appeal to the Board of Trustees for vocational education, and, under the auspices of the National Vocational Education Act, vocational education became a reality. Bowles chaired the department. At age seventy-five, he was named president emeritus, the first in Alcorn's history.

William H. Pipes became the twelfth president of Alcorn in 1945. He was the first president at Alcorn to hold a doctorate degree. He had previously taught at Southern University in Baton Rouge, Louisiana, and was the first black Michigan State University professor. Pipes believed, as had Bell, that the college needed a paved road built from Highway 61. He stressed the need for a better physical plant with the necessary equipment to carry out the mission of a land-grant college. Pipes's aim was to receive an "A" accreditation rating from SACS. Slowly the college began to look like a land-grant college with a major focus on agriculture, home economics. and trades. During Pipes's administration, the main highway was hard-surfaced at last, and faculty salaries finally increased. He served as president for four years and then resigned. He felt that Alcorn had not progressed as quickly as he had desired, so he decided it needed new leadership.

Jesse R. Otis took over the presidency in 1949 as the thirteenth president. Several buildings were constructed during his tenure, including Pritchard

William H. Pipes, twelfth president.

Jesse R. Otis, thirteenth president.

Hall, the Eunice Powell Home Economics Building, and the Home Management House. He employed the first full-time faculty in forestry. For the first time, research became a part of the faculty's function, mostly related to agriculture. He considered the foundations of a land-grant college to be instruction, research, and extension. The Baptist Student Union was also organized. Under his administration, an Alcorn graduate was the first black to be given a teaching fellowship by Cornell University. Enrollment at Alcorn increased to 644 students. He issued a ten-year development plan based upon the needs of black youth at a land-grant college. His proposed program included approximately twenty-five new buildings, both instructional and noninstructional. The plan totaled $5,388. After the Board of Trustees accused him of approving a strike by students, he was discharged of his duties in 1957.

The board immediately appointed Dr. John Dewey Boyd, another Alcorn graduate, as the fourteenth president of the college. He changed an $85,000 deficit to a $50,000 surplus in a short period of time. The number of faculty holding doctorate degrees increased. The curriculum became more varied and organized; the enrollment at the time increased to its highest point ever, at least 24 percent each year; and the physical plant continued to improve. Three divisions were created in the college (arts and sciences, education, and vocational education) in an effort to become a full member of SACS. Buildings were renovated and refurnished, the dining hall was expanded, and three dormitories for women and two for men were built. A new sewage system was acquired, and street and light improvements were made. The college was approved and admitted to full membership in SACS. Sports became

John D. Boyd, fourteenth president.

Walter Washington, fifteenth president.

prominent during his term. In spite of his successes, mandated curfews, quality of food, and other routine operations of the university led to marches, strikes, and other forms of student unrest that plagued his administration. On June 30, 1969, Boyd became the first president to officially retire from the college. Each previous president had quit or was fired.

On July 1, 1969, Dr. Walter Washington became the fifteenth president of Alcorn. This was the beginning of a new era for this historically black land-grant institution. A "commitment to excellence" was Washington's philosophy from his first day on campus as president and throughout the coming years. He was the first black to earn a doctorate degree at the University of Southern Mississippi. His priority as Alcorn's president was to make what he believed to be a good institution into a better one. In spite of uncertain funding, he was successful in holding strong faculty members through faculty development programs that allowed them to go away to earn doctorates and then return to Alcorn. The result was minimum turnover, even with low salaries. He created the Office of the Vice President and appointed two assistants for buildings and grounds. Alcorn was now beginning to attract students from all over the state. Washington wanted strong directors of the academic programs. He revitalized the alumni office to improve relations and increase the flow of information to the public about the achievements of the college.

Washington was deeply concerned about improving Alcorn's image, which led him to many powerful local, state, and national appointments, including

The Walter Washington Administration and Classroom Building, named in honor of Alcorn's fifteenth president.

being the first black to hold a position with SACS, where he served as vice chairman of the Commission on Secondary Schools. His goal of having an experiment station became a reality in 1971. He was instrumental in getting appropriations for more buildings. Under his leadership, the first organizational meeting for the university's foundation was held on July 31, 1973. Alcorn received its charter of incorporation of the Alcorn Agricultural and Mechanical College Foundation on August 27, 1973. Dr. Albert L. Lott donated the first gift to the foundation in the amount of $500. The first large contribution was received from the Alcorn State University National Alumni Association in 1974 in the amount of $67,712.31. Today, contributions have increased overall, including from the national alumni association. (For the public and private contributions to the ASU Foundation, Inc. in 2013, see Appendix 11.) Although Alcorn competed in the marketplace, Washington maintained that the primary product was service. His administrative style indicated his desire to be of service, and, under his leadership, the "new Alcorn" was on the move. In 1974, Alcorn Agricultural and Mechanical College was renamed Alcorn State University. Washington retired in 1994 and died in 1999. (For more about Walter Washington, see *Against Great Odds: The History of Alcorn State University*.)

2

POSSESSING THE WISDOM
FOR EXCELLENCE

Rudolph E. Waters, interim president.

After President Washington, the fifteenth president of Alcorn, retired, Executive Vice President Rudolph Waters was appointed by the Mississippi IHL board to serve as interim president until a new president was selected. Born in Brookhaven, Mississippi, Waters attended the public schools of Brookhaven and Hattiesburg. He received a B.S. degree from DePaul University in Chicago, an M.Ed. degree from Boston University, and a Ph.D. from Kansas State University in 1977. He was married to Dr. Kathleen Waters, and they have one son and one daughter. Waters had served as an invaluable adviser to the fifteenth president and other leading officers at the university. At Alcorn, he previously held the positions of chair, dean of students, dean of instruction, and coordinator of Title III programs. He became vice president at Alcorn in 1970 and later executive vice president. Before coming to Alcorn, Waters served as registrar and dean at Utica Junior College in Utica, Mississippi.

Waters was affiliated with many professional organizations, including the National Association of Collegiate Deans and Registrars, the American Association for Higher Education, the National Education Association, the American Association for University Administration, and the Southern College Personnel Association. He chaired many school evaluations for the SACS and other accrediting agencies. Waters was the first person in Mississippi to coordinate a self-study of black schools and enabled evaluators to visit the schools. He was also a member of the governor's Private Sector Council in the state of Mississippi and served as an evaluator for federal programs in several other states as well. Waters served on the board of directors for the Andrew Jackson Council Boy Scouts of America, the National Society for the Study of Education, and Delta Mu Delta. He was a member of Phi Beta Sigma Fraternity, Inc. and a very committed member of Phi Delta Kappa. Waters was one of Alcorn's greatest lobbyists to the legislature in order to ensure that Alcorn was always at the table and not forgotten in efforts necessary for funding and continuous growth.

Waters and Ralph Payne, the director of Public Relations at the time, were Alcorn's two representatives for the University Press of Mississippi (UPM), the publisher that serves Alcorn and other universities through the publication of scholarly works. UPM has published scholarly works by Alcorn employees, including Josephine M. Posey and Melerson Guy Dunham's publications on the history of Alcorn. After Waters and Payne, there were other university representatives for the press. In 2015, two very capable professors represent Alcorn from the Department of English and Foreign Languages, Drs. Cecile Bunch and Lillie Jones. Both of these individuals have served Alcorn in various capacities with commitment and have also been involved in scholarly efforts to preserve Alcorn's illustrious history.

Waters demonstrated that, at Alcorn, the students were the first priority. He was determined to move forward in a positive direction and, as interim president, he enabled that to happen. He knew that all university offices were critical to the overall success of Alcorn's undergraduate and graduate students. In 2015, among these are the Office of Admissions, directed by Katangela Tenner; the Office of Financial Aid, directed by Juanita Edwards; the Office of Counseling and Testing, directed by Dyann Moses; and the Office of the Registrar, under the auspices of Jimmy Smith, all of which collaborate to ensure that students' entry to the university as freshmen and/or transfer students goes smoothly and continues throughout their tenure as students. The James L. Bolden Campus Union, under the direction of Willie Moses, provides several forms of entertainment for students, including bowling. The students and the student leadership enabled their future and the university's future to be a success. (For past Miss Alcorn State University Queens, see Appendix 12. For past Student Government Association presidents, see Appendix 13.)

One of Waters's famous statements was that "an institution is great not because of its buildings or its beautiful campus, not simply because it's a Harvard or a Yale, but because of its alumni since the alumni epitomize Alcorn's greatness." Faculty continued to pursue terminal degrees and advanced themselves in an effort to ensure the graduation of globally competitive students from the historic Alcorn State University. Waters knew that Alcorn had long been known for greatness, specifically for its agricultural and mechanical component, and that those roots should never be lost; therefore, Waters was one of Alcorn's greatest advocates in carrying out the land-grant mission.

Throughout Waters's career, his wisdom and experiences led him to many successes. He was the commencement speaker in 1993. Waters was highly recognized in all of his pursuits, including Kappan of the Year in 1993, the Hiram Revels Achievement Award in 2011, and many other awards and recognitions. Waters died in September 2014.

Rudolph Waters delivering the Commencement address in 1993.

3

CARRYING THE TORCH
FOR EXCELLENCE

Clinton Bristow Jr., sixteenth president.

Dr. Clinton Bristow Jr. was appointed president in 1995 and was inaugurated as the sixteenth president of Alcorn State University on October 18, 1996. He was born in Montgomery, Alabama, and grew up in the public housing projects in Cleveland, Ohio. He graduated valedictorian, class president, and a football letterman. He received the Doctor of Juris Prudence and the Doctor of Philosophy in education administration and public administration from Northwestern University in Evanston, Illinois. He was married to Joyce Moore Bristow, and they have one daughter.

The inauguration of the sixteenth
president.

Bristow's vision statement was:

My vision is to have Alcorn State University recognized as a prominent
institution for the study of agricultural science, agricultural business, com-
modities/future trading and leading edge technology, and especially robotics
coupled with a strong liberal arts program. Further, as the only historically
Black land-grant institution in Mississippi, Alcorn should be an archive of
teaching effectiveness and a retention model archived at Alcorn for its students and others around the country to study its paradigms and those from
other predominantly Black universities. I envision Alcorn regularly hosting
conferences, colloquies, etc. on student achievement models and sharing
reports with politicians and decision makers.

Bristow kept his word in supporting the land-grant mission of the university
by advocating programs for expanding production and research opportunities in agriculture, implementing a landscaping program, and enhancing and
strengthening academic programs. The Master of Business Administration
(MBA) program in Natchez was also established. Under his administration,
Alcorn's Vicksburg office opened in 2003, and a partnership was also formed
with Hinds Community College to increase enrollment. Eight student residence halls were renovated on the main campus, and funds were secured to
renovate other buildings and build a new housing residence. Bristow's motto
was "Life will always be balanced and successful if the triangle of integrity,

Bristow interacting with students.

Bristow crowns Miss Alcorn, Jenetria Thomas.

industrialization and intelligence is employed." He believed in capturing excellence in all areas of operation. He felt that Alcorn went beyond nurturing and caring and gained a cutting edge by doing so. He labeled Alcorn with the concept that "ASU=CEO: Innovators. Trendsetters. Leaders." Alcorn State University has traditionally possessed unique reputations that have continued through the decades, and many are recorded in the *ASU Mini Facts* newsletter.

In 1998, Alcorn awarded the largest number of master's degrees to African Americans in teacher education. This was published in 2001 by the Frederick D. Patterson Research Institute, located in Fairfax, Virginia. Additionally, 100 percent of the graduates in teacher education passed the National Teacher Examination (NTE). Teacher education candidates were not approved for graduation unless all parts of the certifying test were successfully passed. This enabled them to be immediately ready for the workforce rather than having to continue the certification process after graduation.

The School of Education and Psychology, under the deanship of Josephine M. Posey at the time, was highly acknowledged by the Mississippi Department of Education (MDE), the Mississippi IHL, the National Council for Accreditation of Teacher Education (NCATE), and the Commission on Colleges of SACS for various assessments, annual process reviews, mandated reports, and site visits. SACS cited the School of Education and Psychology as being among the best and the potential shining star for Alcorn. During this time, the collective efforts of Dr. Doris Gary, the associate dean; Drs. Doris McGowan, Alvin Simpson, Malinda Butler, and Johnny Thomas, department chairpersons; Drs. Jan Duncan and LaShundia Carson; and other teacher education faculty, staff, and students across disciplines made it all possible.

Throughout the years, the late Dr. John I. Hendricks contributed untiringly to the overall success of teacher education in accreditation and other areas at

Bristow engaged in professional dialogue with students.

Bristow with the deputy undersecretary of agriculture.

Alcorn State University. Additionally, Drs. Levi Robinson, Robert Smith, and Darlene Dungee, former department chairpersons, and other teacher education faculty, staff, and students during their tenure contributed greatly to the accreditation efforts and other successes.

Alcorn was also number one among the nation's 100 institutions in graduating students with agriculture business and production degrees. The *Mississippi Board of Nursing's 3rd Quarterly 2001 Statistical Report* cited that 100 percent of Alcorn's nursing students took and passed the state licensure examination at the associate and baccalaureate degree levels. The rankings cited were also documented in a June 7, 2001, United States Department of Education publication. The School of Agriculture, Research, Extension and Applied Sciences (AREAS) acknowledged Bristow's support in the School of AREAS's report publication, stating that "President Bristow supported the mission of the Cooperative Extension Program in helping people lead personally satisfying, economically rewarding and socially wholesome lives. This coincided with the land-grant mission of the university in reaching out to people in rural areas and/or communities in providing research, extension as well as teaching in improving ones quality of life."

Dr. Napoleon Moses, the dean at the time and later vice president for Academic Affairs, ensured that the School of AREAS took advantage of every opportunity available to enhance the school, university, and quality of graduates going out into society to represent the state of Mississippi and the world. He always encouraged students to stay in the library, study, and be smart.

Alcorn's library has been a hallmark of knowledge for all. Dr. Blanche Sanders became dean of University Libraries after the retirement of Jessie Arnold, who succeeded long-term director Dr. Epsy Hendricks. University

Computer lab in the J. D. Boyd Library.

Libraries serves as the major storehouse of knowledge in meeting the informational, cultural, and recreational requirements for students. It houses reference and general circulation collections as well as a computer lab and other technological advances. There are various reading areas where students can study in applicable areas. Each director or dean of the library ensured that students were given the opportunities needed to meet the acquisition of knowledge thirst. Alcorn's library was featured in an international newsletter in 2011, where the library has been well represented on several initiatives. The dean of University Libraries was previously referred to as the director.

A Biotechnology Research Center was built in 2000 to improve competition among crops grown by small farmers in Mississippi. One of the major projects of this center was the establishment of the Southern Agriculture Consortium for Underserved Communities (SACUC). This consortium was a joint effort of land-grant institutions, industrial partners, farm organizations, and government agencies. Additionally, the Biotech Application in Vegetable Production Project was implemented focusing on the plant branch of biotechnology research. The research initiatives in agriculture were noteworthy. Dr. Patrick Igbokwe, through the Experiment Station, made many significant contributions to the initiatives. Other initiatives during the time included fuel cell research. Alcorn had its own fuel cell, which used natural gas as a fuel to generate about 6 percent of the electricity used on the Lorman campus. Other fuels were also studied. The Swine Development Center focused on swine research, providing assistance to small farmers in the genetics of swine specifically to increase the number of pigs born.

Biotechnology Research Center.

Agriculture vegetable product.

William Patton grinding cane at the mill of Glenn Dyes in Pike County.

Conservation research was a focus where ongoing research was in place to collect plant growth as well as resident data used to populate the database needed to develop conservation factors in revised universal soil loss equations. Bell peppers, cabbage, cauliflower, potatoes, nectarines, lettuce, and mustard greens were all studied as part of this research. Specialized research study was conducted with sweet potatoes and hot peppers. The Natural Products Initiative was also organized, including collaborative efforts and agreement with the University of Mississippi emphasizing cultivation, harvesting, and processing of selected crops.

In the early 2000s, the School of AREAS continued the land-grant mission. Some of the involvements included:

• Processing sugarcane and syrup at the Mississippi State Fair in Jackson. (A demonstration was done on site on how syrup is made at a cane mill.)

On June 14, 1996, local officials and state legislators were present for the groundbreaking ceremony of the 7-mile-long new four-lane Mississippi Highway 552 from US Highway 61 to Alcorn.

- Providing technical assistance to farmers in at least twenty counties in Mississippi. (These farmers produced about 14 acres of cane for the fair.)
- Sharing alternative crop and livestock income suggestions with farmers, including commercial vegetable production, goats, and hot peppers. (Raising goats and growing hot peppers were considered the best ways to supplement a low income at the time, with goats selling at $1.00 a pound after about eight or nine months and a 1-acre plot of hot peppers turning a $1,000–$1,500 profit.)
- Discussing farming problems with Mississippi and Louisiana farmers, such as the inability to get loans and financing, sponsoring a lending and equipment fair, and focusing on financing opportunities available through agricultural lending agencies.
- Counseling services and nutrition therapy concerning nutrition-related health problems from a community-based partnership between Alcorn and the Claiborne County Health Center known as Nutrition PLUS (Public Learning Utilization System).
- Assisting agriculture students and ensuring that they were highly involved with the United States Department of Agriculture (USDA) through internships.

The university experienced improved graduation rates and led the state in 2005 in retention and graduation. A pre-professional program was implemented to improve graduate and professional school matriculation, and an Athletes-as-Scholars Program in support of all athletic teams was implemented that improved graduation rates for student athletes. The program was spearheaded by former football coach Johnny Thomas, who now serves as chair of the Department of Health, Physical Education and Recreation. The

Lady Braves basketball team, 1996–1997.

Grand opening of the Dr. Clinton Bristow Jr. Dining Facility, named in honor of Alcorn's sixteenth president.

diversity rate improved. Bristow was responsible for many positive changes as president before his untimely death, including the groundbreaking ceremony to celebrate the start of the four-lane Mississippi Highway 552 from US Highway 61 to Alcorn. He died from a heart attack in 2006 while jogging on the football field at Alcorn. The dining facility on campus is named in his honor.

4

CONTINUING THE THRUST FOR EXCELLENCE

Malvin A. Williams Sr., interim president.

Upon the death of President Bristow, the IHL board was on the move again to select a permanent replacement for president of Alcorn State University. Vice President Emeritus Malvin Williams Sr. was immediately appointed to serve as interim president until the process was completed. Prior to becoming interim president, he had served as a math professor and dean and retired as vice president for Academic Affairs. Williams took over the helm full of knowledge concerning the great institution under his leadership. He is married to Delores Williams, and they have three daughters and one son.

Williams received his bachelor of science degree from Alcorn, his master's degree from Arizona State University, and his doctorate degree from Southwestern University in Louisiana. As interim president, Williams demonstrated true commitment to keeping the university operating efficiently on a daily basis. He was very concerned about promoting a positive image of Alcorn State University and worked hard toward that end. Williams was a long-term member of the Council for Higher Education Accreditation (CHEA). He received several honors and recognitions for his service as he represented Alcorn and other institutions as a part of CHEA.

Williams took over the presidency just in time to begin the implementation of the five-year strategic plan for 2006–2010 that was submitted by Bristow. Among the operating principles were:

- Utilizing the Ayers desegregation settlement to build for tomorrow through new programs and facilities (the Ayers desegregation settlement was the result of a case filed by Jake Ayers Sr. in 1975 in an effort to address inadequate funding in Mississippi claiming discrimination in the funding formula for the state's three historically black colleges);
- Meeting the diverse higher education needs of the southwestern region of Mississippi, the bordering parishes in northeastern Louisiana, and beyond. This included primary services to students throughout the country and ensuring additional graduate programs in specific areas of need;
- Proactively providing outreach programs and services geared toward meeting the educational, economic, recreational, and cultural needs of the immediate community, the region, and the state;
- Serving families with limited resources and helping small family farmers improve their standard of living through agriculture and extension programs;
- Moving toward advanced technologies, high-value agriculture, health, and nutrition; and
- Continuing the development of programs in areas of need for the Natchez and Vicksburg sites.

By 2007, Alcorn was still a part of the Ayers desegregation settlement and became the first one of the state's historically black institutions to meet the nonblack enrollment goal under the Ayers case. By 2007, Alcorn had received $283,000 from the Ayers desegregation settlement.

Williams strove to ensure that this strategic plan was a major focus and did not wait until a new president was selected to start. He ensured that the university emphasized strong undergraduate programs and worked toward enhancing graduate programs. He operated in line with the documented vision of Alcorn being a land-grant university that prepared students well for

The Extension Program aids with relief after Hurricane Katrina.

graduate and professional schools. Students were prepared to be responsible citizens with a strong work ethic. He enabled faculty, staff, and students to commit to public service as exemplified through Bristow's "Communiversity" Outreach Initiatives and Extension Programs. For example, in 2005 Bristow ensured that Alcorn students assisted Katrina victims during the disaster caused by the hurricane and were involved in other similar areas of support.

A major goal was to make Alcorn the epicenter of development for its region through efforts such as researching, publishing, receiving grants, and other similar scholarly initiatives. Some examples are as follows.

- Dr. Ella Anderson, the director of the Students in Free Enterprise (SIFE) Program, has worked untiringly with the university's SIFE team since its inception. This team focuses on empowerment of the individual and the communities through education and application of life-changing learning skills. The team focuses on restoration and empowering through education, leadership, and devotion to service. The 2009–2010 team consisted of twenty-five members in seven different majors. Specific categories of interest are active health, hydroponics, environment sustainability, teenage pregnancy, income determines outcome, ethics in the workforce, entrepreneurship workshops, market economics, and team sustainability. SIFE focuses on excellent projects, high moral values, unity, fund-raising activities, recruitment, and a winning spirit among its members. Anderson's hard work resulted in her being inducted into the Enactus Hall of Fame at the Enactus United States National Exposition in 2015 for successfully leading Alcorn's students to winning projects with the organization since 1999. She serves as the Sam M. Walton Faculty Fellow primary adviser with Enactus. Enactus is a community of student, academic, and business leaders interested in entrepreneurial action in making the world a more sustainable place for all of us. The breakdown for Enactus is:
  - ○ **en**trepreneurial
  - ○ **act**ion
  - ○ **us**

Students hold a candlelight vigil in remembrance of 9/11.

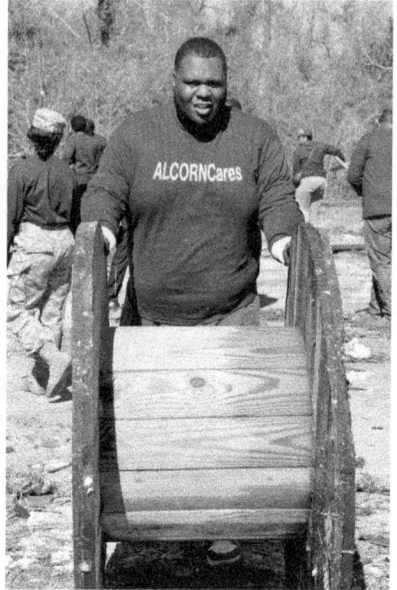

Students aid with relief in Hattiesburg after a tornado struck the area.

- Dr. Bettaiya Rajanna directs Alcorn State University's Minority Health International Research Training (ASU-MHIRT) Program. This program ensures that Alcorn students in the areas of biological/biomedical sciences are successful in their fields. Research training is held for ten weeks in India each summer. Students are involved in several research activities under senior faculty scientists who are recognized as leaders in research programs at their institutions. Each Alcorn student is trained on independent research projects. The experiences are excellent in enabling most students for the first time to study outside the United States. The experience enabled Keiera Ducksworth from Taylorsville, Mississippi, to win the Best Presenter Award at the annual Biomedical Research Conference for Minority Students, among other recognitions.
- The Louis Stokes Mississippi Alliance for Minority Participants (LS-MAMP) is one of the major programs implemented at Alcorn to increase minority representation in the field of science and engineering. Students receive knowledge in communication skills and learn various computer application skills to be used in the scientific, mathematical, or engineering curriculum. It also offers tutorial services for students. This program, established in 1991 and directed by Site Coordinator Dr. Troy Stewart, professor of chemistry, housed a group of very capable faculty and staff members who ensured that the goals and objectives of the program were accomplished.

Multicultural Festival.

- Alcorn State University was one of thirty-one minority-serving institutions to be selected for the Reading First Teacher Education Network (RFTEN). Directed by Delores Williams, RFTEN supported the university's mission to provide well-rounded, quality educational programs. As a participant, Alcorn is committed to preparing highly competent minority teachers of reading in scientifically based reading research (SBRR) strategies. RFTEN was launched in 2003 with a $4.5 million grant from the United States Department of Education.
- Global Programs, directed by Dr. Dovi Alipoe, supports students abroad. It presents opportunities and brings nationwide collaboration through various exchange programs, including language institutes. The mission of the program is to facilitate global engagement through relevant international content, activities, and knowledge in order to advance internationalization. This office contributes positively to the overall operation of the university and benefits its faculty and students. The purpose is to facilitate global engagement throughout the university with events such as the Multicultural Festival, whereas the vision was to coordinate technical assistance efforts for developing middle-income countries by building and enhancing effective university involvement in international affairs. In 2015, the office has realized this vision and is positively moving forward in its implementation.

Faculty and staff members are the lifelines to the students as students pursue their careers. Faculty and staff are continuously engaged in teaching, research, service, and professional development in order to stay on the cutting edge of knowledge as they work with the students in various classes and

Alcorn students and faculty on a field visit during an academic study tour in Nicaragua.

other areas. They are continuously involved in scholarly initiatives, including writing grants and proposals, publishing articles and books, attending and presenting at national and international conferences and workshops, servicing the local communities and surrounding states, and other professional engagements. The students are also involved. In 2011, one of Alcorn's students, Vera Zholondz from Russia, was named Mississippi's Undergraduate International Student of the Year.

Faculty and staff receive awards for being outstanding in their areas of expertise and other related areas, including the Mississippi IHL Black History Award, and the IHL Higher Education Appreciation Day Working for Academic Excellence (HEADWAE) Award, among others. (For student and faculty HEADWAE Award recipients, see Appendix 14.) Many were selected to professional boards, leadership programs, and task forces in their professional settings. Many foreign employees received significant honors from their native countries enabling all awards to be inclusive in the quality of Alcorn employees.

Throughout Alcorn's history, faculty and staff have continuously striven to ensure that the strategic plan for each period of time is enhanced and carried out professionally. Faculty and staff become eligible for promotion in rank from instructor to assistant professor, to associate professor, to professor and/or tenure after having served the institution at least five years in each rank. Their overall involvement in applicable areas determines whether they are successful in acquiring these promotions. Faculty members, as well as staff members and students, have been recipients of the Intellectual Renewal Grant, which enabled them to attend certain meetings, trainings, and conferences in an effort to keep them abreast of the latest in their areas of expertise or training. (For Intellectual Renewal Grant recipients, see Appendix 15.) The Writing Center in the

The Alcorn Enactus team at the United States Enactus Competition in 2014 in Cincinnati, Ohio.

Model United Nations Students Club at the National Association of African American Honors Programs Conference.

Department of English and Foreign Languages began offering services of faculty tutors in spring 2008, which have been very valuable. The Saturday Science Academy, whose goal is to address the disparity in the number of African Americans in science, technology, engineering, and mathematics (STEM-related) courses, also had a positive influence on student success.

The Faculty Senate chairperson, Dr. Yolanda Jones in 2015, who succeeded Dr. Dickson Idusuyi after he rendered several years of valuable service, and the Staff Senate chairperson, Donna Hayden in 2015, meet and keep faculty and staff abreast of issues impacting them in an effort to keep all employees on scholarly levels. Because of the dedication of faculty and staff collectively, Alcorn's citations and rankings have been noteworthy, such as the following:

- Alcorn was cited as having one of the best master's degree programs at a university in the South;
- Alcorn ranked seventh in the nation in the number of African American baccalaureate graduates in engineering-related technologies;
- According to *Black Issues in Higher Education*, Alcorn was ranked tenth in the number of African American baccalaureate graduates in math;
- Alcorn was cited among the top twenty Historically Black Colleges and Universities (HBCUs) by *Diverse Issues in Higher Education*.

Williams ensured that students continued to gain these experiences from exposure to many scholarly initiatives such as the honors curriculum, internships, cooperative education seminars, and lecture forums, as well as involvement in professional, civic, and social organizations. (For a list of student organizations, see Appendix 16.) He embraced Bristow's "profile of an Alcornite," which included demonstrating general education competence and

The Delta Epsilon Chapter of Delta Sigma Theta Sorority, Inc. helps raise funds for relief in Haiti after a devastating earthquake.

Professional conference hosted by Alcorn.

being competent in one's discipline, having a strong work ethic, being a good citizen, and being well-groomed. Williams ensured that the profile remained very active as the strategic plan for 2006–2010 continued to unfold.

The Department of Agriculture was awarded patents. One was a patent for discovering a nonpharmacological means for reducing cardiovascular disease risk through the use of a vegetable crop called waterleaf. At a reception held in honor of the people who made the discovery, Williams voiced that it was the first patent of its type in the university's history.

As a new president was being sought, Williams continued to ensure that all students obtained a unique and enriching experience in preparing them in their field of study. He ensured that each unit's plan complemented the institutional strategic plan.

5

Addressing Challenges toward Excellence

George E. Ross, seventeenth president.

After the death of President Bristow and after Dr. Williams served as interim president, Alcorn was again on the search for a permanent president. Dr. George E. Ross was selected as the seventeenth president of Alcorn in 2007, but he was forced to delay responsibilities until January 2008 because of medical challenges. He received his bachelor's and master's degrees from Michigan State University in business administration and a Doctorate of Education from the University of Arkansas. He did further study at Harvard University.

Ross, along with his wife Elizabeth Ross, experienced a week of inaugural events on and off campus, including a parade in his hometown of Utica, Mississippi. During his inauguration, he spoke of the challenges as well as the opportunities facing the 137-year-old institution at the time. He stressed being cognitive of the struggling economy as well as the status of support for higher education. Additionally, he shared information about the comprehensive academic planning study that was being done on the campus entitled Alcorn 20/20 that would identify the future direction of the university. He indicated that individuals on and off campus would be contributing to this study and stressed that the study would indicate what the university should and should not be doing. He shared that his number one priority was to maintain a high level of academic excellence and a commitment to diversity. He was confident that Alcorn would reach the destiny as one of the greatest universities in the United States and that he would be a part of such a destiny. Inauguration speakers referred to the appointment of the new president as the start of a new era at Alcorn and challenged him to be the best that he could be. Ross expressed his humbleness for the trust and confidence shown in him. He said that he was committed to an Alcorn that was fair and valued the views of faculty, staff, students, and alumni.

Alcorn State University signed a partnership in education with Central Michigan University. This partnership was designed to foster and address educational opportunities through cooperative efforts that would benefit both institutions. Ross outsourced some operations of the university and contracted some consultants and firms for several aspects of university support such as strategic planning, technology, human resources, and food services.

Under Ross's administration, over sixty employees were terminated in accordance with the state's "at will" law. This action led to internal unrest.

Ross ensured the continuation of successful programs and projects in an effort to enhance the quality of education received by the students. Funds from grants and gifts contributed much to this reality. Some funding sources included, but were not limited to, Entergy; the USDA; local, state, and national foundations; international grants; the humanities; capacity building grants; and some special initiatives of US Representative Bennie Thompson. Ross stressed that the university's faculty scholars across disciplines should submit proposals for funding on a routine basis. Examples of some of the larger funded grants received by Alcorn State University before, during, and after Ross's administration include:

- The Mississippi Math and Science Partnership (MMSP) with Alcorn State
  University providing support for pre-K–12 school districts, higher education

The inauguration of the seventeenth president.

communities, and other collaborative groups to improve the areas of mathematics, science, engineering, and technology. The grant funded $3.5 million for five years.

- The United States Nuclear Regulatory Commission awarded Alcorn $200,000, which was announced by Representative Thompson. The purpose of the funds was to help with the start up of Alcorn's Grand Gulf Nuclear Power Station applied science degree in radiation safety education and training. This collaboration is between Alcorn, Grand Gulf, and the local community colleges and school districts.
- Alcorn received several $100,000 grants from Entergy Mississippi, of which $50,000 promoted scholarship support to radiation technology majors and $50,000 was for student internship opportunities. In addition to scholarships and internships, the grants also supported a mentorship program. Entergy also extended a Homeland Security Grant in the amount of $234,995 to the School of Business to continue work on assisting small minority businesses.

- Alcorn received $1 million to conduct biofuel research and bolster new growth in the biofuel research industry in the state, giving Alcorn's faculty and students new opportunities in this field of science.
- The Department of Chemistry received funds from the HBCU-UP grants. They were $500,000 from the National Science Foundation (NSF), an additional $165,000 from the NSF, $498,000 from the USDA, $640,000 from the Department of Homeland Security (DHS), and $72,000 from the Mississippi Department of Transportation (MDOT).

Ross supported the Office of Pre-Professional Programs, which houses the honors program and has, since its inception, been a major advocate for students. In 2015, the Office of Pre-Professional Programs is directed by Dr. Thomas Sturgis, and Dr. Wandra Arrington is the assistant director and coordinates the honors program. Pre-professional programs prepare students to enter specialized studies specifically in the areas of law, engineering, dentistry, nursing, physical therapy, pharmacy, and other professions. The director, assistant director, and other staff members have provided opportunities that enable the students to encounter rewarding and enriching experiences that equip them to exit as scholars in pursuing educational heights.

Alumni Bells were installed in the Oakland Memorial Chapel and each day ring at intervals with the "Alcorn Ode." These bells were dedicated in October 2009 and installed in the four-faced clock tower atop the chapel and can be programmed to play other musical selections. The chapel has served Oakland College and Alcorn State University since it was constructed as a campus landmark and a center of religious activities. Portions of the building were also used as laboratories, classrooms, and student rooms. It was a prayer hall for Oakland College and has served Alcorn for various religious and nonreligious activities since 1871. The first degree issued in Mississippi was conferred in Oakland Memorial Chapel. It is one of the original buildings remaining from Oakland College that was built by slaves. The iron stairs of the chapel came from Windsor Plantation, once an antebellum home near the campus that was destroyed in 1890 by fire. The chandelier is a replica of the original assembled and hung in New Orleans in 1958. The chapel was renovated in 1958, but the building is almost unchanged. The pews, in 2015, are the original ones. The chapel was officially listed on the National Register of Historic Places in 1975.

Alcorn State University honored the life and legacy of Steve Latreal "Air II" McNair throughout the fall 2009 football season. Alcorn fans packed the stadium for four seasons to be mesmerized by the performance of Steve and were not disappointed. He was quarterback from 1991 to 1994 and provided great leadership in that position. He received Southwestern Athletic Conference (SWAC) Offensive Player of the Year for four years and *Sports Illustrated*

Oakland Memorial Chapel.

The Alumni Bells were dedicated October 17, 2009.

Steve "Air II" McNair in action.

Susan Cayton Woodson.

Offensive Player of the Year during his time at Alcorn. He was named SWAC Offensive Player of the Week four times. He made unbelievable achievements during his freshman year, and he broke many passing records, earning Freshman of the Year honors. He led the team to the first SWAC Championship since 1984. In 1993, Steve "Air" McNair was nominated for the Heisman Trophy. Although he did not receive it, the honor of being nominated was great, being the highest honor to be received by an athlete in the SWAC. He graduated in 1995 and proceeded to play professional football with the Houston Oilers, Tennessee Titans, and Baltimore Ravens. He died July 4, 2009, from a mysterious incident where he was shot to death. His life and legacy will forever remain in the hearts of all who knew him. He was inducted posthumously into the SWAC Hall of Fame in December 2009.

Hiram Revel's great-granddaughter Susan Cayton Woodson donated a gift to Alcorn including a Seth Thomas mantle clock that was given to Revels when he was senator by Jefferson Davis in 1870. Other items included:

- Two oil portrait paintings of Revels's daughters, Susie Sumner Revels Cayton and Madge Revels Cayton;
- An oil portrait painting of Senator Revels by artist Benjamin Goss;

The Seth Thomas mantle clock that
Hiram R. Revels received in 1870 as a
gift from Jefferson Davis, president of
the Confederate States of America.

Medgar Wiley Evers Heritage Village Complex.

- An oil painting of Susan Cayton Woodson by artist Jan Spivey Gilchrist; and
- A stone bust of an African woman by nationally known sculptor Woodrow Nash.

Extreme gratefulness to Revels's granddaughter and family was expressed for their generosity. Susan Cayton Woodson died in January 2013 in Chicago at the age of ninety-four.

During Ross's tenure, knowledge and character became a common thread. There was an increase in student enrollment, an increase in support from alumni and friends, the development of strategic and master plans, and the construction of a $47 million, 1,002-bed residential student housing complex. It included four dormitories and an amenities building featuring a convenience store, fitness center, computer labs, and leasing offices, becoming one of the largest constructions in the university's history. Ross was the first president to invite employees to the President's Home for a faculty convocation luncheon. Student orientation was also once held at the President's Home.

Through the Office of Academic Affairs, where Josephine Posey served as interim vice president, some changes were made. Faculty and staff began receiving free meal tickets rather than be on their own for lunch during the university's opening Faculty Convocation; faculty adjunct and overload pay

Faculty and Staff Convocation held at the President's Home.

increased; efforts were made to enhance salaries across all academic disciplines; Thanksgiving break for students changed to one week instead of three days; school/departmental achievements were submitted monthly to the Office of Public Relations for public knowledge; and the university's vision and mission statements were revised and approved by IHL under the guidance of the Barthwell Group contracted by Ross on strategic planning. The Barthwell Group is a multidimensional management consultant firm based in Detroit, with clients throughout the United States. The group was founded under the leadership of Dr. Akosua Barthwell Evans, who is the chief executive officer (CEO). This group conducted strategic planning workshops after being engaged to guide the strategic planning process for the university. Groups were involved in dialogue on their vision for the future of the university and opinions on the strengths and weaknesses of the university. The series of meetings, small group sessions with some of them initiated by Dr. Wanda Newell, and workshops yielded the revised vision and mission statements and applicable core values and goals.

As Ross's tenure came to a close upon his resignation, he expressed appreciation for advice, voluntary assistance, and financial support of Alcorn. He focused on the economic storm clouds and the merger recommendations enforced in Mississippi that had questioned the future of Alcorn State University. He indicated that the university's commitment to seeking innovative ways to broaden and continuously improve would secure its place as a leading institution of higher learning. When he left Alcorn, the commissioner of higher education and president of the IHL board saluted him for his service to the university and the state. He stepped down in 2010 to return to Michigan as president of Central Michigan University, which he left to initially come to Alcorn.

6

DEMONSTRATING FAMILY AND RELIGIOUS VALUES TOWARD EXCELLENCE

Norris A. Edney Sr., interim and acting president.

Dr. Norris Allen Edney Sr. served as interim president of Alcorn State University from 2010 to 2011 and acting president from 2013 to 2014. University issues were not new to him, and he knew how to overcome them. He strove diligently to keep the university operating efficiently on a daily basis. Edney holds an associate's degree from Natchez Junior College, a B.S. in biology from Tougaloo College, a Master's of Science in teaching from Antioch College, and a doctoral degree in conservation from Michigan State University.

He is married to Lillian Edney, and they have three sons. He spent most of his career at Alcorn State University, where he successfully carried out the various roles and responsibilities expected of him in teaching as well as in administration. Prior to retiring in 2000, he had served as professor, dean of Graduate Studies, and dean of the School of Arts and Sciences. He served as president of the Mississippi School Board Association and president of the SWAC, where he was also inducted into the SWAC Hall of Fame.

Among Edney's awards are the Natchez Junior College Alumnus of the Year, Outstanding Science Award recipient, first annual White House Initiative Faculty Award for Excellence in Science and Technology, National Association for Equal Opportunity in Higher Education honoree, Research Scientist of the Year Achievement Award, and the SWAC Distinguished Service Award, to name a few. He is a life member of Alpha Phi Alpha Fraternity, Inc.

Edney has authored more than thirty publications. Upon appointing him as interim president, IHL Commissioner Hank Bounds said, "As a former professor and dean, Dr. Edney will be able to meet faculty, staff and students' needs on a personal level during this transition period." Bounds was indeed correct in his thoughts. During Edney's first tenure as president from 2010 to 2011, he reaffirmed to the Alcorn State University family that Alcorn could still remain the university that we all knew—the university of family and community, the university of dedication and commitment, the university of love, the university of scholars, the university of hospitality, the university of academic integrity, the university of sincerity, the university of many historical beginnings, and the university with a land-grant mission. He strove to ensure collaborative efforts in making positive things happen, and he took no personal credit.

Edney's main goals as interim president were to ensure that together:

- Alcorn succeeded in all accreditation initiatives;
- Alcorn's land-grant mission was supported;
- Alcorn's degree programs met the needs of students and the professions pursued by them;
- Alcorn's student enrollment increased through continuous active recruiting efforts;
- Alcorn provided more opportunities for students to encounter activities that were meaningful and would develop all-around citizens;
- Alcorn remained fiscally sound in carrying out university operations;
- Alcorn's salaries were more competitive with other institutions;
- Alcorn recruited and maintained qualified administrators, faculty, and staff; and
- Alcorn's thrust for excellence enabled graduates to exit the university with enthusiasm ready to send others to their alma mater.

During his first tenure as interim president, Edney was instrumental in the success of many university operations, including the achievement of accreditations and/or reaffirmations. One of his priorities when he was appointed was to ensure that the SACS reaffirmation, chaired by Dr. Donzell Lee, including the development of the required Quality Enhancement Plan (QEP), and the National Collegiate Athletic Association (NCAA) recertification, chaired by Dr. Peter Malik, were successfully accomplished. Edney employed Dr. Josephine Posey as his special assistant, with the various accreditation initiatives as a major focus. She contributed untiringly to the success of the scheduled accreditations as well as other university operations.

Edney believed that Alcorn remained among the best and would continue to be among the best. He witnessed that, through all obstacles, regardless of how steep they appeared, God's favor always shined on Alcorn and Alcorn always crossed the hurdle. The on-site SACS team was highly complementary of Alcorn's visit and the QEP, which focused on improving the writing abilities of students. In 2015, Dr. Cynthia Scurria, chairperson of the Department of English and Foreign Languages and QEP director, is committed to continuous success in implementing the QEP. (For the QEP, see Appendix 17.) Alcorn eagerly anticipated a favorable decision by SACS at its meeting in December 2011 in Orlando, Florida, and got it!

Some of the scheduled campus accreditation visits were held after the permanent president was selected; however, Alcorn's employees were already well prepared to pass each of the accreditations with no difficulty. The other accreditations initiated or accomplished during Edney's first tenure included the Council on Social Work Education (CSWE), chaired by Dr. Dorothy Idleburg, where Alcorn passed benchmarks I, II, and III and received initial accreditation for the first time in the university's history, and the recertification of the robotics and automation program by the Association of Technology, Management, and Applied Engineering (ATMAE), chaired by Dr. Kwabena Agyepong. Edney did not believe that you rest on your accomplishments but that you continue to strive and move ahead and accomplish even more.

Edney revamped the Campus Police Department by hiring experienced, certified, and trained officers and replacing damaged vehicles. Melvin Maxwell served as chief. In 2015, Douglas Stewart serves as chief of Campus Police. Full ambulance service was made available and accessible to the infirmary to ensure the timely addressing of medical emergencies. Edney also worked hard to ensure that an assessment of degree offerings revealed opportunities to meet the expectations of students in their chosen field of study. Enrollment increased, and students graduated from the university with enthusiasm and excitement as they transitioned to advanced studies and/or the world of work. Alcorn State University remained financially stable as the overall operations of the university were being carried out.

In 2010, Mississippi's public four-year institutions saw an approximate 5.75 percent increase in degrees awarded during the various commencements. The eight institutions awarded an estimated 15,500 degrees. Dr. Alfred Rankins Jr., who served as IHL assistant commissioner for Academic and Student Affairs, shared that changes to some system policies, campus practices, and university focuses could have contributed to that increase. He also indicated that universities would have to adjust in order to continue to be competitive and productive in the future. He further shared that universities needed to be fluid enough to respond to inevitable changes in the educational environment by taking a hard look at the degree programs being offered. Alcorn has continued to evaluate and modify departmental curricula to ensure that degree offerings are serving the purpose of the students and preparing them for their future. In May 2011, Alcorn graduated approximately 685 students during commencement.

A new fitness center was opened and operated in the James L. Bolden Campus Union. General College was restructured to include the Newtie Boyd Center for Academic Support. The late Dr. Newtie Boyd, after whom the center was named, was a former employee at Alcorn State University. He served as director of General College for Excellence. The Newtie Boyd Center ensured that the students were provided with general knowledge in the areas of English, reading, writing, creative arts, social science, natural science, and mathematics. It was also responsible for providing students with an orientation to the university, for monitoring their progress, and for making recommendations when students were ready to proceed to their major department.

Edney made an effort to put smiles on the students' faces and to boost the morale of faculty and staff. He focused on what was best for Alcorn State University, and he did that with dignity, integrity, and respect. A major issue that Edney had to address was the School of Nursing's exam policy, which led to negative publicity. He handled and enabled disgruntled prospective graduates to graduate. (The issue was with the timing of the policy.)

After the permanent president was selected, Edney expressed the following departing thoughts at an appreciation function as he ended his first tenure:

> Accomplishments during my tenure would have been impossible without your true commitment and dedication to success. With your help and guidance, we were able to achieve modest but significant goals. Our gratitude is

boundless. Although major challenges remain, there is no shred of doubt that Alcorn will weather the storms that lie ahead as it has done in the past. With documented accomplishments during my term as interim president, evidence abounds that Alcorn will continue to excel towards higher heights. Please extend the same cooperation and support to the new president as he takes on the leadership helm at this great institution.

His specific accomplishments as interim president are captured in a publication that he initiated and his executive assistant, Karen Shedrick, entitled *Simply Sharing*. (For *Simply Sharing* publications, see Appendix 18.) This publication was coordinated by Jerry Domatob, chairperson of the Department of Mass Communications, with an assisting committee. After the permanent president took over the helm, the Mississippi IHL commissioner asked Edney if he would remain as a special consultant to the new president, and he accommodated the request. He later served as interim dean of the School of Arts and Sciences and later the interim dean of the School of Nursing. He was instrumental in Alcorn's School of Nursing being located in Natchez at its inception. As interim dean, he ensured continuous success in the overall operations of the departments under the auspices of each school involved until the permanent deans were selected.

7

PURSUING EXCELLENCE WITHOUT EXCUSE

M. Christopher Brown II, eighteenth
president.

Dr. M. Christopher Brown II began his tenure as the eighteenth president of
Alcorn State University in January 2011. He succeeded President Ross, who
resigned to become president of Central Michigan University, and Interim
President Edney. Brown came to Alcorn as the youngest president to serve at
a historically black institution of higher learning. He possessed great inter-
personal skills and was viewed by faculty, staff, and students as energetic,
down to earth, and approachable.

His inauguration was held April 15–17, 2011. Activities associated with the inauguration were held in Vicksburg and Natchez and on the main campus in Lorman. The theme for the inauguration was "Alcorn Bravery: Engaging Possibilities, Ensuring Excellence." The investiture and celebration of Brown as president of Alcorn State University also saluted the years of existence of Alcorn and its rich tradition and history by honoring the past and investing in the future as Alcorn celebrated 140 years of education and service.

Brown labeled Alcorn as the greatest university in the world and pledged to lead it well through his service. He promised that Alcorn would remain a first-class institution under his watch. He was a former dean of the College of Education at the University of Nevada in Las Vegas and had held several appointments at various universities and institutions since 1995. He earned his bachelor's and master's degrees from South Carolina State University and the University of Kentucky, respectively. He was born an only child and raised by his grandmother. He shared that a decision had to be made during his birth to save either him or his mother. His grandmother would not make that decision; instead, she said, "Let's pray." The power of prayer has allowed him and his mother to be among the living in 2015.

Brown held a general assembly and introduced members of his administration. He kept all existing university institutional officers in the same position for the remainder of the academic term, but changes were later made. The changes and/or additions made were the positions of executive vice president and provost, senior vice president for University Operations, vice president for Student Success and Enrollment Management, special assistant for University Initiatives, director of Educational Equity and Inclusion, and presidential ombudsman for Administrative Affairs. The vice presidents for Media and University Relations and Institutional Advancement remained the same. He also met with the student leadership during his early months as president because he believed strongly in student involvement, becoming cognizant of student concerns and addressing them conscientiously. He continued the thrust of internship experiences for students and was involved in extending these opportunities for them and acquiring funds to support these initiatives through selected grants. The university's land-grant mission, in line with the Morrill Act of 1890, was implemented through various projects. One project in particular was the Small Farm Outreach Project. One of the major objectives of the project was to develop and implement a statewide program in an effort to decrease the number of socially disadvantaged farmers and assist eligible farmers who desired assistance in various areas of operation.

Brown immediately addressed the economic dilemma by negotiating $9.7 million to be appropriated to Alcorn earmarked for safety and environmental purposes. Alcorn acquired a revenue bond in 1996 in order to construct, equip, and furnish a residence hall on the Natchez campus specifically for nursing students. The project was completed in 1997, and the $680,000 bond was paid off in 2011. Allocation of funds to effectively run the university became a major focus. All schools have individual budgets for operating expenses. The Division of Finance and Administrative Services, with Carolyn Dupre as vice president in 2015, oversees all financial transactions of the university across disciplines. Financial requests, whether by faculty, staff, or students, are transacted through this division. Budget analysis and allocations were historically assessed in the best interest of the university, although issues with university funding are annually encountered. A large unexpected fund came through a $4.2 million endowment from the legacy of President Washington, made through a Title III Endowment Challenge Grant Program by Washington in 1986.

The university held the first Presidential Encampment during the fall 2011 Faculty Convocation. Brown introduced this name as a forum to convene the university and community family in discussion on where we are and where we are trying or want to go as a team through collaborative initiatives. The 2011 Presidential Encampment, a new name for discussions during past convocations, had as a theme "Envisioning Our Destiny, Charting Our Direction." The overall theme for the fall 2011 convocation was "Alcorn Bravery: Leading a Community of Excellence."

During the first month of Brown's administration, he stressed recruitment and set up a new student scholarship in the amount of $1,000 to be given to any current Alcorn State University student who could recruit and ensure enrollment of a new, first-time student beginning fall 2011. Alcorn exceeded the enrollment goal that was set for the 2011–2012 academic school term. The target was 4,100, and the overall fall head count reached 4,391 registered students. This represented the highest recorded head count in Alcorn's history. Faculty, staff, and students were continuously encouraged to be actively involved in the recruiting process.

The initiatives of University College, which houses the Newtie Boyd Center for Academic Support, enabled students who were recruited to succeed at various levels. In 2012, under the leadership of Dr. Edward Vaughn, dean, and Dr. Olayinka Oredein, associate dean, Alcorn decentralized advising of freshmen students. Many of the responsibilities for advising and academic services were allocated to the students' individual academic departments; however, the Newtie Boyd Center for Academic Support works closely with the academic departments to ensure proactive approaches to advising and student services. The major role of the center became that of developing programs and services for freshmen and sophomore students. A retention specialist position was created, and in 2015 a web-based student performance monitoring system called GradesFirst was launched. This system provides automated student services and communication among faculty, academic advisers, and students.

In 2015, Dr. Valerie Thompson became the dean of University College. Thompson stressed that any commitment to success in any area reaffirms the enduring commitment of everybody affiliated with the Alcorn family on a daily basis, including students, instructors, professors, administrators, and staff. Her very capable staff and coordinators of the six key areas (Upward Bound, Academic Advising, Summer Developmental Program, First and Second Year Experience, Student Support Services, and Retention Specialist) all work cooperatively in support of excellence in University College. The First Year Experience Program, now called the First and Second Year Experience Program for freshmen and sophomores, has been very instrumental in ensuring that students get a head start in college expectations of an entering student. This connection ensured that students acquired the academic and social skills needed to succeed and have a positive experience from the time they arrived on campus.

It is evident that during his early months as president, Brown had to move fast—a search for a new head football coach was in progress, along with an upcoming SACS team visit in addition to his inauguration. Coach Melvin Spears Jr. had been selected to lead the Braves football team. After an unsuccessful first year, the university was once again searching for a permanent head football coach. Coach Todd McDaniel was appointed interim head football coach until a permanent coach was selected. After a search committee reviewed over fifty applications, Jay Hopson was selected as head football coach. His selection put Alcorn in a unique history-making limelight since he was the first white coach to lead the Braves football team and also the first white football coach in the history of the SWAC. The public's opinion and perceptions toward this move varied. More than 100 alumni and fans were excited when they were introduced to Coach Hopson at a meeting. Some of the comments made were highlighted in the *Vicksburg Post* soon after his selection:

- "I think he's going to bring a lot of good things to Alcorn. He's looking to the future and he's gotten a good staff. That's the good thing because you're no better than the people you hire. I'm looking for good things, but people are going to have to be patient and let him build."—Lenell Henry
- "I am happy about Hopson's hiring and I hope Hopson will help improve the scholastic atmosphere of the school as well as boost the football program and bring back the winning tradition."—Willie Adams

Coach Jay Hopson.

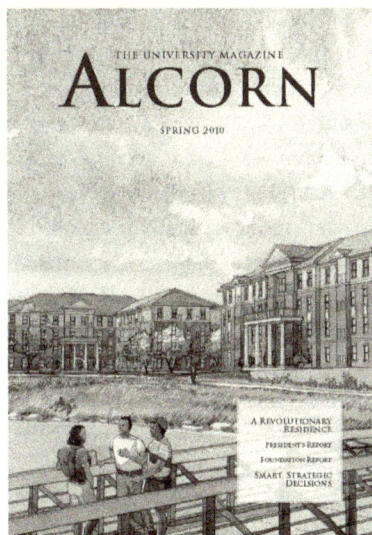

Cover of the first university magazine, *Alcorn*.

- "I had the confidence that the selection committee would get the person we needed. He's from Vicksburg and rooted with his family. He's a quality person and I'm excited about it."—Santa Carpenter
- "I'm here to support him. I've known Jay for years. I'm a friend of his family. I watched him play football and I know he will do well. And we're going to go to the games."—Linda Moss
- "I think he's going to do real well. He played quarterback at Warren Central. He was never affected by pressure."—George Hunt
- "I'm very excited about what we've got. He's doing the right things and saying the right things."—Lakesha Batty, president of the Vicksburg Warren Chapter of the Alcorn State University National Alumni Association
- "He's a very spiritual man. He is very grounded in his faith and you need that if you are going to lead and develop young men. He will do well in his life and on the field. Regardless of what happens, he will win because God is with him." —Manny Murphy

Many current students on the campus were positive about the selection. Some individuals believe that students today don't view race as a big deal as in the past and that time has really brought about such a change. Others, however, criticized the decision to hire a white coach and believe that a black coach could do the same. Brown defended his decision by letting it be known that the best coach was selected from the pool received. He addressed the long-anticipated wait in filling the position as being indicative of a deliberate design for a winning program for Alcorn State University.

Brown also filled another coaching position as a result of the promotion of Coach Larry Smith to director of Athletic Development. Smith had served as head men's basketball coach for Alcorn since the 2008 season and spearheaded several basketball camps. As a student at Alcorn, Smith led Alcorn to a perfect season in 1979. Following Smith's tenure, Coach Luther Riley was selected to lead the team. Riley had won four state championships and was named Mississippi Coach of the Year as a high school coach in Jackson, Mississippi, among other honors, before becoming Alcorn's head basketball coach. He held the first Celebrity Basketball Camp in summer 2011. This camp gave young boys ages five to seventeen basketball and life skills training in an effort to enable them to be successful. In summer 2011, Lady Braves Basketball Head Coach Tonya Edwards held the first Basketball vs. Childhood Obesity Developmental Camp focusing on the fundamental skills needed to play at all levels and introducing students to the basics of nutrition. Additionally, the Braves baseball team became champions in the SWAC in spring 2011 under Baseball Head Coach Barret Rey, who was named SWAC Coach of the Year.

The basketball legend Coach Davey "The Wiz" Whitney paved the way for men's basketball at Alcorn. Among his many honors was being inducted into the National Collegiate Basketball Hall of Fame (NCBHOF). He enabled Alcorn to become the first HBCU to win a National Invitation Tournament (NIT) game and the first HBCU to win an NCAA tournament game. (For more about Coach Davey "The Wiz" Whitney, see *Against Great Odds: The History of Alcorn State University*.) Coach Whitney died in May 2015. A memorial was held in his honor at Alcorn State University in June 2015. He was eighty-five years of age.

The Division of Marketing and Communication is the lifeline of Alcorn for ensuring effective internal and external communications to the community, city, state, and nation. In 2015, Clara Ross Stamps serves as vice president. The university has received numerous awards and continues to receive accolades for publications produced by staff in the division. Four university magazines, *Alcorn*, have been produced through Marketing and Communication in 2010, 2011, 2012, and 2013. The magazines have received awards and recognition from the Council for Advancement and Support of Education (CASE) and the College Public Relations Association of Mississippi (CPRAM). In 2013, the *What Matters?* video received first place, and an "Investment in Knowledge and Character" brochure and the president's Scholarship Birthday Celebration Invitation both earned third-place awards. The Special Merit Award was also given for the "Get in the Game" football brochure.

Brown on the Alumni Tour.

Brown attended the annual Alcorn State University National Alumni Association Mid-Winter Conference for the first time in spring 2011. This conference brings alumni from across the country to a location in Mississippi or out of state to reunite and take care of the business of the Alcorn State University National Alumni Association, collectively and individually supporting Alcorn State University. This conference is held each year during the last weekend in February. (For a list of Mid-Winter Conferences, see Appendix 19.) Brown also scheduled and implemented national alumni tours, where he visited alumni chapters and discussed and found out firsthand their concerns and how the alumni and the university could work together to ensure that Alcorn would be the best that it could be. He was the first president to designate his birthday celebration for the purpose of a fund-raiser for student scholarships. A fortieth birthday reception was held in his honor, with the donations going to the ASU Foundation, Inc. The first significant contribution to the foundation received by Brown was from alumni Willie "Rat" McGowan Sr., former head baseball coach at Alcorn, and his wife Doris McGowan, former department chairperson, in the amount of $10,000.

Alcorn State University held the first Heritage Convocation in spring 2012. The legacy and descendants of Alcorn as a land-grant institution were honored and various renowned individuals were recognized. During spring 2012, Alcornite Myrlie Evers, the widow of Medgar Wiley Evers '52 and a civil rights activist, was employed at Alcorn as a distinguished scholar-in-residence. Students and faculty members had an opportunity to interact with her through lectures and archival research projects. The legacy of Medgar Evers

Statue of Medgar Wiley Evers.

was honored through the unveiling of a statue, the largest known in history, depicting his leadership, courage, commitment, and stamina as a fellow Mississippian and graduate of Alcorn State University. He became involved in civil rights as a student at Alcorn. The new student housing complex and the library auditorium at Alcorn are named in his honor. The Medgar Evers Statue Campaign was initiated by alumnus John Jones, who strove to ensure that the statue became a reality.

During spring 2011, Governor Haley Barbour signed a bill naming certain sections of Highway 552 in Claiborne and Jefferson Counties the Dr. Walter Washington Memorial Parkway. The allocated segments extend to the intersection of US Highway 61 beginning at Alcorn State University. Washington was the longest-tenured president of Alcorn State University, serving twenty-five consecutive years, making significant contributions locally, regionally, nationally, and internationally, and leaving a great legacy at Alcorn State University. Additionally, a legend, Dr. Isaac Thomas, a retired pharmacist in Laurel, Mississippi, was very instrumental in Alcorn's history in early efforts to move the highway project toward reality. He and his wife, Mattie McCann Thomas, are both dedicated and committed Alcornites.

During Brown's first commencement in 2011, past United Negro College Fund (UNCF) president and former US House of Representatives Majority Whip William "Bill" H. Gray III was given an honorary Doctor of Humane

Dr. Walter Washington Memorial Parkway.

Letters degree. Gray was the highest-ranking African American leader in the history of the US House of Representatives. At commencement, Brown challenged the 2011 graduates to get successful jobs and give back to their alma mater. He started each graduate off by giving them their first dollar at graduation. He held a baccalaureate service the evening before commencement. Graduates all repeated the alumni pledge at commencement, which was written by Dr. Connie Larkins Williams upon the request of Dr. John Walls Jr., then president of the Vicksburg Warren Alumni Chapter. Departmental/school graduation activities were incorporated into commencement week, including pinning ceremonies, a teacher induction ceremony, and other scholarly activities. He believed strongly in student engagement, and the director of Student Engagement, Devina Hogan, ensured that they were involved in commencement as well as other unique activities throughout the academic year. Compared to today when commencement is held on Saturday, in May 1928 commencement was held on a Wednesday. (For the 1928 Commencement Day program, see Appendix 20.)

Students often expressed appreciation for services rendered and specifically for their scholarships. For example, Cameron Jenkins, who recently authored his first book, and Jadtrl Heard expressed graciousness as to how foundation scholarships aided them. They encouraged alumni and others to contribute annually. Additionally, the music department gives a Presser Foundation Scholar Award. Recipients are elated over these acknowledgments. (For a list of Award of Excellence recipients, see Appendix 21.) Students know

Cameron Jenkins delivers the valedictory address at Commencement.

Jadtrl Heard.

that it is through these initiatives that they are able to move toward graduation and enjoy their graduation ceremony, one of the highlights of a student's tenure at Alcorn State University, with pride.

Having met all requirements for graduation, students are excited about continuing into advanced degree programs and/or entering the world of work, hopefully in their area of training. Excellent speakers inspire the graduates at commencement exercises. Graduates are encouraged to seek new truths and make the appropriate application of existing knowledge for the betterment of humankind. They are further encouraged to pursue advanced studies and to join an alumni chapter near them. Once they graduate, many advance to higher degrees, including a doctorate or the highest degree applicable in their profession. (For a list of commencement speakers, see Appendix 22.)

During some commencement exercises, selected individuals continue to be given honorary degrees, such as Jesse Morris Jr., son of the late Drs. Jesse and Alpha Morris, who attended most alumni meetings with his mother. Alpha Morris, former chairperson for the Department of Social Sciences, and Jesse Morris, former director of the Division of Agriculture, were long-time educators at Alcorn State University. They worked beyond measure in so many areas of university functions, received many awards, and supported Alcorn continuously during their lifetimes. (For more about Jesse and Alpha Morris, see *Against Great Odds: The History of Alcorn State University*.) Commencement was held once a year in May, although Alcorn once had summer commencements. (For an excerpt of the 1952 summer commencement program, see Appendix 23.)

Several partnerships were initiated between the university and other entities. In spring 2012, Alcorn partnered with the Children's Defense Fund to

Bettaiya Rajanna receiving the Presidential Award.

Willie "Rat" McGowan receiving the Athletic Heritage Award.

offer Freedom School to enhance literacy skills of K–12 students. A partnership was established with the People to People Ambassador Program. This program represented the world leader in global educational travel experiences. It allowed long-term dialogue on issues relevant to higher education and promoted cultural and international enrichment.

Many awards were given during Brown's tenure at Founders Day, convocations, and other functions, including the Presidential Award of Excellence. (For a list of Presidential Award of Excellence recipients, see Appendix 24.) Other awards included the Presidential Citation Award, Academic Award, Agricultural Heritage Award, Athletic Heritage Award, Access Heritage Award, Torch of Justice Award, Hiram Revels Award, Levi J. Rowan Heritage Award, Alcorn Bravery Award, and Oakland Memorial Chapel Award. Brown was named 2013 Male HBCU President of the Year by the Center for HBCU Media Advocacy, Inc.

In spite of the many accomplishments during Brown's tenure, he resigned abruptly in December 2013 in the midst of allegations concerning university purchasing practices.

Edney was asked again to take over as acting president until a permanent president was selected. He served a brief period from December 2013 to March 2014. Although Edney was not cognizant of how long he would serve, he moved quickly carrying out the responsibilities expected of him in the position. He took every moment seriously and served until the nineteenth president, Dr. Alfred Rankins Jr., was announced March 4, 2014. Edney strove daily to ensure that the administrators, faculty, staff, students, alumni, and the entire Alcorn community knew that Alcorn was well and alive and would not go backwards. He was a problem solver and did not envision issues surfacing that could not be resolved with the right mind-set. He took on this tenure with the same enthusiasm and commitment that he had before. He always had as a major focus to return the Alcorn spirit that once existed among the students, faculty, and staff at the university. He demonstrated that everybody was somebody. The positive demeanor around the campus began to become evident, and several university improvements were made across all areas of operations.

Edney encouraged all to work hard and pray daily for Alcorn State University and to remember that the future lies in us as well as in our students, and the future would be bright and prosperous if we put everything in the right perspective by putting God first. "If we put Him first, everything else will fall in place! With Him all things are possible if we only believe!" He stressed that everybody should make each year the best year ever with spirits as high as ever for Alcorn State University. "We can do it!"

8

Advancing to a New Height of Excellence

Alfred Rankins Jr., nineteenth president.

Since the retirement of the fifteenth president, Walter Washington, Alcorn has had four permanent presidents and three interim or acting presidents, with Edney serving twice. After Brown's resignation, the sentiments of the alumni became more evident than before as to what Alcorn needed in its next president. The major descriptions were:

- An Alcornite, preferably from Mississippi, with an understanding of the university's history;
- An individual with a spouse/children and a commitment to stability;

- A person who has an agriculture background with an understanding of the land-grant mission; and
- A person who could turn vision into action.

Bounds and the Board of Trustees indicated that they listened to the will of Alcornites and appointed Dr. Alfred Rankins Jr. as the nineteenth president of Alcorn State University. A presidential search was not implemented as with most recent presidents. Bounds shared that since Alcorn had gone through so much transition in recent years, policy allowed the board to act quickly when it is in the best interest of the university. Rankins was appointed to Alcorn as a president who fit the description sought by alumni in addition to having worked with the IHL. The deputy commissioner for Academic and Student Affairs for the IHL was announced as president of Alcorn March 4, 2014. In a letter to faculty, Bounds stressed that Alcorn was a special place and needed and deserved a special leader who could successfully lead the Alcorn family. He also stressed that Alcorn was special because of the influence that the university had made at the local, state, and national levels. In Rankins's role at IHL, he had administrative oversight over many operations and managed a budget of $14 million. He advised the IHL board on academic programs, faculty affairs, and student access, readiness, and success, as well as policy and planning.

Others also commended the appointment of Rankins, as recorded in an article published by the university. Graduate student Kaelon Walker, of Oklahoma City, Oklahoma, said, "I felt his sense of pride and ownership for Alcorn." He described Rankins's response to one of his questions: How long will you be here?, "His answer, although simple, was a genuine and honest response—'As long as Alcorn will have me.' I feel strongly that he is right for us and more than capable of leading us forward." For Roderick Patterson, a freshman with military obligations majoring in plant and soil science, the person holding the position of president must understand "To whom much is given, much is required. I appreciate that he is concerned about us as students and that he promises to support us." Nontraditional student Barney Rankin, age fifty-six, agreed with Patterson and Walker: "We need President Rankins ASAP. He is the right fit for Alcorn and has my vote of confidence and support. He understands our successes and challenges and has pledged to become part of the solution."

Students were not the only ones excited about the appointment. Cedric Thomas, Braves football defensive back coach, also spoke highly of Rankins and his tenure at Mississippi Valley State University. "He [Rankins] made a difference at MVSU. The collaboration between the administration and athletics

Karen Shedrick.

led to an increase in academic support and mandatory study halls, improving APR for student-athletes." For Wade Tillery, project manager for the Office of Sustainability, it is important to have a leader who will listen and respond to concerns of the Alcorn family. "This is not a one-way street," says Tillery. "It's great that President Rankins is not a micro-manager and that he believes in putting our students first and having transparent communications."

A native of Greenville, Mississippi, Rankins received a Bachelor of Science degree from Alcorn State University and both Master of Science and Doctor of Philosophy degrees from Mississippi State University in agriculture-related fields of study. Rankins is married to Juandalyn Rankins, and they have one daughter and one son.

From the time of Washington's presidency, Karen Shedrick remained the administrative assistant or executive assistant to each president. No other administrative assistant or executive assistant to the president had served as continuously as she had. Shedrick received her bachelor's and master's degrees from Alcorn State University and was awarded the School of Business Alumnus of the Year Award in 2013. She served as administrative assistant/executive secretary to the president from 1994 to 2011 and executive assistant to the president since 2011. Prior to then, she was the secretary/receptionist in the Office of the President. She received many thank-yous and accolades from contacts external and internal to the university, including one

United Nations Conference on Sustainable Development.

from Commissioner of Higher Education Hank Bounds after Alcorn hosted an IHL board meeting in 2009. (For the letter from Commissioner Hank Bounds, see Appendix 25.)

Prior to becoming president at Alcorn State University, Rankins served as acting president of Mississippi Valley State University, where one of his concerns was student recruitment and retention. He reallocated resources to support this, and there was an increase in the enrollment of first-time freshmen. Other areas of emphasis as interim president were student support services, business operations, planned giving, and the engagement of alumni. Therefore, he brought experience in various categories to his role as president of Alcorn State University. He acknowledged his appointment in writing to alumni, sharing that challenges lie ahead, but together they could be faced and we would go above the call of duty for our great university. He had to hit the ball and move fast for, with only two and a half months left before commencement, much had to be done, with minimum time to do it.

During Rankins's first year as president of Alcorn State University, many accomplishments were evident. Alcorn hosted a United Nations conference twice, one for a lecture series on global food security and one for sustainable development. The thirty-fourth annual Alcorn Jazz Festival featured ten-time Grammy Award winner Arturo Sandoval. The Mississippi Coalition of Partners in Prevention Seminar was held at Alcorn, and members of the Mississippi Senate Agriculture Committee visited the campus. Alcorn had a student perform with the National HBCU Choir in Washington, D.C., and the Gospel Choir performed with award-winning artist Dottie Peoples.

Rankins was selected to serve on the Board of Trustees of SACS for the class of 2016. Additionally, he was instrumental in Drs. Robert Carr Jr., dean of the School of Education and Psychology, Associate Dean Malinda Butler, and Department Chairpersons Helen Wyatt and Johnny Thomas experiencing a successful campus visit pursuing a new accreditation with the Council for Accreditation of Educator Preparation (CAEP). This accreditation will enable Alcorn to become the first university in the state of Mississippi and the first HBCU in the nation to receive such accreditation from the accrediting agency in the area of education. Carr was courageous and ambitious to lead such an accreditation task as this one; however, during Alcorn's last NCATE visit, he courageously and ambitiously built Alcorn's teacher education assessment system, and it received high praise from NCATE team members. The CAEP's decision on accreditation will be officially announced fall 2015.

As a young professional, Carr's experiences are broad based, having worked at the state department level as a certification officer for the Mississippi Department of Education, director of Student Teaching at Jackson State University, education liaison for Alcorn's Vicksburg Expansion Program, dean of Education at Langston University in Oklahoma, and back to Alcorn as the dean of the School of Education and Psychology. He modernized technology in the School of Education and Psychology through the implementation of smart classrooms. He is very knowledgeable in many accreditation areas and was very instrumental in ensuring that Alcorn received a favorable status with not only educational accreditation but with the NCAA, where he addressed standards requiring analyzing and interpretation of data and tied them in with the mandates of the NCAA as with other specialized accreditations.

As Rankins continued positive strides, Alcorn, through the School of Education and Psychology, was chosen as the latest site for the World Class Teacher Academy (WCTA); Alcorn partnered with Natchez in offering the 2015 Entrepreneur Academy; and it was instrumental in beginning the construction of a new Product Development Center in agriculture to support, guide, and equip the development of creative ideas in the School of AREAS. Another great accomplishment that had been on the table for a while came to fruition—waiving out-of-state fees for students. Alcorn initiated the All for Alcorn Student Recruitment Program and the Braves Kids Club, and it was awarded a grant to fund an Athletic Academic Success Program (AASP).

The first two notaries, Cora Fuller and Shundera Stallings, were officially appointed for Alcorn. Rankins implemented the 1098-T form for the purpose of providing better customer service. The 1098-T is an information tax document to aid taxpayers in determining whether they are able to claim a

Cover of the thirty-fourth annual Jazz Festival.

tax deduction or one of the education tax credits. A hospitality and gaming management program was also offered.

Students were awarded the 2014 Mississippi Professional Educators Scholarship. Students also received scholarships from the Mississippi Farm Bureau's Young Farmers and Ranchers Scholarship Foundation. Alcorn was selected to receive a portion of $250,000 donated by Nissan for its science, technology, engineering, and math (STEM) programs. Alcorn also received the STEM Degree Completion Award from the Association of Public and Land-Grant Institutions Council (the 1890 Award in Research, Teaching, and Innovation). Rankins implemented the FACES initiative, which focused on facilities advancement, academic excellence, customer service, enrollment growth, and student success.

Rankins reading to children in the Child Development Laboratory Center during Week of the Young Child.

Additionally, Alcorn hosted the first Agricultural Enhancement Camp for high school students and an Ag-Academic Camp for agriculture and technical training for youth ages six to twelve. Rankins formed the Alcorn State University Customer Service Task Force, which includes students, alumni, faculty, and staff, and Alcorn hosted the second annual Center of Excellence in Research Symposium. Since his appointment, Alcorn celebrated the fifty-year anniversary of the Upward Bound TRIO Program; 100 years of service by the Cooperative Extension Program; and the Week of the Young Child, where Rankins read to the children at the Child Development Laboratory Center.

Alcorn received additional awards through Marketing and Communication at the annual CPRAM conferences. Alcorn was selected as one of the top five universities to present at the National IDeA Symposium of Biomedical Research Excellence, and a ribbon-cutting ceremony was held for the relocation of Health and Disability Services to Rowan Hall.

President Rankins selected Myrlie Evers as the 2014 commencement speaker, and Alcorn alumna Dr. Jacqueline Walters, a nationally celebrated board-certified obstetrician and gynecologist and one of the stars of Bravo's hit reality series *Married to Medicine*, as the 2015 commencement speaker. He gave the Alcorn State University National Alumni Association

Health and Disability Services relocates to Rowan Hall.

an excellent update at the 2015 annual Mid-Winter Conference held in Biloxi, Mississippi.

Keeping in coherence with the land-grant mission, Rankins appointed Dr. Ivory Lyles as interim dean of the School of AREAS (interim was later dropped from his title). Lyles came on board, as other agriculture deans in the past, realizing that the foundation of Alcorn State University was rooted in its agricultural component. He succeeded Dr. Barry Bequette as dean, who also served as the director of Land Grant Programs. Lyles, in 2015, is engaged in several legislative priorities that are being considered for the school, including the restoration of agriculture program funding; a meat processing facility in De Kalb, Mississippi; agriculture facility renovation and repair; small loan programs; and shitake mushroom research and production expansion. Lyles has kept the School of AREAS constantly moving in a positive direction from the very beginning of his appointment. Several funded grants contributed to this reality, including:

- The USDA awarded Alcorn's School of AREAS $300,000. This grant was funded for the purpose of developing a comprehensive plan for the establishment and operation of a policy institute. This institute would focus on rural communities and small farmers and ranchers as they build new sustainable economic opportunities in Mississippi. The grant was through the competitive grants program for Outreach and Assistance for Socially Disadvantaged Farmers and Ranchers.

Myrlie Evers delivering the commencement address.

- The USDA awarded more than $1.9 million in grants to promote the agricul-
ture sciences and research professions ($929,901 was received through the
1890 Institution Research, Extension and Teaching Capacity Building Grant to
advance research, extension, and teaching in food and agriculture sciences, and
$977,673 was received through the 1890 Facilities Grant Program to improve
food sciences and equipment). These grants came from the FY 2010 Consolidated Appropriations Act supported by Senator Thad Cochran. The university
has received many other USDA grants for various areas of agriculture, including the USDA/1890 National Scholars Program, which was a partnership

between the eighteen historically black land-grant institutions and the federal government and was opened to high school seniors and first- and second-year college students, including community and junior college transfer students.

- Alcorn received a $17.9 million grant for a TRI-Mississippi Project, a collaboration between Claiborne, Franklin, and Jefferson Counties and Alcorn to build bridges with support from the department's Transportation Investment Generating Economic Recovery (TIGER) 2014 Program.
- Alcorn received a Capacity Building Grant in the amount of $386,187 from the USDA to investigate "3D fruit through imaging technologies to automatically detect bruised fruit."
- Alcorn's Department of Advanced Technologies received a grant of $409,123 for three years from the Department of Defense's Office of Naval Research for a dual face recognition system for human identification applications. The project enhances role authentication, right authorization, law enforcement, environment surveillance, activity accounting, and suspect monitoring and tracking.
- Alcorn was awarded a $671,548 grant for night vision colorization.
- Alcorn was awarded $338,027 to address thermal face recognition. The identity patent application regarding the thermal face recognition is in progress.

General repairs and renovations, infrastructure upgrades, Americans with Disabilities Act (ADA) modifications, housing, and campus safety and security across disciplines are all ongoing to make Alcorn the best that it can be. The initiation of *The Voice*, a publication highlighting the School of AREAS, under Lyles's deanship speaks volumes for AREAS.

Celebrating the 1890 land-grant institutions' 125 years of existence with the theme "Providing Access and Enhancing Opportunities in Agriculture" was a major function. The many activities surrounding this celebration commemorated a history of changing lives through education, research, and community engagement. Alcorn's history tracks back to the Morrill Acts named after Justin Smith Morrill, who focused on a higher education system that would go beyond just the acts, but teach agriculture and mechanical skills as well. The Morrill Act of 1862 granted land for states to establish public universities. The Morrill Act of 1890 supported states with segregated schools. This funding was created for black colleges ("Negro" land-grant universities). Alcorn, however, did receive funding from the 1862 act, enabling it to be known as the oldest public historically black land-grant institution in the United States and the second-oldest state-supported institution of higher learning in Mississippi. The celebration included a National 1890 Day of Wellness where all attendees were invited to participate in a walk/run route across the campus. The consortium that officially represents the 1890 institutions appointed Dr. Dalton

ISSUE 2
FALL 2015

INSIDE THIS ISSUE:

Introducing Dr. Ivory W. Lyles 1

Agriculture and Family and Consumer Sciences Alumni Hall of Fame 3

Spotlight: Alumni Zelmarine Murphy and Dr. Willie F. Jackson 5-6

Stories: Students enjoy the School of AREAS First Harvest Festival 7

Alcorn's Department of Advanced Technologies Hosts Entergy Day 8

Alcorn Advanced Technologies/Health Physics Students' Successful Journey 9

Jones Appointed to the Southern Region Program Leadership Committee 10

Grants Awarded in Fall 2015 11

Earmarked Grants 12

Personnel Changes Congrats on Years of Service 13

Dates of Importance for 2015

Alcorn
SCHOOL OF AGRICULTURE, RESEARCH, EXTENSION & APPLIED SCIENCES

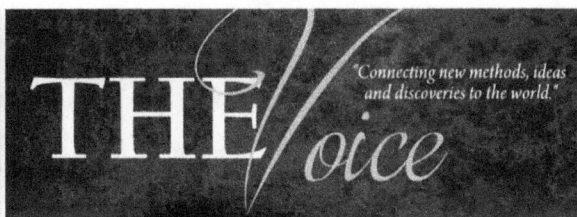

THE Voice

"Connecting new methods, ideas and discoveries to the world."

Greetings from

Dr. Ivory W. Lyles
Dean and Director of Land-Grant Programs

Dear Alumni, Students and Faculty,

"We are prone to judge success by the index of our salaries or the size of our automobiles rather than by the quality of our service and relationship to mankind," said the Rev. Martin Luther King Jr.

Today, you get the benefit of a conversation I had with one of my neighbors a few months back. He told me about his car not starting the evening before, and how upset he was with the situation. After waiting over an hour, an older guy stopped and gave him a boost. As he was putting his jumper cables back into the truck, my neighbor offered to pay; however, the guy replied "you owe me nothing." He insisted, "I need to pay something." "No," the guy reiterated. "Back in Vietnam, someone helped me out of a worse situation – that's when I lost my legs - and that guy told me to just pass it on. Just remember, whenever you get the chance, you pass it on."

So, this story shows us that how we serve others and the relationships we have with others is a much more significant way to measure our success. Within the School of Agriculture, Research, Extension and Applied Sciences, I hope we are measuring our success by how we serve our students, alumni and friends. Surely, we are measuring success by the strength of our relationship with our contributors, vendors, and supporters.

Everyday upon entering campus, I am reminded that we have an obligation to pass on the blessings that have been provided to us. So the next time a student, friend, faculty or stranger needs your assistance, please remember, "just pass it on."

Purple and Gold Forever,
Dr. Ivory W. Lyles
Dean and Director of Land-Grant Programs
School of AREAS

125 Years of Service
1890 2015

125 Years of Providing Access and Enhancing Opportunities

Cover of *The Voice*.

McAfee, a former dean, to the American Distance Educators Consortium in 2011. Other areas of focus were food and nutrition, tobacco-use prevention, community resource development, a research farm and technology transfer center, and a small farm incubator farm.

Through the School of AREAS, the Cooperative Extension Program focuses on opportunities for first-generation students and other students,

Alcorn students engaged in poultry processing.

health and obesity issues, safe and nutritious food, social and economic mobility of families, a safe environment, and engaging youth in STEM–related studies, among other unique experiences. Cutting-edge research is conducted in an effort to create new knowledge in the various agriculture areas for continuous progress. Alcorn's Experiment Station has offered very strong support for the various efforts incorporated through the School of AREAS. Major research has focused on horticulture, poultry, fruit, beef cattle, wine, and dairy cattle. Alumnus Delmar Stamps, Jessie Harness, and others ensure continuously that Alcorn's Department of Agriculture is not left out at the local, state, and national levels.

Additionally, during Rankins's first year as president, Alcorn won the SWAC championship in football and was honored as Black College Football National Champions. Alcorn also received the SWAC tennis championship under Coach Anthony Dodgen. The basketball court in the Davey L. Whitney Department of Health, Physical Education and Recreation Complex was named after Coach Shirley Walker, the retired Alcorn Lady Braves head

Braves Football team, 2014 SWAC Champions.

coach who left an impeccable mark in the history of women's basketball. She won 493 games in thirty seasons at Alcorn, and twelve regular season and six SWAC tournament titles. She served on many SWAC and NCAA committees and received a Lifetime Achievement Award from the national level. Her husband, Coach Lonnie Walker, a former Alcorn basketball player who later coached at Alcorn, was inducted into the SWAC Hall of Fame in 2011.

Changes in personnel in selected areas of employment were made. For example, Drs. Donzell Lee and John Igwebuike both served in interim positions for approximately a year and were appointed permanently. Lee, who replaced Dr. Samuel L. White when he retired as vice president and former dean of the School of Arts and Sciences, became the provost and executive vice president for Academic Affairs, and John Igwebuike, who replaced Lee, became vice provost for Academic Affairs, with Kimberly Buie as his administrative assistant.

Lee had previously served in various positions at Alcorn, including director of the Honors Program and department chairperson for the Department of Fine Arts, associate vice president for Academic Affairs, vice provost for Academic Affairs, and dean of Graduate Studies. During Alcorn's convocation, he received the Academic Heritage Award. He chaired the SACS reaffirmation process for three SACS evaluations, with Patricia Keys working untiringly as his executive assistant each time. He also had two cochairs

Coach Shirley Walker.

working along with him for each evaluation. During the first evaluation, Josephine Posey and Epsy Hendricks were cochairs; during the second, Posey and Napoleon Moses served as cochairs; and, during the third, Drs. Noland Boyd and Igwebuike served as cochairs. Accreditations were successfully accomplished with accolades. Lee and his team did a great job during each of the evaluations.

Igwebuike had previously served as assistant professor of business and as associate dean. He serves as the athletic representative for Alcorn and contributed to the success of the NCAA recertification process in 2012, which was cochaired by Dr. Peter Malik, assisted by Josephine Posey. (Malik did an outstanding job with this reaffirmation process.) Igwebuike also contributed to the success of the SACS reaffirmation in 2011 and the business accreditation in 2013. Together, Lee and Igwebuike were transitioned from interim to permanent positions in order to move Academic Affairs forward with the collaborative efforts of deans and chairs as they worked with faculty, staff, and students in ensuring success. (For academic schools and major support divisions, see Appendix 26.)

Alcorn continues to serve the surrounding communities, the state of Mississippi, the region, and the nation in graduating exemplary students and scholars in multiple professional fields. The history of Alcorn validates that Alcorn graduates are leaders throughout the world. Serving the people since 1871, striving for excellence in all fields of study is a major focus. Alcorn strives to graduate students who are useful, proficient, efficient, productive, and of high moral character in an atmosphere that is conducive to high ideals of scholarship and democratic living.

In 2015, there are plans to relocate the Office of the President, which for decades had been housed in the Walter Washington Administration and Classroom Building, to the newly renovated Bowles Hall. Other offices will also be transitioned to Bowles Hall, namely Academic Affairs; Marketing and Communication; ASU Foundation, Inc.; and Institutional Research and Assessment. This move is scheduled to take place after June 30, 2015.

Rankins and other permanent and interim/acting presidents worked with their leadership to continuously make Alcorn better than it was before. (For leadership of permanent, interim, and acting presidents since 1994, see Appendix 27.) He has accomplished much to date, and Alcorn is definitely looking forward to greater achievements as we collectively keep at the fore-front Alcorn's commitment to excellence. The author of the next published history of Alcorn State University will capture additional accomplishments of President Rankins and other noteworthy historical data related to Alcorn's history. The information included in this publication ended June 30, 2015.

9

STUDENTS: SUCCEEDING
WITH EXCELLENCE

Alcorn is nationally recognized, employs understanding professors, promotes positive collaborative relationships, and has graduated generations of successful alumni, among other reasons students choose to attend. When students apply to the univeristy and are accepted, Alcorn employees at every position realize that the students are first priority at the institution.

Students attend freshmen and/or transfer orientation and are given a student handbook to follow as a guide in order to ensure that their new environment experiences are rewarding. The Office of Career Services gives them a four-year career plan. (For the 2014–2015 four-year career plan, see Appendix 28.) Sessions are held to discuss the handbook and a student's overall expectations. Students encounter excitement in the learning and living environment. Alcorn's radio station keeps students and the Alcorn community updated and informed on university occurences. Many students become involved in extracurricular activities organized through various units on campus and encounter other recreational activities in the campus union such as playing cards, table tennis, and bowling. In 2015, students can dine at Pizza Hut in the campus union. Although these recreational activities are available, students realize that their number one priority as a student is to study hard, apply scholarly skills needed to survive in a global society, and receive a degree from the university. Relationships are developed that create a sense of community. The Honors Convocation, held each semester, honors students who have performed well in their academic field, where some receive presidential scholar honors and others are recognized as dean's scholars.

The student enrollment during the 2014–2015 academic year is 3,518 compared to almost 3,000 during the 1994–1995 academic term. In 2011, the enrollment actually reached 4,018 students and has declined slightly each year since. In 2015, the enrollment is 3.7 percent white, 91.8 percent black,

Honors Convocation.

and 4.5 percent other. Of this percentage, there are 34.8 percent male and 65.2 percent female. (For other Alcorn enrollment by ethnicity, gender, residency, level, age, and full-time equivalent from 1999 to 2005, see Appendix 29.) A longtime former director of Financial Aid, Laplose Jackson, occasionally used the phrase, "We welcome overflow." Student Support Services (SSS) contributed greatly to overall student success. Regina Rankin, a former director of SSS, incorporated innovative programs as a major focus in leading students to success and involved the total student population when applicable. One of her favorites was "SSS: Your GPS to Success."

Admission requirements for entering Alcorn State University as an undergraduate are that prospective students must take the American College Testing (ACT) Program Examination or the Scholarship Achievement Test (SAT), and they must have their scores submitted to the Office of Admissions. In order to be admitted, the prospective student must also do the following:

- Complete the College Prep Curriculum (CPC) and maintain a minimum GPA of 3.2;
- Complete the CPC with a minimum 2.5 GPA and score at least 16 on the ACT or at least 790 on the SAT;
- Rank in the upper 50 percent of their class and score at least 16 on the ACT or at least 790 on the SAT;

Pizza Hut located in the campus union.

- Complete the CPC with a minimum 2.0 GPA and score at least 18 on the ACT or at least 870 on the SAT; and/or
- Satisfy NCAA standards for student athletes who are "full qualifiers" under Division I guidelines.

If a prospective student does not meet one of the five requirements, an interview is scheduled with the student that will include a computerized exam known as Accuplacer. The results will determine the student's status and the next steps to be taken.

In order for a transfer student to be admitted, an official transcript showing credits, grades, and a statement of honorable dismissal should be sent directly to the Office of Admissions at Alcorn from the college or university previously attended. Credit is given for all coursework with a grade of "C" or above. ACT or SAT requirements must be satisfied, and the student must have a GPA of 2.0 on a 4.0 scale. Admission requirements for all other students vary according to specific criteria, such as the admission of former students, international students, special students, veterans, and graduate students. Many of Alcorn's graduates continue on to graduate school at the university under the governance of a graduate council and receive master's and/or education specialist degrees. Once completing advanced degrees at Alcorn, some continue their educational thrust at other universities for a more advanced degree.

The availability and addition of new degree offerings allow students more choices and the possibility of being able to study in their preferred discipline. Students voice that this weighs greatly in their decision to attend Alcorn State University. They want to be sure that Alcorn offers the degree that they want

J. D. Boyd Library.

before engaging in the application process. During the recruitment process, students are made aware of what the university has to offer, and many of the degree choices of the prospective students are often available. Mississippi has an articulation agreement between the IHL board and the Community and Junior College Board. This agreement governs required offerings impacting both entities. Generally, prospective students have reviewed this prior to preparing to make a decision about college. If the first choice is Alcorn and Alcorn does not offer their choice, they will pursue their second choice. Degree offerings play a great role in the college or university decision; however, Alcorn State University can usually accommodate the major for most students who apply. (For academic degree programs in 2015, see Appendix 30.) Once admitted, students are encouraged to stay in close contact with their adviser and to take advantage of all student support services.

Through their resource guides, students are instructed on processes such as calculating grade point average, contacts for major offices, a campus map, and other necessities to ensure student success. They are made aware of the university calendar. (For the 2015 university calendar, see Appendix 31.) The calendar today is quite different from the past. (For the 1888 calendar, see Appendix 32.)

Parents also receive a guide addressing areas such as campus safety and health and community resources. In 2005, the Newtie Boyd Center for Academic Support added an electronic newsletter for parents distributed to them via email. Parents and students should be on one accord as it relates to student entrance and expectations. Financial aid is available for eligible students in the form of scholarships, grants, loans, and work-study. Once getting settled

Computer Camp

Peanut Butter and Jelly Theater Group performed at Alcorn this summer

Mississippi Alliance for Minority Participation/Summer Bridge/MAMP

ASU Upward Bound

Summer Youth Program Participants

Ag Hope
(Gospel Concert)

Summer programs.

in classes, university life becomes a reality to the students. Many of them realize that the library has to become one of their best friends. (For the 2012 J. D. Boyd Library annual statistics, see Appendix 33.)

Most Alcorn students enjoy the university environment once they become accustomed to the transition from high school to college and being away from home if they don't commute. Summer programs are also available for

On January 20, 2005, the Alcorn Concert Choir performed at the second inaugural ceremony of President George W. Bush.

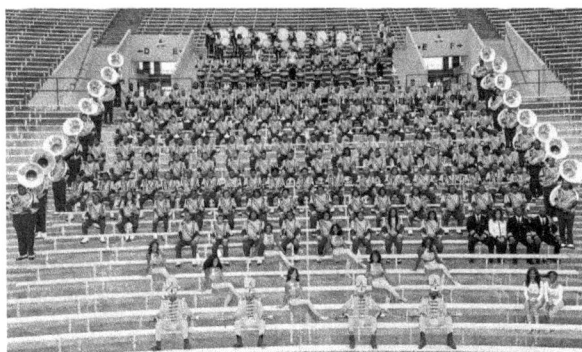

Sounds of Dyn-O-Mite Marching Band.

Longtime band director Samuel Griffin alongside current band director Renardo Murray.

The models of Beaute' Noire.

K-12 students. In 2015, food services are vastly changed. Students have more choices than students had in the past and they enjoy the options available. In 2015, food services are under the auspices of Sodexo; however, former Alcorn students will never forget Bernadine Coleman and Dorothy Hunt for their role in food services for many years.

In sports, football tends to dominate most of students' interests; but they attend other sporting events as well. Student athletes are challenged to compete and win on the field just as they, along with other students, are challenged to win in the classroom. Some students join sororities, fraternities, and other organizations on campus, and others display special talents as members of one of the choirs; the band, which was nominated Best HBCU Marching Band by the Center for HBCU Media Advocacy, Inc.; a modeling squad; the debate team; or other groups.

Students observe faculty and staff and expect them to be scholarly as well. Faculty publications, attendance at professional meetings, and involvement in scholarly endeavors serve as positive examples for students. Students are provided with much excitement on holidays such as getting into the holiday spirit where faculty, staff, and students enjoy the Christmas tree lighting ceremony. They also support Alcorn nursery students and international students during holidays and special occasions.

Funding for the experiences encountered by students once they are registered are enabled through several avenues, such as grants, selected funds from the foundation, Title III, state funds, and local and/or regional contributions. (For a sample analysis of the operating budget summary of IHL appropriations, see Appendix 34.) Activities under Title III, coordinated by Dr. Lola Brown, and Sponsored Programs, directed by attorney Alfred Galtney, change from one period of time to another, and budget allocations also vary because of economic reasons. For example, in 2007 the total Title III allocation was $3,381,115, compared to $2,991,023 in 2010; however, 2010 included an additional $1,036,938 from the Student Aid and Fiscal Responsibility Act (SAFRA) accounts. Student tuition in 2015 ranges from $6,500 to $7,500 based on where the student is housed or if the student is commuting. (For a sample of the Fall 2013–Spring 2014 tuition breakdown, see Appendix 35.) Additionally, during their tenure at Alcorn State University, students are involved in significant partnerships with external entities, including other colleges and universities. Among the many partnerships are the following:

- America Reads Mississippi (ARM): This partnership includes Alcorn State University, Mississippi State University, Delta State University, Jackson State University, and other state agencies. It focuses on tutoring pre-K through middle school students in the areas of reading and stresses that attitude is everything. The monthly ARM newsletter summarizes their role through its title, *Tutors with a Mission*. The partnership services approximately eighty-five school districts statewide.
- The Mid-South Partnership for Rural Community Colleges: This partnership includes Alcorn State University, Mississippi State University, community colleges, rural communities, businesses, and industries. It was funded through the Phil Harden Foundation and the Ford Foundation. This was a collaborative effort covering the states of Alabama, Arkansas, Louisiana, Mississippi, and Tennessee. The partnership's two major goals were to encourage economic growth in rural towns to help them reclaim their future and to strengthen the role of the community college and economic development. It had four initiatives of focus:
  - University degree programs;
  - Rural community partners;
  - Leadership and professional development; and
  - Policy research.

There were other partnerships benefiting students, including the Mississippi Teacher Fellowship Program and Achieve Mississippi.

Students are given an opportunity for open dialogue through student leadership roundtable discussions with advisers, faculty, staff, and administrators. These discussions help students resolve issues as well as develop leadership abilities. Activities leading up to graduation present a high level of excitement as students pursue job options. For example, Teacher Recruitment Day often enabled teacher education majors to have a job before graduating. After graduation, some students receiving a B.S. degree express an interest in the

Commencement 2015.

Ronald E. McNair Post-Baccalaureate Achievement Program, which focuses on preparing eligible participants for doctoral studies through involvement in research and other scholarly activities as well as other advancement opportunities. Alcorn's placement services are most valuable in assisting students in their various transitions upon graduating.

Most Alcorn students, whether undergraduate or graduate, are able to overcome barriers and succeed because they are determined to meet their goal and accomplish their purpose for being students at Alcorn. They want to follow in the footsteps of Alcorn legends and be men and women who refuse to be defeated. Shawn Anderson '96 stated that "Alcorn gave me the foundation—a solid set of people skills and an understanding of many disciplines to step out in the world and succeed." Myra Hoskin '95 said that "Alcorn is small enough to offer one-on-one attention and large enough to provide many avenues for involvement." Health and Disability Services is always on alert to address student illnesses and health needs. The university also has a disaster recovery plan.

Graduates exit ready for the world of work and prepared to go out into society representing themselves, their families, their community, Alcorn State University, the state of Mississippi, and the world with excellence. People fifty or more years from now need to know that Alcorn has always striven for excellence since its founding on May 13, 1871, and will continue to do so.

10

ALUMNI: SUCCEEDING WITH EXCELLENCE

Alcorn alumni, who traditionally refer to themselves as Alcornites or Braves, have demonstrated their love and devotion to their alma mater in various ways. The Alcorn State University National Alumni Association was organized in 1890 to support the goals and objectives of the university in the areas of student and alumni recruitment, programs, and activities, promoting the highest standards of excellence and supporting these areas financially. Through the association, alumni are kept informed and encouraged to stay connected to the university. They are made aware of any issues impacting the university positively or negatively. Members are expected to engage fully in preserving the rich heritage of the university. (For the Alcorn State University National Alumni Association history, see Appendix 36.)

Alumni dedication and commitment to Alcorn are exemplified through their support of scholarships, fund-raising efforts, and other avenues of support in enhancing the overall mission of the university. The association serves as the liaison between the university and the many alumni throughout the world. The association's role includes maintaining a continuous line of communication with alumni. In 2015, alumna Janice Gibson, who worked closely with alumnus Charles Davis when he was director of Alumni Affairs, has done a great job maintaining this connection with the National Alumni Association as director for Development and Alumni Affairs.

Alumni chapters throughout the world support the spirit of Alcorn succeeding against great odds. (For the Alcorn State University National Alumni Association's current chapter presidents, see Appendix 37.) Members work very hard within their chapters, whether it is hosting a conference or other endeavors. For example, the closest conference held near Alcorn's campus was in Vicksburg, Mississippi, in 2012. Walter Sheriff, the chapter president at the

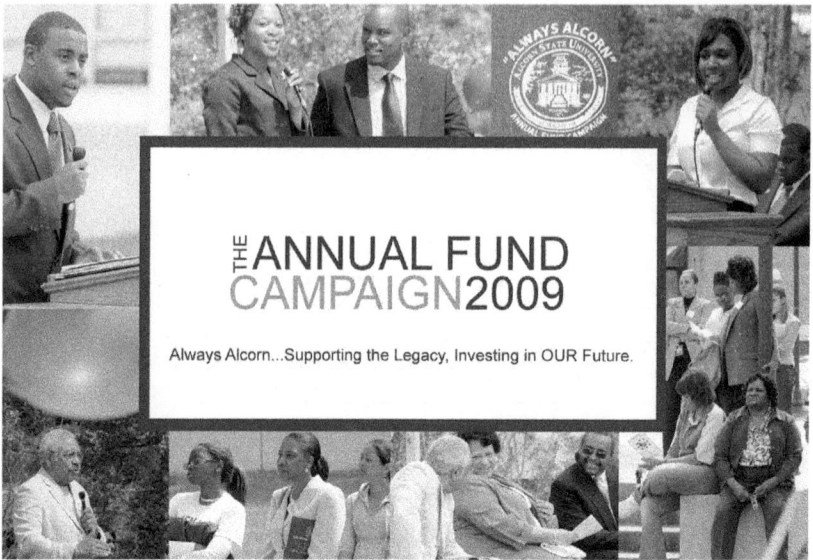

ANNUAL FUND CAMPAIGN 2009

Always Alcorn...Supporting the Legacy, Investing in OUR Future.

Always Alcorn Annual Fund Campaign.

time, and the chapter members ensured that attendees would long remember it. This is the sentiment of Alcornites once they have attended a Mid-Winter Conference.

There have been nineteen presidents of the Alcorn State University National Alumni Association. (For a list of Alcorn State University National Alumni Association presidents, see Appendix 38.) The 2012–2014 and 2014–2016 alumni boards, under the leadership of President James Stubbs, have worked diligently, as have all previous presidents and board members, to ensure that the goals and objectives of the National Alumni Association are met. The immediate past president, Percy Norwood, also worked very hard as a leader, along with his national officers. Past president and attorney James McDonald, the youngest National Alumni Association president, served after the untimely death of President Freddie Owens. (For a list of Alcorn State University National Alumni Association officers from 2008 to 2015, see Appendix 39.)

The National Alumni Association also has its own foundation, chaired by past national president Dr. John Walls, which has awarded scholarships to needy students as well as contributed to other requests deemed significant to the overall operations of the university. It has been operated with transparency and integrity and has been a blessing to many of Alcorn's students and other university requests as applicable.

Walter Sheriff, former Vicksburg
Warren Alumni Chapter president.
Courtesy of Walter Sheriff.

Dr. John Walls Jr. '68, chairman of the National
Alumni Association Foundation, and Vice Chairman
Matthew Thomas Jr. '65 presented to President
Alfred Rankins Jr. a $10,000 gift for student
scholarships.

Alcornites gather as an association at least four times a year: at an August
board meeting, a December board meeting, the annual Mid-Winter Conference in February, and Alumni Reunion Weekend in May. These meetings
are in an effort to dialogue about the university and to receive input on
issues and any university concern of Alcornites with a common interest to
support Alcorn State University. The Mid-Winter Conference, the largest
gathering of the four, takes place in various states in February of each year.
Alumni plan years ahead to attend this particular conference regardless of
where it is held. It is more like an overall reunion where classes also plan
their own meetings.

Alumni are recognized in many capacities for their contributions to their
local chapters, the community in which they live, and Alcorn State University.
All of these efforts support the fact that, as graduates of Alcorn, Alcornites
succeed against great odds confronting them and make a difference in the
world. Alumni are recognized by their selection for the Hall of Honor in the
categories of alumni, service, and athletics and for the most prestigious award,
Alcornite of the Year. (For a list of Hall of Honor inductees, see Appendix 40.
For a list of Alcornite of the Year recipients, see Appendix 41.)

Alcornites are involved in scholarly initiatives at all levels. For example, some
are authors who publish books and other documents. Examples are Beulah

Alumni Reunion Weekend.

Alumni House Bed and Breakfast.

Walker, Carolyn Williams Parker, Buford Spann, Ladonna Smith-Cook, Brenda Waters, John Plump, Katina Rankin, Mike Windham, and Montrell Green.

The National Association for Equal Opportunity in Higher Education (NAFEO) also recognizes Distinguished Alumni of the Year, and Golden Classes are recognized each year by Alcorn State University. Golden Classes, composed of alumni who graduated fifty years ago at the time, are honored at the annual commencement exercises held in May. These graduates participate in the commencement ceremony and receive their golden diplomas along with all other graduates. Seeing their excitement and

Golden Class at Commencement in 2010.

enthusiasm throughout graduation is unforgettable. Records indicate that Golden Classes have been recognized and have participated in graduation since 1933, with seventy-six graduating in 2015. (For a list of Golden Classes, see Appendix 42.)

Many parents have ensured that all or almost all of their children attended Alcorn. Examples include the following:

- The Jones family, where five siblings graduated from Alcorn: Wiley F. Jones '64, Roger D. Jones '68, Clifford E. Jones '69, John H. Jones '71, and Daniel L. Jones '73;
- The Smith family, where seven siblings graduated from Alcorn: Mildred Smith Neil '50, Cora Smith Carter '58, Mary Smith Johnson '58, Grace Smith '62, Vernice Smith McKnight '64, Beatrice Smith Young '64, and Shirley Smith Alexander '68 (for a brief background on the Smith's family desire to educate by Beatrice Smith Young, see Appendix 43);
- The Jackson family, where twelve siblings graduated from Alcorn: Elnora Jackson Bobo '72, Mary Jackson King '72, Polly Jackson Wright '73, Walter Jackson Jr. '74, Kathy Jackson Davis '75, Sara Jackson Harper '75, Brenda Jackson Patterson '79, Rita Jackson Winn '80, Omega Jackson '81, Karen Jackson Hairston '83, Leslie DeWayne Jackson '85, and Joy Jackson '90; and
- The Johnson family, where thirteen siblings graduated from Alcorn: Marilyn J. Lynn '59, Earlean J. Scarbrough '59, Robert Johnson Jr. '60, Walter Johnson '63, Emanuel L. Johnson '63, R. C. Johnson '65, W. C. Johnson '68, H. C. Johnson '70, Bernard J. Johnson '73, Mary B. Johnson '74, Evelyn C. Johnson '76, Carl Johnson '78, and Nathaniel C. Johnson '83.

There are many other families of Alcornites who fall into the category of having a high number of siblings to graduate from Alcorn such as the Prater family and the Johnny B. Barnes family. In addition to the siblings mentioned, spouses, in-laws, nieces, nephews, cousins, uncles, and aunts also attended and/or graduated from this great institution.

Alumni are always on the move. Alumnus Dr. Charles Tillman's family operation, the T-6 Farm, was very instrumental in the success of an Alternative Crop Field Day coordinated by the agriculture extension agent. This day included a tour of the beef cattle facility, catfish pond, and the feeder pig operation as well as the sweet sorghum syrup site. Tillman is former chair of the Department of Agriculture.

The Alcorn spirit remains high, and Alcornites demonstrate it continuously. It is expressed very well in a song written by Jessica Hayes Williams '76, entitled "Alcorn Spirit." (For the "Alcorn Spirit" song, see Appendix 44.) James Holloway, better known as "Chicken," stood out beaming with the Alcorn spirit through his actions, along with alumnus Andre Young. Holloway died in 2015 and will be long remembered as a die-hard Alcornite.

Alcorn alumni have demonstrated scholarly accomplishments beyond just the traditional. Alumna Dr. J. Janice Coleman has served the university and alumni in various capacities. Her creativity as a scholarly artist led to several unique creations. Among these was the design of an Alcorn quilt. Many alumni who have seen the quilt have offered to purchase it, but Coleman plans to raffle it and donate the profits to support student scholarships for Alcorn State University. The quilt is truly a masterpiece. (For a description of the Alcorn Quilt centerpiece, see Appendix 45.) She has a deep interest in the origin of many Alcorn historical facts such as the Himes family. Her research revealed much about the Himes family and Estelle Charlotte Bomar Himes, the wife of J. S. Himes, who actually wrote "The Alcorn Ode" with music by Mattie Foote Rowan. Coleman's interest and enthusiasm in her historical findings are both astonishing and noteworthy. She has been the recipient of several awards for artistic and creative initiatives, including the Mississippi Humanities Council Teachers Award in 2010–2011.

Alumna Marilyn Shelton was very devoted to coordinating the annual Alumni Day that was initiated in 2004. She always ensured that the day was full of meaning and served a valuable purpose. Oldest and youngest alumni were recognized, and chapters brought amenities and materials to hand out that reflected their counties. Displays often included scrapbooks, photographs, posters, banners, and other valuables. Shelton and her committee did an excellent job with this function annually. (For the Alcorn Alumni Day agenda, see Appendix 46.)

Dr. Charles Tillman, owner of the
T-6 Farm.

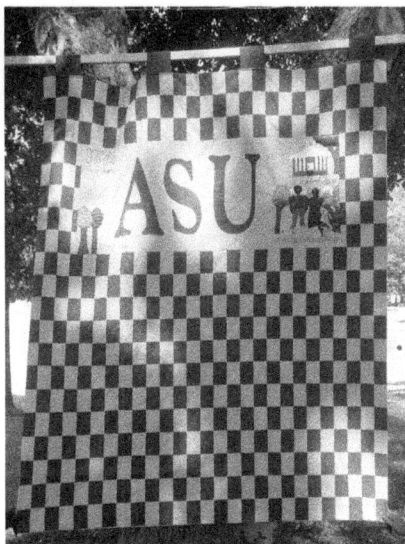

The Alcorn Quilt. Courtesy of J. Janice Coleman.

One of the major university activities that alumni from almost every aspect of society cherish is football. Although all sports are important to the athletic success of the university, football tends to dominate. Through the years, under the lead of several different coaches, the various teams would be up and down in their losses and wins. Some led to championships, some led to general wins, and others led to complete losses. A familiar voice usually heard announcing the game is that of alumnus Emanuel Barnes, who in 2015 serves as vice president of Student Affairs, previously serving in various related positions, rendering great service in each one.

Several married couples who graduated from Alcorn very seldom miss football games—rain or shine, sleet or snow. One couple is Helen Milloy and Kermit Milloy from Covington County, Mississippi. They have been responsible for many students attending Alcorn State University, including their own children and the children of relatives and friends. They tailgate at each home game and many away games, and welcome everybody to join them and talk, eat, and drink all they want. Some tent gatherers were regulars, and some just passed through. Many stopped to get delicious teacakes that were baked by Helen's mother, who, along with her father, Calvin, sent all four of their children to Alcorn. Her mother looked forward to baking the teacakes for each game because she knew that her children, Josephine, Helen, John, and Connie; their spouses; and other relatives and friends would be at the tailgating site.

Braves Football.

During the Steve McNair era, the Milloys bought a bus and named it "Air Express," and the Covington County (Mount Olive) delegation was always present. The Milloys have not missed a home game since the mid-1980s, and before then they attended almost every game each season, but not every game. A poem was presented at a program on NFL National Signing Day April 22, 1995, in Vicksburg, Mississippi, as people waited to see who Steve and Tim, one of Steve's older brothers, would sign with. (For the poem "A Dedication to Tim and Steve McNair," see Appendix 47.) In 2015, the oldest of the McNair brothers, Fred, who also played at Alcorn, serves as assistant head football coach at the university. This couple, along with many other couples, strongly supported the games in various ways and took pride in enjoying the togetherness and witnessing others having a great time as they exemplified that old Alcorn spirit.

The Department of Health, Physical Education and Recreation received a fitness grant through the specific efforts of alumnus Dr. Garry Lewis, a faculty member in the department. A health and wellness fair is also held annually coordinated by Cassandra Thompson, the department's administrative assistant.

Buildings, stadiums, and floors were named after selected alumni/coaches during recent years. The baseball stadium was named after Willie "Rat" McGowan, a retired living legend who served Alcorn for forty years. Coach McGowan was a four-year letterman in football, received all-conference honors in each of his four seasons, and was named Most Valuable Player.

Jack Spinks–Marino Casem Stadium.

He was the recipient of the first Jack Spinks Award in 1968. He retired having garnished 702 victories. He was the longest-tenured coach in the SWAC, receiving the SWAC Coach of the Year award four times, and was named to the Alcorn Hall of Fame in 1998.

The baseball field was named in honor of the late William "Bill" Foster, one of the finest left-handed pitchers in Negro National League history. Foster was elected to the National Baseball Hall of Fame March 5, 1996. He served as dean of men and head baseball coach at Alcorn from 1960 until his death in 1978. Coach Marino Casem's name was added to Jack Spinks Stadium. Coach Casem was known as the "Godfather" and left Alcorn in 1986 to become athletics director at Southern University in Baton Rouge. (For more about Coaches Willie "Rat" McGowan, Coach William "Bill" Foster, and Marino Casem, see *Against Great Odds: The History of Alcorn State University*.)

Occasionally, former Alcorn athletes return to Mississippi and host camps for youth. One example includes but is not limited to the Green Bay Packers' Donald Driver, who also won the *Dancing with the Stars* Season 14 Mirror Ball Trophy. The *Philadelphia Inquiry* (1994) wrote that Alcorn had "a gritty football team that sent 68 players to the National Football League . . . which was an achievement for a small school in a rural area of Mississippi." (For professional athletes that attended Alcorn, see Appendix 48.) The A-Club has been very devoted in addressing and supporting the initiatives of Alcorn sports through various initiatives. (For the history of the A-Club, see Appendix 49.)

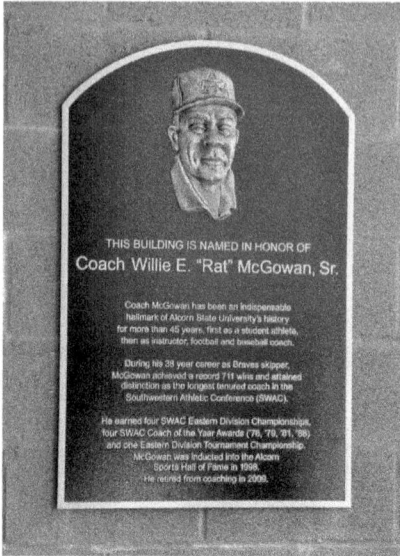

Plaque naming the baseball stadium in honor of Willie E. "Rat" McGowan Sr.

Plaque naming the baseball field in honor of William Hendrick "Bill" Foster.

The 1871 Club was introduced to alumni at the cost of $1,871 per year, per member. The club has thirty-two seats and twelve swivel bar stools that provide an excellent view of the field. It has food and beverage services and private restroom facilities, and includes reserve parking services and amenities and benefits such as a distinctive 24KT gold lapel pin, a membership certificate, an 1871 Club car decal, a members-only embroidered polo shirt, a free gift at each game, recognition in and a copy of the football program book, VIP parking preferred purchaser, weather-protected (priority) seating, gourmet catering and select beverage options, in-suite HD flat-screen televisions, coat closet/coat check, charitable tax deduction, invitations to club-member-only events, and priority to purchase classic game tickets, away-game football tickets, and single-game home football tickets. Several alumni have joined this prestigious club. Vice President Marcus Ward and his staff work untiringly through the Division of Institutional Advancement coordinating the efforts of the 1871 Club and other university foundation initiatives and have experienced continuous success.

Alcorn has had several athletic directors during the past years, including two females who served as interim directors at selected points during the transitions—alumna LLJuna Weir, who is currently director of Educational Equity and Inclusion/Title IX coordinator, and Brenda T. Square, who is currently the director for Auxiliary Services. The head coaches for the various

"Enjoy the suite life at Spinks-Casem Stadium"

WWW.ALCORN.EDU/FOUNDATION

1871 CLUB

THANK YOU 2013 MEMBERS!!!

DR. KENNETH BEAL	DR. W. B. HOPSON, JR.	MR. MARCUS WARD
DR. NORRIS EDNEY	MR. WILBERT JONES	MR. MALVIN WILLIAMS, JR.
MR. ROBERT GAGE IV	MR. WILLIE "RAT" MCGOWAN	MRS. EXIE WILLIAMSON
MR. JAMES HOPSON	MRS. ANNIE OWENS	MR. HARPER WILSON
MRS. PAT HOPSON	MS. E. CHERYL PONDER	

MR. MARINO "THE GODFATHER" CASEM
MRS. VERNA JACK "THE RIPPER" SPINKS
DR. M. CHRISTOHER BROWN II

Membership in the 1871 Club provides the perfect way to enjoy Braves football with all the amenities and luxury you would expect. Club membership is ideal for those who expect the absolute best. The Club offers unsurpassed benefits and deluxe amenities that redefine comfort.

MEMBERSHIP:

$1,871.00 per seat/per year

(includes food, beverages and reserved parking space)

Must be football season ticket holders

FOUNDATION@ALCORN.EDU   601.877.6693

1871 Club.

sports—soccer, softball, volleyball, baseball, basketball, football, cross country, track and field, golf, tennis, and bowling—have all served the university committedly through the years.

As indicated in the previous history, *Against Great Odds: The History of Alcorn State University* (1994), the university was a part of the Capitol City

Zelmarine Murphy, also known as "Mama Brave."

Classic for years; however, Alcorn declared independence from the Capitol City Classic in 2012. This move was favored by most Alcornites because it ensured more revenue for Alcorn State University. This decision was made after much debate and dialogue among the stakeholders involved during the Brown administration.

One alumna, Zelmarine Murphy, became known among athletes and others as "Mama Brave." It actually started more than twenty years ago during the Washington administration, but became more prevalent in later years. When attending games today on and off campus, she is referred to by some athletes as "Mama Brave." When walking into a hotel where the team is staying, a yell usually surfaces from some players acknowledging her, and she hears, "Hey, Mama Brave!" One football player said, "She be at all the games . . . she's just like our mama." Murphy has been a continuous supporter of Alcorn, along with many other alumni, in the areas of athletics, academics, and other aspects of university operation.

Alcornites love to get together and talk about how Alcorn made them what they are today and give praise to their alma mater continuously. They wear purple and gold with pride. Many alumni attend Purple and Gold Day annually in Jackson, Mississippi, to advocate to state representatives and senators for full and adequate funding and support. Janice Gibson, alumnus Robert Simmons, and other alumni dedicate themselves to this being a great day for Alcornites. Many activities take place on that day, including special presentations and a lunch where interaction with legislators and other state officials take place. (For the 2015 Purple and Gold Day agenda, see Appendix 50.) Another annual recognition for athletes is the Sports Hall of Fame ceremony, where alumni are honored in selected areas for their roles in athletic success. (For Sports Hall of Fame inductees, see Appendix 51.)

Alcorn was and is fortunate to have had alumni serve in significant positions and be a voice at the table in many situations for Alcorn, including athletics, academics, and others; for example, Representatives or Senators Alyce G. Clarke, Albert Butler, Willie Simmons, Karl Gibbs, Gregory Holloway Sr., Chuck Middleton, Orlando Paden, and Adrienne Wooten in the legislature and all Alcornites who have served in the legislature in some capacity. Charles McClelland, chairman of the College Board, was the 2012 Alcornite of the Year and has received many other awards and recognitions. Their voices were heard often in the boardrooms and were clear when it came to the well-being of Alcorn State University. Our nineteenth president, Alfred Rankins Jr., was also a positive voice for Alcorn in his role as deputy commissioner for Academic and Student Affairs for the Mississippi Board of Trustees of State Institutions of Higher Learning. It is evident that Alcorn's alumni have always qualified and served in positions that ensured continuous success against great odds in support of excellence.

Through the years, alumni faced many challenges. One of the biggest challenges was a proposal to restructure the National Alumni Association. A very ambitious, hardworking, and committed alumnus, Samuel Washington, and a dedicated committee presented a proposal to restructure/reorganize the National Alumni Association for better operations. The proposal was submitted, approved, debated, and interpreted in many different ways. After going back and forth with discussion, the plan was never implemented, although concerns had surfaced for years regarding moving the association to a new and higher level of excellence.

Today, more than 25,000 alumni throughout the nation enjoy the fruits of having received a quality education from Alcorn State University, named HBCU of the Year in 2012. Although the university has struggled against great odds, alumni have proven that they can succeed against these odds as long as they continue to support excellence in all of their endeavors. One of these endeavors to ensure support was through the Tom Joyner Foundation Matching Challenge, which was very valuable to Alcorn in enhancing fundraising efforts among alumni. Through the Tom Joyner Foundation, Alcorn was named School of the Month in November 2013. Not only do Alcornites have a positive image of their alma mater, others' opinions are powerful as well. (For opinions about Mississippi's best-kept secret, see Appendix 52.)

One writer put it this way in talking about Alcorn: "You have the choice to go wherever you want to go. There are many ways of getting there. Begin by believing in God! Believe in his future for you! Then you can make it." Many throughout Alcorn's history made that choice and kept God at the head of their lives and made it.

Additional Noteworthy Historical Facts and Photos

There have been so many significant occurrences at Alcorn since 1994, it is impossible to detail them all; however, this list is an effort to capture some of the other historical facts and photos, not necessarily in a particular order of occurrence.

- Alcorn received 100 percent priority accountability from the State Auditor's Office (2002).
- George White, a 2009 graduate of Alcorn, was appointed by President Obama as US Marshal for the Southern District of Mississippi.
- Alcorn received the Higher Education Excellence in Diversity Award (2012).
- An Alcorn Pilgrimage honored Hiram Rhodes Revels by visiting and placing a wreath on his grave (2013).
- Alcorn ranked #1 in social mobility and research among all Mississippi public comprehensive, regional, and master's universities (2013).
- Alcorn hosted the first Mission Mississippi "Glowing for Christ" church service in Oakland Memorial Chapel (2013), coordinated by the organization's president, alumnus Rev. Neddie Winters.
- Alcorn was a winner in the Retool Your School Program from the Home Depot Mid-South Region.
- Director of Inventory Jerry Sims received the first Bill Pope Property Award from the Mississippi Association of Governmental Purchasing and Property Agents (MAGPPA).
- Alcorn and the Natchez Festival of Music produced the opera *Porgy and Bess* by George Gershwin in Natchez, Mississippi (2005).

- Alcorn students placed second in the Quiz Bowl competition and received $25,000 from the Honda Campus All-Star Challenge (2008).
- The Department of Mass Communications received the Statewide Silver Award for its newscast (2008).
- Alcorn helped raise funds for alumnus Jerry Brooks in his battle with a rare disease, ALS, with Alcorn's president, Alfred Rankins Jr., accepting the Ice Bucket Challenge.
- Kimberly Morgan was the first and only Alcorn graduate to be crowned Miss Mississippi (2007).
- Dr. Chandra Minor became Mississippi's first African American female orthodontist.
- Alcorn received first place in the 2014 Broadcast Sports Program's Spirit Story Category in the Mississippi Associated Press Broadcasters Contest.
- Alcorn alumna Brittany Noble-Jones was one of the first reporters to interview Michael Brown's mother after the controversial Ferguson, Missouri, shooting, and was named Journalist of the Year by the National Association of Black Journalists (2015).
- Alcorn alumna Dr. Jacqueline Walters is the founder of the 50 Shades of Pink Foundation.
- Dr. Willie Fred Jackson and LaPlose Jackson are the oldest surviving former employees of Alcorn State University.
- Summer school started at Alcorn for college credit in 1924.
- Alcorn first became accredited in 1926.
- Alumna LaShunda Anderson was the first African American woman to receive a doctorate at Louisiana State University in agronomy, environmental planning and management.
- Alcorn student Tracy Catchings was recognized by the Mississippi Association of Colleges for Excellence in Teacher Education from Alcorn State University (2012).
- Two Alcorn students, Brandy Johnson and Woodrow Price, served as state presidents of the Student National Education Association.
- Nissan donated two high-tech robots to the Department of Advanced Technologies (2013).
- Wiley Jones, longtime business manager for Alcorn State University, was the first black from the state of Mississippi to serve on the Board of Directors of the Southern Association of College and University Business Officers (SACUBO).
- Alcorn opened a new Technology Transfer Center in Mound Bayou, Mississippi.
- Alcorn students transition to Penn State to complete a doctorate degree in the Alcorn State–Penn State Bridges to the Doctorate Program.
- Alcorn's School of AREAS displays a mounted two-headed calf for learning purposes that was donated to Alcorn in 2014. The animal died shortly after being born on an Adams County cattle farm.

- Alcorn was recognized by the US Census Bureau for the census efforts and helping to paint a new portrait of America.
- In 2010, the Vicksburg Hospital Medical Foundation supported local Alcorn students in the areas of chemistry, physics, and biology with a cumulative financial impact of $350,000. The foundation also supported other areas under certain eligibility requirements.
- The Farmers Market Voucher Project originated with Alcorn's Extension Program and was conducted in partnership with the Mississippi Department of Agriculture and Commerce.
- Alcorn sponsors a Summer Ecology Workshop for K–12 teachers, annually coordinated by Dr. Alex D. W. Acholonu.
- Alcorn is the only HBCU in Mississippi with a building for the Wesley Foundation, where students retreat for fellowship, prayer, and worship.
- Alcorn was the first university to receive endowment money from the Ayers desegregation settlement.
- Alcorn alumna Alyce G. Clarke was the first black female in the Mississippi House of Representatives, representing District 69 in Hinds County.
- In 2002, Alcorn was recorded in the *Black Voices Quarterly* magazine as having the highest percentage of athletes to graduate.
- The 2012 graduate students were the first graduating class to actually be hooded during the commencement exercises.
- Alcorn's School of Business was granted its first official initial accreditation by the Accreditation Council for Business Schools and Programs (ACBSP) in 2010.
- Alcorn hosted the GEAR-UP Mississippi Program for tenth graders in Mississippi several times. The program provides enriching experiences to students attending an approved GEAR-UP high school in Mississippi.
- Hilton Miller '98, from Pike County, was appointed federal administrative judge in New York and had previously received a lifetime federal administrative appointment in Ohio, making him one of the youngest federal judges in the nation.
- Alcorn's Fire Department received a new state-of-the-art fire truck.
- Dr. Robert Sizemore, biology professor at Alcorn, was named one of the editors of the *Journal of Cell and Developmental Biology*, a peer-reviewed journal and one of the nation's most outstanding publications in the discipline.
- Dorothy Cole-Gary '81 was selected National Head Start Association Administrator of the Year in 2012.
- Alcorn was among five colleges and universities that were the first-time recipients of the Plant Genome Research Award advancing the understanding of plants of economic importance such as corn, rice, soybeans, tomatoes, and wheat.
- African American scholar and former Alcorn teacher George B. Vashon was denied admission to the Allegheny County Bar because of race; after 163 years,

justice was served through the efforts of his great-grandson, which led to winning recognition for Vashon from the Pennsylvania Supreme Court.

- Alcorn won the 2010 SWAC Softball Championship.
- Alcorn's laundry closed in 2013 and services were outsourced.
- The MBA program and the nursing program housed in Natchez, Mississippi, offer selected degrees through distance learning.
- The Vicksburg Expansion Program offers selected courses through distance learning.
- Alcorn and Chamberlain Hunt Academy held a joint Founders Day Celebration in 2013.
- Roberta Laing received the Golden Opportunity Scholar Award from the Golden Opportunity Institute of American Society of Agronomy (ASA), the Soil Science Society of America (SSA), and the Crop and Social Sciences of America (CSSA).
- Phillip West was the first black mayor in Natchez, Mississippi, since Reconstruction.
- The Alumni House Bed and Breakfast opened on campus in 2012.
- Alcorn is now a proud brewer of Starbucks Coffee.

For more noteworthy historical facts and photos, see *Against Great Odds: The History of Alcorn State University.*

President George H. W. Bush delivering the Commencement address in 1989.

Jack Parnell, deputy secretary of agriculture, pictured at the Poultry Research Facility with Dr. Samuel Donald during a visit to campus.

State Representative Alyce G. Clarke (second from left) pictured with Dr. Rudolph Waters, vice president; Majorie Sellers, instructor and senior class sponsor; and Emanuel Barnes, dean of Student Affairs.

Planting of a magnolia tree as part of the 1890 land-grant colleges and universities centennial celebration at Alcorn.

Reverend Joseph Bartee at the 1993 football stadium dedication.

Walter Washington and his wife, Carolyn.

Groundbreaking ceremony for the new Extension and Research Complex held December 11, 1996.

Reverend Jesse Jackson and Congressman Bennie Thompson visit Alcorn.

The Honors Student Organization, founded in 1971, promotes leadership, citizenship, and academic excellence. Its purpose is to encourage both academic and scholarly achievement as well as facilitate meaningful service.

President Rankins and family.

AFTERWORD

As we look to the future of Alcorn State University, with great anticipation of continued success, Alcorn has survived for almost 145 years and will continue to survive. As a group of protesters chanted during an Ayers case rally, "We don't believe He (God) brought us this far to leave us!" (*Against Great Odds: The History of Alcorn State University*). Today, in 2015, Alcorn has come too far to go back.

Administrators, faculty, staff, students, alumni, friends, and local, state, and national supporters and all concerned must continue to band together and ensure that Alcorn will continue to succeed against great odds. Great odds that were obstacles in the past, that are obstacles today, and that will continue to be obstacles tomorrow will always be present, but, together, we can overcome them and continue to progress as an institution.

For example, Alcorn has struggled to receive adequate funding since 1871 and this will continue, but Alcorn will succeed; a proposal to downsize Alcorn and other universities will continue to surface, but Alcorn will succeed; the mandates of the Ayers case may never be fully realized or implemented, but Alcorn will succeed; the original plan for the growth of Alcorn and its land-grant function through the wealthiest funding formula may never be fully allocated, but Alcorn will succeed; all capital improvements for Alcorn may never be fully witnessed, but Alcorn will always succeed.

The love and devotion today are as strong as they were 144 years ago. Young men and women will continue to arrive on the campus seeking wisdom and knowledge for a better life and future for years and years to come as we look toward a prosperous and successful future. The tradition of success will not fold regardless of the struggle and regardless of the difficulty of the road being traveled because Alcornites once crossed a cattle gap to get to the campus!

APPENDIXES

1   University Goals and Core Values

2   University Mission and Vision Statements

3   Minutes from Sunday School Assemblies in 1959 and 1960

4   Minutes from Meetings with the President in 1921 and 1922

5   Accreditations

6   Why We Love Alcorn: Top 100 Reasons

7   University Buildings

8   Athletics Coaches as of 2015

9   Inaugural Programs of the Last Five Permanent Presidents

10 Mississippi Institutions of Higher Learning Board of Trustees at the Time of Inauguration of the Last Five Permanent Presidents

11 Public and Private Contributions to the ASU Foundation, Inc. in 2013

12 Miss Alcorn State University Queens

13 Student Government Association Presidents

14 HEADWAE Award Recipients

15 Intellectual Renewal Grant Recipients

16 Student Organizations

17 Quality Enhancement Plan

18 *Simply Sharing* Publications

19 Mid-Winter Conferences

20 1928 Commencement Day Program

21 Award of Excellence Recipients

22 Commencement Speakers

23 1952 Summer Commencement Program

24 Presidential Award of Excellence Recipients

25 Letter from Commissioner Hank Bounds

26 Academic Schools and Major Support Divisions as of 2015

27 Leadership of Permanent, Interim, and Acting Presidents from 1994 to 2015

28 2014–2015 Four-Year Career Plan

29 Alcorn Enrollment by Ethnicity, Gender, Residency, Level, Age, and Full-Time Equivalent

30 Academic Degree Programs as of 2015

31 2015 University Calendar for June

32 1888 University Calendar

33 2012 J. D. Boyd Library Annual Statistics

34 Analysis of Operating Budget Summary of IHL Appropriations

35 Fall 2013–Spring 2014 Tuition

36 Alcorn State University National Alumni Association History

37 Alcorn State University National Alumni Association Chapter Presidents as of 2015

38 Alcorn State University National Alumni Association Presidents

39 Alcorn State University National Alumni Association National Officers from 2008 to 2015

40 Hall of Honor Inductees

41 Alcornite of the Year Recipients

42 Golden Classes

43 Excerpt from "A Desire to Educate"

44 "Alcorn Spirit" Song

45 Alcorn Quilt Centerpiece

46 Alcorn Alumni Day Agenda

47 A Dedication to Tim and Steve McNair

48 Professional Athletes

49 History of the A-Club

50 2015 Purple and Gold Day Agenda

51 Sports Hall of Fame Inductees

52 Mississippi's Best Kept Secret

1. University Goals and Core Values

Goals

Student-Centered

Offer students an engaging, transformative learning and living environment, empowering them to become globally competitive, socially and environmentally sensitive, and technologically competent leaders.

Academic Excellence

Enhance academic excellence and become nationally recognized as a premier comprehensive land grant university offering engaging intellectual experiences and collaborative research opportunities.

Shared Governance and Professionalism

Assess processes to ensure that honest and transparent communications, merit-based systems, and accountability prevail.

Enhancement of Infrastructure and Technology

Develop and implement a strategy to ensure that the technology and infrastructure exist to achieve the University's vision and mission.

Enhancement and Diversification of Resources

Enhance resources and diversify sources of funding through partnerships, creative fundraising strategies, leveraging its intellectual property, and entrepreneurship.

Diversity

Engage all stakeholders in developing an environment which embraces diversity of thought and encourages the acceptance of differences.

Community Outreach and Engagement

Strengthen community outreach and engagement efforts by encouraging continuing education, expanding community partnerships, and developing new service and outreach programs.

Core Values

Student-Centered

Our students are our greatest assets. We value every student. We encourage leadership development by mentoring our students and enabling them to participate in our decision-making processes.

Academic Excellence

We uphold the highest, rigorous academic standards. We expect excellent scholarship, preparation, and performance from every student and faculty member.

Shared Governance

The University provides an open and honest environment. Communications are thorough, truthful and present all of the facts. We value transparency in decision-making and communications. We encourage every stakeholder to be aware of our opportunities, challenges, and resources. Policies are merit-based, fair, and broadly communicated.

Professionalism

Everyone accepts full responsibility for personal performance and actions, maintains high moral standards, and complies with effective performance appraisal processes. We expect honesty, objectivity, and fairness in all transactions among our stakeholders. We pride ourselves on our strong commitment to a rigorous work ethic.

Diversity

We value the global nature of our society. Everyone is respected. We promote diversity of thought and encourage the acceptance of cultural diversity. We believe that diversity stimulates a dynamic intellectual environment, creativity, and innovation. We believe that everyone has something to offer.

Outreach, Engagement, and Community Service

We are committed to improving communities, locally and globally. We encourage students, faculty, and staff to apply their knowledge to build stronger, healthier, economically viable communities.

Institutional Pride

We treasure our legacy, our commitment to excellence, our development of leaders, and our service to others. These attributes imbue us with great pride in Alcorn State University. We respect the assets and resources of our University and use them prudently. We provide our students, faculty, and staff with the necessary infrastructure and technology to succeed while maintaining a safe, secure, and nurturing environment.

2. UNIVERSITY MISSION AND VISION STATEMENTS

The mission and vision statements for the university were revised and approved by the IHL Board of Trustees (March 2009).

MISSION STATEMENT

Alcorn State University, a Historically Black College and University, is a comprehensive land-grant institution that celebrates a rich heritage with a diverse student and faculty population. The University emphasizes intellectual development and lifelong learning through the integration of diverse pedagogies, applied and basic research, cultural and professional programs, public service and outreach, while providing access to globally competitive academic and research programs. Alcorn strives to prepare graduates to be well-rounded future leaders of high character and to be successful in the global marketplace of the 21st century.

VISION STATEMENT

Alcorn State University will become a premier comprehensive land-grant university. It will develop diverse students into globally competitive leaders and apply scientific research, through collaborative partnerships that benefit the surrounding communities, states, nation, and world.

3. Minutes from Sunday School Assemblies in 1959 and 1960

Sunday October 11, 1959

The Alcorn A&M College Sunday School assembled at 9:30 conducted by Mr. Monroe Ballard. Song - Blessed assurance, Jesus is mine, Scripture from 1st Corinthen and prayer. Song - Just as I am, without one plea. Then the classes past to their respective places for the lesson discussion.

The report of the classes:

Class	mem. pres.	collection	taught by
Primary	2	$.30	Jessie James
Freshman	72	3.81	Delphine Williams
Sophomore	48	1.85	(mr) Gerald Clay
Junior	43	1.79	Lue Ella Jorden
Senior	22	1.94	Mae Lia Hart

Total present 187
Total collection $8.69

The program supposing to be render by the senior class was ommitted today.

We will be dismiss will a song and the benediction.

Mr. Monroe Ballard, Supt
Abbie Lena Jones, Sec.
(Miss) Erlexia Lewis, Piania

Sunday   October 23, 1960

    The Alcorn A. + M. College Sunday School
was called to order by the Superintendent
Mr. Emmanuel Lang at 9:45 A.M.
The denation was as follows:
Song.... Jesus Keep Me Near the Cross
Responsive Reading and Prayer
   by Mr. Emmanuel Lang
Song.... Fairest Lord Jesus

The classes then passed to their respec-
tive places for discussion of the
lesson entitled "Our Need of God."
    The Report of the Classes:
The Primary Class: members present
7   Collection $.31   taught by
Miss Dora Prater
   The Freshman Class: members present
56 Collection $2.30   taught by
Miss Shirley Thompson.
   The Sophomore Class: members present
32 Collection $1.25 taught by Miss
Oline Young
   The Junior Class: members present
25; Collection $1.22 taught by Miss
Alice Hillard.
   The Senior Class: members present
21 Collection $.91   taught by Mr.
Andrew Dupré Jr.
   Total present — 141
   Collection — $6.00, $5.85

4. MINUTES FROM MEETINGS
WITH THE PRESIDENT IN 1921 AND 1922

2

Alcorn A and M. College. Alcorn Miss. May 16, 1921.

The Faculty of Alcorn A and M. College met on the evening of the above named date pursuant to adjournment, with Dr. L.J. Rowan presiding

Prayer was offered by Prof. J.A. Ramsey.

Minutes of the last meeting were read by Secty. and on motion by Mrs. R.S. Grossley the same was adopted.

Then the Report of the auditor for the month of April 1921 per report. On motion by Prof. J.C. Holmes the report was adopted.

Report on Senior Banquet was presented by Prof. J.A. Ramsey, as to amount spent for same. The amount was reported was fifty dollars & 03/—. On motion of Dr. A.A. Gordon the report was adopted, with the understanding that the above amount to be proportioned out among the members of the Faculty. The apportionment to each member one dollar + 27/— and Mrs. Garrett requested to collect same.

There being no further business before the Faculty. We adjourned.

L.J. Rowan   President.

A.D. Snodgrass   Secty.

49

Alcorn A and M College. Alcorn Miss May 5 - 1922

On the above named date the Faculty of Alcorn
College met pursuant to adjournment with Dr L J Rowan
in the chair. Prayer was offered by Dr. A D Snodgrass
Minutes of previous meeting were read by Sec.
and on motion by Prof. J.C. Holmes the minutes
were adopted, the minutes of the meeting before
the last, having been deferred, were now read
and on motion by Rev. M. N. Craig, the same were
adopted.

The then listened to Miss Hall report for April
1922 (See report.) On motion by Prof. J.C. Holmes
the same was adopted.

The of Miss Marcus Harrall versus Mr Nathaniel
Williams for unbecoming conduct at Dining Hall
was brought before the Faculty. The testimony showed
that Miss Harrall had used very abusive language
to Williams — and that Williams had slapped Harrall.
After due consideration the Faculty Indefinitely
suspended Williams on motion by Dr. R. A. Gordon
Prof. J.C. Holmes made motion to Indefinitely
Suspend Marcus Harrall. On motion by
Prof. P. R. Conner motion was tabled —
A. D Snodgrass gave notice that the motion
to table would be taken up at next meeting

No further business Faculty
adjourned —

L J Rowan President
A D Snodgrass Sec.

5. ACCREDITATIONS

Alcorn State University is accredited by the Commission on Colleges of the Southern Association of Colleges and Schools (SACS) to award the Associate, Bachelors, Masters, and Specialist in Education degrees.

- The Bachelor of Science in Nutrition and Dietetics is accredited by the American Dietetics Association (ADA).
- The Associate of Science in Nursing degree, the Bachelor of Science in Nursing degree, and the Master of Science in Nursing degree programs are accredited by the Accreditation Commission for Education in Nursing (ACEN).
- The School of Business is accredited by the Accreditation Council for Business Schools and Programs (ACBSP).
- Alcorn State University is an accredited institutional member of the National Association of Schools of Music (NASM).
- Alcorn is an accredited institutional member of the National Association of Industrial Technology (NAIT).
- Alcorn is an accredited institutional member of the American Association of Family and Consumer Sciences (AAFCS).
- The teacher education program is currently accredited by the National Council for the Accreditation of Teacher Education (NCATE). The upcoming approval of the new accreditation will then designate Alcorn's teacher education program to be accredited by the Council for the Accreditation of Educator Preparation (CAEP).
- The Bachelor of Science in Social Work is accredited by the Council on Social Work Education (CSWE).

6. WHY WE LOVE ALCORN: TOP 100 REASONS

7. UNIVERSITY BUILDINGS

Building Name	Year Constructed
Administration Building	1929
Administration Classroom	1977
Agricultural Science Building	1977
Airstrip Building	1974
Alice Tanner Hall	1955
Amenities Building (renamed Barnes and Noble at Alcorn State University)	2011
Apartment "A"	1961
Apartment "B"	1961
Baseball Stadium (renamed Willie E. "Rat" McGowan Sr. Baseball Stadium and William "Bill" Foster Field)	2007
Beef Facility (renamed Johnnie B. Collins Beef Research Facility)	1984
Belle Lettres Hall	1830
Biology Lab	1976
Biotechnology Building	2008
Boar & Sow Pen	1971
Bowles Hall	1929
Burrus Hall	1968
Campus Union Building	1963
Central Rec. & Storage	1961
Cottage "D"	1961
Cottage D-2	1961
Cottage D-3	1961
Cottage D-4	1961
Cottage D-5	1961
Cottage D-7	1961
Cottage D-8	1961
Cottage D-9	1961
Cottage D-10	1961
Cottage D-12	1965
Cottage D-13	1965
Cottage D-15	1965
Cottage D-16	1965

Cottage D-17	1965
Cottage D-21	1955
Cottage D-22	1955
Dairy (renamed David C. Carter Dairy)	1967
Dining Hall (renamed the William H. Bell Dining Hall)	1953
Dormitory "A"	1961
Dormitory "AR"	1961
Dormitory II	1830
Dormitory III	1830
Dr. Clinton Bristow Jr. Dining Facility	2008
Eunice Powell Hall	1955
Extension and Research Building	1999
Facilities Management	1996
Faculty Garden (renamed Matt Thomas, Jr., Garden Apartments)	1972
Farm Vehicles Building	1969
Farrowing House	1971
Fine Arts Building	1963
Gym & Auditorium (renamed E. E. Simmons Gymnasium)	1959
Harmon Hall	1929
Hay Barn	1981
Health & P. E. Complex (renamed Davey L. Whitney Classroom Health, Physical Education, and Recreation Complex)	1975
Home Management House (renamed Dorothy Gordon Gray Home Management House)	1956
Honors Dormitory	2001
Industrial Technology	1981
Infirmary (renamed Felix Dunn Infirmary)	1962
J. D. Boyd Library	1969
Lanier Hall	1939
Laundromat	1987
Laundry	1953
Library and Science Building	1959
Maintenance Building	1928
Math and Science Building	1997
Mechanical Arts Building	1959
Medgar Wiley Evers Heritage Village Complex	2010
Men's Tower (renamed W. S. Demby Men's Tower)	1973

Microbial Poultry Lab	1974
New Men's Dormitory (renamed Albert L. Lott Hall)	1962
New President's Home	1999
New Women's Dormitory (renamed Mabel Thomas Hall)	1962
Nursing School (renamed Cora S. Balmat School of Nursing)	1985
Oakland Chapel	1830
Orchard Building	1994
Poultry Facility (renamed Luther Alexander/E. S. Burke Poultry Research Laboratory)	1987
President's Home	1830
Press Box	1981
Quonset 20 x 96	1961
Quonset 20 x 96	1961
Quonset 20 x 96	1961
Revels Hall	1967
Robinson Hall	1965
Rowan Model House	1830
Safety Center (Police and Fire Station)	2000
School of Nursing Dormitory	1998
Service Station	1947
Silo (14 x 30) S-1	1953
Stadium Dress, Facility	1981
Storage Building (Nursing)	1986
Vegetable Shed	1971
Vehicle Storage & Machine	1967
Water Treatment Plant	1968
Women's Tower (renamed Cleopatra D. Thompson Women's Tower)	1973

8. Athletics Coaches as of 2015

Baseball	
Bretton Richardson	Head Baseball Coach
Oscar Reed	Assistant Baseball Coach
Frank Schaeffer	Pitching Coach
Men's Basketball	
Montez Robinson	Head Men's Basketball Coach
Terrance Chatman	Assistant Men's Basketball Coach
Alexander Ireland	Assistant Men's Basketball Coach
Cabral Huff	Assistant Men's Basketball Coach
Women's Basketball	
Courtney G. Pruitt	Head Women's Basketball Coach
Alexis Green	Assistant Women's Basketball Coach
Ta'Neil Lewis	Assistant Women's Basketball Coach
Football	
Jay Hopson	Head Football Coach
Fred Kaiss	Offensive Coordinator
Tony Pecoraro	Defensive Coordinator
Fred McNair	Assistant Head Coach/Quarterbacks Coach
Cedric Thomas	Defensive Back Coach
Wes Turner	Linebackers Coach/Videographer/Football Ops
Derek Nicholson	Defensive Line Coach
Shannon Harris	Wide Receivers Coach
Ryan Stanchek	Offensive Line Coach
AJ Antonescu	Tight Ends Coach
Kenry Tolbert	Graduate Assistant, Defensive Line
William Prince	Equipment Manager/Strength and Conditioning
Roderick Young	Athletic Trainer
Men's Golf	
Andrew MacBean	Head Golf Coach

Women's Soccer	
Samuel Dr. Nwaneri	Head Soccer Coach, Interim
Softball	
Josef Rankin	Head Softball Coach
Men's and Women's Tennis	
Anthony Dodgen	Men's and Women's Head Tennis Coach
Kersten Vanem	Graduate Assistant
Men's and Women's Track and Field/Cross Country	
Brian Johnson	Head Men's and Women's Track and Field/Cross Country Coach
Volleyball	
JarQuita Copeland	Head Volleyball Coach

9. INAUGURAL PROGRAMS OF THE LAST FIVE PERMANENT PRESIDENTS

THE
INAUGURATION
OF THE
PRESIDENT

ALCORN AGRICULTURAL AND MECHANICAL COLLEGE
LORMAN, MISSISSIPPI
MARCH 6, 1971

ALCORN AGRICULTURAL AND MECHANICAL COLLEGE

INAUGURATION OF

WALTER WASHINGTON

AS THE

FIFTEENTH PRESIDENT

OF THE COLLEGE

March 6, 1971

2:30 p.m.

College Gymnasium

Lorman, Mississippi

GREETINGS

The Honorable John Bell Williams
Governor, State of Mississippi

The Honorable Charles L. Sullivan
Lieutenant Governor, State of Mississippi

Elliot Travis
President, Alcorn Student Government Association

E. T. Hawkins
President, National Alcorn Alumni Association

Porter L. Fortune
*Chairman of the Presidents' Council and
Chancellor, University of Mississippi*

William D. McCain
President, University of Southern Mississippi

John M. Claunch
President, George Peabody College for Teachers

Calvin S. White
Dean of Instruction, Alcorn A. & M. College

MUSIC

Introduction to Act Three from Lohengrin . . . Wagner-Drumm
The Alcorn A. & M. College Wind Ensemble

THE INAUGURAL ADDRESS

Felix C. Robb
Director, Southern Association of Colleges and Schools

THE INVESTITURE OF THE PRESIDENT

M. M. Roberts

Board of Trustees, Institutions of Higher Learning, State of Mississippi

Assisted By
E. E. Thrash
*Executive Secretary and Director
Board of Trustees, Institutions of Higher Learning, State of Mississippi*

THE INAUGURAL RESPONSE

Walter Washington
President of The College

MUSIC

Ride On, King Jesus . . . . arr. Harry T. Burleigh
Dorothy J. Allen, *Contralto*
Sophomore Music Major

ANNOUNCEMENTS

ALMA MATER
(Audience)
ALCORN ODE

Beneath the shade of giant trees,
  Fanned by a balmy southern breeze
Thy classic Walls have dared to stand
A giant thou art in learning's band;
O, Alcorn, dear, our mother, hear
  Thy Name We praise, thy Name we sing.

Thy name thy sons have honored far;
  A crown of gems thy daughters are;
When country called, her flag to bear,
The Gold and Purple answered, "here"
  O, Alcorn dear, our mother, hear
  Thy Name we praise, thy Name we sing.

Far as our race thy clan shall need—
  So far to progress thou shalt lead
Thy sons, with clashing arms of trades;
In useful arts full garbed, thy maids;
  O Alcorn, dear, we proudly bear
  Thy standard on to victory.

                                        —Mrs. J. S. Himes

BENEDICTION

The Most Reverend Joseph B. Brunini
Bishop, Natchez-Jackson Diocese

RECESSIONAL

Grand Processional . . . Don Haddad
The Alcorn A. & M. College Wind Ensemble

The Inauguration of
*CLINTON **BRISTOW**, JR.*
Sixteenth President of
Alcorn State University
October 18, 1996

PROLOGUE CONCERT

Didn't My Lord Deliver Daniel   arr. Carl Hawood
University Concert Choir
William J. Borovina, Director

Sonata No. 3 in D Major, K. 381   Wolfgang A. Mozart
Allegro
Andante
Allegro molto
·Tony Gordon and Donzell Lee, Piano

The Lord Is My Light   Olly Speaks
Ernest A. Fields, Baritone
Tony Gordon, Piano

THE INAUGURAL CEREMONY

Rudolph E. Waters, Executive Vice President, Presiding

PROCLAMATION FANFARE
ACADEMIC PROCESSIONAL

Academic Procession   Clifton Williams
University Wind Ensemble
Samuel S. Griffin, Conductor

PRESENTATION OF COLORS

ROTC Color Guard

INVOCATION

The Reverend Neddie Winters
Pastor, Hope Springs Missionary Baptist Church
Jackson, Mississippi

INTRODUCTION OF THE PRESIDENT'S FAMILY
AND SPECIAL GUESTS

GREETINGS

The Honorable Eric Clark
Secretary of State, State of Mississippi

Maconnia C. Chesser
President, Alcorn Student Government Association

Robert W. Bowles
President, Alcorn National Alumni Association

Walter Washington
President Emeritus, Alcorn State University

Robert C. Khayat
Chairman, Presidents' Council and
Chancellor, University of Mississippi

The Honorable Fred L. Banks, Jr.
Supreme Court Justice, State of Mississippi

Malvin A. Williams
Vice President for Academic Affairs

Belinda R. Havard
President, Faculty Senate

Barbara J. Bailey
President, Staff Senate

Robert B. Donaldson
Public Building Commission, City of Chicago

MUSIC

Glorious Everlasting　　　　　*M. Thomas Cousins*
University Concert Choir
William J. Borovina, Director

INVESTITURE OF THE PRESIDENT
AND
PRESENTATION OF THE UNIVERSITY MEDALLION
Cassie Pennington
Vice President
Board of Trustees of State Institutions of Higher Learning

Assisted By
Thomas D. Layzell
Commissioner of Higher Education
Board of Trustees of State Institutions of Higher Learning

PRESENTATION OF THE PRESIDENT

INAUGURAL ADDRESS
Clinton Bristow, Jr.
President of the University

MUSIC
Music for a Ceremony   John J. Morrissey
University Wind Ensemble
Samuel S. Griffin, Conductor

ANNOUNCEMENTS

THE ALCORN ODE

BENEDICTION
Reverend Winters

FANFARE
ACADEMIC RECESSIONAL
Marche Romaine   Charles Gounod
University Wind Ensemble
Timothy W. Chambers, Conductor

Dr. George E. Ross

PRESIDENTIAL INAUGURATION

Seventeenth President

of

Alcorn State University

The Installation

of

GEORGE EUGENE ROSS

As Seventeenth President of
Alcorn State University

ORDER OF CEREMONY

Presiding, James McDonald, Esq.
President, National Alumni Association

THE ACADEMIC PROCESSION
AND THE PLATFORM PARTY

THE PRESENTATION OF THE COLORS
AND THE NATIONAL ANTHEM

THE INVOCATION
The Reverend Vera Stamps
Director, ASU Wesley Foundation

WELCOME
Inneka Minor
Miss Alcorn State University

CHOIR SELECTION
Alcorn State University Concert Choir

SALUTATIONS
Mr. Johnny Franklin, Education Policy Advisor to the Honorable Haley Barbour,
Governor of the State of Mississippi
Ms. Amy Whitten, President, Board of Trustees,
State Institutions of Higher Education
Mr. Eddie Davenport, President, Student Government Association
Dr. Dickson Idusuyi, President, Faculty Senate
Dr. Gwendolyn Boyd, President, Faculty Assembly
Mrs. Donna Hayden, President, Staff Senate

INVESTITURE OF THE PRESIDENT
AND
PRESENTATION OF THE UNIVERSITY MEDALLION

Dr. Aubrey K. Lucas
Interim Commissioner of Higher Education

Ms. Amy Whitten
President, Mississippi Board of Trustees of State Institutions of Higher Learning

THE INAUGURAL ADDRESS
PRESIDENT GEORGE EUGENE ROSS

THE ALCORN ODE

THE BENEDICTION
Reverend Vera Stamps

RECESSIONAL OF THE PLATFORM PARTY

Following the Inaugural Ceremony, there will be a reception on the upper level of the
Davey L. Whitney Complex

Alcorn Bravery:

ENGAGING POSSIBILITIES,
PURSUING EXCELLENCE

Inauguration

OF THE 18TH PRESIDENT

M. CHRISTOPHER BROWN II, PH.D.

ALCORN STATE UNIVERSITY
CELEBRATING 140 YEARS

THE *Investiture* OF
DR. M. CHRISTOPHER BROWN II
AS THE EIGHTEENTH PRESIDENT OF
ALCORN STATE UNIVERSITY

Dr. Samuel L. White, Presiding
Vice President of Academic Affairs
Alcorn State University

Prelude   **Mr. Tony Gordon**
Organist

THE INAUGURAL PROCESSIONAL
    War March of the Priests (from Athalie), Felix Mendelsohn-Bartholdy
         Alcorn State University Symphonic Band
Samuel Griffin, Conductor

POSTING OF COLORS   **ASU ROTC Braves Battalion**

THE HERITAGE ANTHEM   **Audience**
"Lift Every Voice and Sing" (by James Weldon Johnson)

Lift every voice and sing,
'Til earth and heaven ring,
Ring with the harmonies of Liberty;
Let our rejoicing rise
High as the listening skies,
Let it resound loud as the rolling sea.
Sing a song full of the faith that the dark past has taught us,
Sing a song full of the hope that the present has brought us;
Facing the rising sun of our new day begun,
Let us march on 'til victory is won.

THE SUMMONS TO INVESTITURE   **Dr. Rudolph E. Waters**
Executive Vice President Emeritus, Alcorn State University

Order My Steps   **Alcorn State University Concert Choir**
(by Glenn Burleigh)   Ms. Donna Schaffer, Director

—— **ENTRANCE OF THE EIGHTEENTH PRESIDENT** ——

INVOCATION   Rev. Reginald M. Buckley
                          Executive Pastor, Cade Chapel Missionary Baptist Church
                                                            Jackson, Mississippi

Always Remember   **Mr. Tony Gordon**
(by Andre Crouch)   Department of Fine Arts

WELCOME AND OCCASION   **Dr. Malvin A. Williams Sr.**
                                Former Interim President, Alcorn State University

—— **GUBERNATORIAL AND LEGISLATIVE PROCLAMATIONS** ——

THE GREETINGS AND SALUTATIONS TO THE PRESIDENT

from the United States Congress	**Congressman Bennie G. Thompson**
from the Mississippi Senate	**Senator Willie L. Simmons**
from the Mississippi House of Representatives	**Representative Alyce Griffin Clarke**
from the County of Jefferson	**Ms. Brenda T. Buck**
from the City of Port Gibson	**Mayor Fred Reeves**
from the City of Natchez	**Alderwoman Joyce Arceneaux-Mathis**
from the City of Vicksburg	**Mayor Paul E. Winfield**

The Heavens are Telling   **Alcorn State University Concert Choir**
(from The Creation by Franz Joseph Haydn)   Ms. Donna Schaffer, Director

THE GREETINGS AND SALUTATIONS TO THE PRESIDENT (continued)

from the Board of Trustees	**Mr. C. D. Smith**
from the 17th President	**Dr. George E. Ross**
from the Alumni	**Mr. Percy O. Norwood Jr.**
from the Faculty	**Dr. Dickson Idusuyi**
from the Staff	**Mrs. Donna Hayden**
from the Students	**Ms. Tasheena Galmore**

Make Them Hear You   **Alcorn State University Men Chorale**
(from Ragtime by Stephen Flaherty)   Mr. Charles Wesley, Director

THE GREETINGS AND SALUTATIONS TO THE PRESIDENT (continued)

from the American Association of State Colleges and Universities	**Dr. F. King Alexander**
from the Association for Public Land-grant Universities	**Dr. George Cooper**
from the National Association for Equal Opportunity	**Dr. Boyce C. Williams**
from the Thurgood Marshall College Fund	**Dr. N. Joyce Payne**
from the Mississippi Association of Colleges and Universities	**Dr. Donna H. Oliver**

Alleluia   Ms. Conesha Washington, Soprano
(from Exsultate, Jubilate, Wolfgang Mozart)

THE GREETINGS AND SALUTATIONS TO THE PRESIDENT (continued)
from the President's Mentors   Dr. Wayne J. Riley
from the President's Colleagues   Dr. Walter M. Kimbrough
from the President's Civic Community   Senator Steven A. Horsford
from the President's Former Students   Dr. Ronyelle Betrand Ricard
from the President's Friends   Dr. Anthony A. Pittman
from the President's Family   MGySgt Rodney Brown, USMC

Special Tribute

TO THE 18th PRESIDENT'S MATERNAL GRANDMOTHER
Mrs. Evelyna Smith Brown (1923 - 2004)

THE PLEDGE OF COMMITMENT   Dr. Samuel L. White

We, the faculty, staff, students, alumni, friends, and supporters of Alcorn State University, pledge
our commitment to the Eighteenth President of the University: *Dr. M. Christopher Brown II.*

We acknowledge the awesome tasks embedded in your presidential assignment; therefore, we pledge
ourselves to support your leadership and vision as you endeavor to advance the University's mission
of teaching, research, and service to the citizens of this state, our nation, and the world.

We proffer our prayers to assist you in making manifest the ambitions of Alcorn State University.
May the Almighty be with you as you lead this great institution to a new pinnacle in its history
with *Alcorn Bravery: Engaging Possibilities, Pursuing Excellence.*

THE PRESIDENTIAL CHARGE   Dr. Hank M. Bounds
                          Commissioner of Higher Education, Mississippi Board of Trustees
                                        of State Institutions of Higher Learning

All Good Things Will Be Added Unto You   Alcorn State University Concert Choir
(by Shelton Becton)   Ms. Donna Schaffer, Director

—— THE INVESTITURE OF THE PRESIDENT ——

Presentation of the Rector's Regalia   Dr. Mark Keenum
                                              President, Mississippi State University

Presentation of the Chain of Office   Dr. Bettye H. Neely
                                              President, Mississippi Board of Trustees
                                              of State Institutions of Higher Learning

Presentation of the University Mace   Dr. Alpha L. Morris
                                    Faculty Marshal/Chair and Professor of Social Sciences

Assisted by Mrs. Karen R. Shedrick, Executive Assistant to the President

---

THE PRESENTATION OF THE EIGHTEENTH PRESIDENT   Dr. Norris A. Edney
                                              Immediate Past Interim President,
                                              Alcorn State University

THE INAUGURAL ADDRESS   Dr. M. Christopher Brown II
                                              18th President
                                              Alcorn State University

THE ALMA MATER   Audience
"The Alcorn Ode" (by Mrs. J. S. Hines)   Mr. Charles Wesley, Conductor

Beneath the shade of giant trees,
Fanned by a balmy southern breeze
Thy classic walls have dared to stand
A giant thou art in learning's band;
O, Alcorn dear, our mother, hear
Thy name, we praise, thy name we sing.

RETIRING OF COLORS   ASU ROTC Braves Battalion

THE INAUGURAL RECESSIONAL
                              Grand March (from Tannhauser), by Richard Wagner
                              Alcorn State University Symphonic Band
                              Mr. Samuel Griffin, Conductor

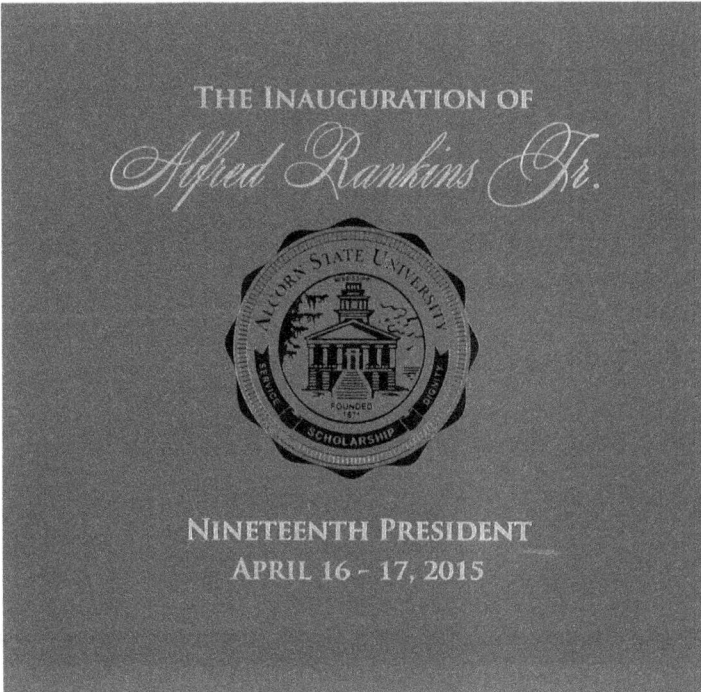

THE INAUGURATION OF

Alfred Rankins Jr.

NINETEENTH PRESIDENT
APRIL 16 – 17, 2015

Investiture Ceremony
ALFRED RANKINS JR.

FRIDAY, APRIL 17, 2015
DAVEY L. WHITNEY HPER COMPLEX
2:00 P.M.

Dr. Donzell Lee, Presiding
Provost and Executive Vice President for Academic Affairs

Prelude

The Inaugural Academic Processional   Mr. Barry E. Kopetz
Olympus

Posting of Colors   Alcorn State University ROTC

ENTRANCE OF THE 19TH PRESIDENT AND FIRST LADY

Invocation

Reverend Chauncey L. Jordan
Pastor, Hill of Zion Missionary Baptist Church
Bolton, Miss.

Greetings

Ms. Cortni Cooper
Miss Alcorn State University

The Honorable Roger Wicker
United States Senator

Musicial Selection

Ms. Kimberly Morgan-Myles
Miss Alcorn State University (2004-2005)
Miss Mississippi (2007)

The Investiture of the President

Dr. Jim Borsig
Commissioner of Higher Education
Mississippi Board of Trustees of
State Institutions of Higher Learning

Mr. Aubrey Patterson
President of the IHL Board of Trustees

Assisted by:
First Lady Juandalyn Rankins

THE INAUGURATION OF DR. ALFRED RANKINS JR.   29

The Inaugural Address

Dr. Alfred Rankins Jr.
19th President

The Alma Mater

"The Alcorn Ode"
Mrs. J. S. Himes

Benediction

Reverend Chauncey L. Jordan

Retiring of Colors

Alcorn State University ROTC

Postlude
War March of the Priests, (arr. by Felix Mendelssohn)

10. Mississippi Institutions of Higher Learning Board of Trustees at the Time of Inauguration of the Last Five Permanent Presidents

Walter Washington

Members with Terms Expiring May 7, 1980
Verner S. Holmes, Seventh Congressional District
Boswell Stevens, First Congressional District
R. C. Cook, State-at-Large
W. M. Shoemaker, Fifth Congressional District

Members with Terms Expiring May 7, 1976
Milton E. Brister, Fourth Congressional District
Thomas N. Turner, Third Congressional District
M. Paul Haynes, Northern Supreme Court District
Ira L. Morgan, Second Congressional District

Members with Terms Expiring May 7, 1972
W. O. Stone, Central Supreme Court District
M. M. Roberts, Sixth Congressional District
H. H. Hederman, State-at-Large
Leon Lowery, La Bauve, Trustee
William H. Mitchell

Officers of the Board
W. O. Stone, President
E. E. Thrash, Executive Secretary

Clinton Bristow Jr.

Thomas D. Layzell, Commissioner
J. Marlin Ivey, President

Cassie Pennington, Vice President
Nan McGahey Baker
Thomas W. Colbert Sr.
William Crawford
Ricki Garrett
James Klumb
James W. Luvene
D. E. Magee, M.D.
J. P. Mills
Virginia Shanteau Newton
Carl Nicholson

George E. Ross

Aubrey K. Lucas, Interim Commissioner
Amy Whitten, President
Scott Ross, Vice President
Ed Blakeslee
L. Stacy Davidson Jr.
Bettye H. Neely
Bob Owens
Aubrey Patterson
Alan W. Perry
Christine Pickering
Robin Robinson
Douglas W. Rouse
C. D. Smith Jr.

M. Christopher Brown II

Hank M. Bounds, Commissioner
Bettye H. Neely, President
Robin Robinson, Vice President

Ed Blakeslee
L. Stacy Davidson Jr.
Bob Owens
Aubrey Patterson
Alan W. Perry
Christine Lindsay Pickering
Scott Ross
Douglas W. Rouse
C. D. Smith Jr.
Amy Whitten

ALFRED RANKINS JR.

Jim Borsig, Commissioner
Aubrey Patterson, President
Alan W. Perry, Vice President
Ed Blakeslee
Karen L. Cummins
Ford Dye
Shane Hooper
Bob Owens
Hal Parker
Christine Lindsay Pickering
Robin Robinson
Douglas W. Rouse
C. D. Smith Jr.

11. PUBLIC AND PRIVATE CONTRIBUTIONS TO THE ASU FOUNDATION, INC. IN 2013

PUBLIC AND PRIVATE CONTRIBUTIONS 2013

$1,715,834 M
CONTRIBUTIONS TOTAL

DONATIONS FROM FRIENDS AND FAMILY

$530,696
TOTAL ALUMNI GIFTS 2013

$115 K+
FOUNDATIONS GIFTS

$259,311

BUSINESSES & CORPORATIONS ENDOWMENT

$228,495

$548,725
Total Investment income throughout the year

ORGANIZATIONS SUPPORT ⟶ $33,412.00

12. MISS ALCORN STATE UNIVERSITY QUEENS

1926–1927	Henriene Simpkins Knaives	1944–1945	Gwendolyn N. Demarks
1927–1928	Emma W. Howard	1945–1946	Janice Snodgrass Waters
1930–1931	Albertine Townsend Reid	1946–1947	Kathryn Moore Jones
1931–1932	Lillian O. Palmer	1947–1948	Catherine Anderson Taylor
1932–1933	Annie Lee Patton	1948–1949	Margie Price Funchess
1933–1934	Ruby Reed Hammond	1949–1950	Helen Johnson Pointer
1935–1936	Gladys Noel Bates	1950–1951	Annie Ruth Johnson Stephney
1936–1937	Ruby Reed McDaniel	1951–1952	Bernice Moore Gamblin
1937–1938	Lula Kelly O'Neal	1952–1953	Beatrice Bryant Moses
1938–1939	Louise King Lawson	1953–1954	Erronteen Horton Evans
1940–1941	Lula B. Stewart Robinson	1954–1955	Mary Bacon Carpenter
1941–1942	Dorothy Hayes Overstreet	1955–1956	Levernis Eiland Crosby
1942–1943	Mattie Bious Reed	1956–1957	Vera Hendricks Bryant
1943–1944	Thelma Miller Owens	1957–1958	Ethel Wilson Powe

1958–1959	Annie Stewart Flemings	1987–1988	Marilyn Kline Marshall
1959–1960	Aneice Knight Cross	1988–1989	Guy Spears Green
1960–1961	Dora Prater Simpson	1989–1990	Lisa Gilmore
1961–1962	Vera Mae Moore Bullock	1990–1991	Cathy Hughes Ways
1962–1963	Veronica Levison Richardson	1991–1992	Wendolyn Young
1963–1964	Laura Brown Nelson	1992–1993	Jessica Johnson Muhammad
1964–1965	Berneyye V. Dillon Steptoe	1993–1994	Rukeyser Thompson
1965–1966	Barbara Bacon Epps	1994–1995	Michelle Graves
1966–1967	Esther Jenkins Henderson	1995–1996	Jenetria Thomas Howard
1967–1968	Lucille Smith Reese	1996–1997	April Smith
1968–1969	Ora Dean Marshall Cardwell	1997–1998	Sabrina Palmer
1969–1970	Rebecca Shaw	1998–1999	Jennifer Page
1970–1971	Jacqueline Barnes Cammon	1999–2000	Kenisha Shelton
1971–1972	Shirley Barnes	2000–2001	Kristi Brown
1972–1973	Victory Dillon Mumford	2001–2002	Sherita Bailey
1973–1974	Carolyn Gamblin Eubanks	2002–2003	Tiffany Lloyd
1974–1975	Hazel Connard Robinson	2003–2004	Shaqueta Wells Murphy
1975–1976	Barbara Henderson	2004–2005	Kimberly Morgan
1976–1977	Patricia Lott Smith	2005–2006	Adrienne White
1977–1978	Brenda Jackson Patterson	2006–2007	Trena Boyd Williams
1978–1979	Debbie Morris	2007–2008	Courtney Bolton
1979–1980	Ethel Bryant	2008–2009	Inneka Minor
1980–1981	Cynthia Dalcourt Longs	2009–2010	Jessica Hinton Hawkins
1981–1982	Betty Tucker Lockhart	2010–2011	Tuandria Smith
1982–1983	Venita Bowie	2011–2012	Arkayla Ellis
1983–1984	Cora Graham Peavie	2012–2013	Airnecia Mills
1984–1985	Watosa Marshall Sanders	2013–2014	Carmen Gibson
1985–1986	Carla Cleveland Kirkland	2014–2015	Cortni Cooper
1986–1987	Monique Jackson		

13. STUDENT GOVERNMENT ASSOCIATION PRESIDENTS

1957–1958	Paul Rucker	1963–1964	Henry Baker
1959–1960	Creevy Harness	1964–1965	Gilbert Smith
1960–1961	James Smith Jr.	1965–1966	Joshua Hill
1961–1962	Willie Bullock	1966–1967	Eddie Tate
1962–1963	Joseph Lloyd	1967–1968	Marvin Arrington

1968–1969	Herman Thomas	1992–1993	Willie Kennedy III
1969–1970	Randolph Walker	1993–1995	Tracy Dace
1970–1971	Elliot Travis	1995–1996	Marsha Graves
1971–1972	Verba Edwards	1996–1997	Maconnia Chester
1972–1973	Joseph Shields	1997–1998	Georgette Crossman
1973–1974	Irvin Bullet	1998–1999	Tara Smith
1974–1975	Ronald Hickombottom	1999–2000	Kim Hooper
1975–1976	Lillie Blackmon	2000–2001	Mario McCann
1976–1977	Larry McMillian	2001–2002	Felichia Fields
1977–1978	Robert Simmons	2002–2003	Derrick Donald
1978–1979	Andrew Nichols	2003–2004	Raqayya Forbes
1979–1980	David Gilbert	2004–2005	Levenia Baker
1980–1981	Terry Thames	2005–2006	Chavez Carter
1981–1982	Jewel Lockhart Jr.	2006–2007	Larry Duncan
1982–1984	Glenn Baham	2007–2008	Vernon Dandridge
1984–1985	Michael Glenn	2008–2009	Eddie Davenport
1985–1986	Dwight Manzy	2009–2010	Ryan Martin
1986–1987	Timothy Lewis	2010–2011	Corey Cooper
1987–1988	Rev. Elliot Parker	2011–2012	Brandon Rook
1988–1989	Karen McLaughlin	2012–2013	Marcus Mercy
1989–1990	James McDonald	2013–2014	Avery Ford
1990–1991	Valerie Carter	2014–2015	Zackeus Johnson
1991–1992	Michael Edwards		

14. HEADWAE AWARD RECIPIENTS

Students are listed first, followed by faculty honorees.

1989	Antonio Phillip Newman	1994	Janice Marie Johnson
	Kenneth Laverne Simmons Sr.		Joscelyn A. Jarrett
1990	Diana Jackson	1996	Madra Natarsha Dorsey
	Josephine M. Posey		Powhatan L. Fluker
1991	Glenda Danette Day	1997	Lemuel D. Oliver
	Frances C. Henderson		Belinda R. Havard
1992	Pamela Love	1998	Cecilia Newsome
	Ella M. Anderson		Troy J. Stewart Sr.
1993	Angela Sherrea Stewart	1999	Demetria Shanta White
	Alpha Lockhart Morris		Minnie Gloria Hawkins

2000	Clarence Gibson	2009	Demark Cole
	Donzell Lee		Wesley Lloyd Whittaker
2001	Kitonya Grushon White	2010	Fabian Wiley Jr.
	Patrick Emeka Igbokwe		John G. Igwebuike
2003	Carlos Buford	2011	Crystal Denise Glenn
	Kim Welch Hoover		Jan E. Duncan
2005	LaKeshia Nicole Myers	2012	Marnisha La'Karra Hatch
	J. Janice Coleman		Sandra Lee Rogers Barnes
2006	Jamal L. James	2013	Lawrence E. Warren
	Darryl Vanrich Grennell		Sidney Taylor Hawkins
2007	Archie Taylor-Price	2014	Anastasia Tuset
	Larry Konecky		Kimball Putman Marshall
2008	Antonio Cooper Jr.	2015	Nanette Boyd
	Pamela Theresa/Evans Felder		Lixin Yu

15. Intellectual Renewal Grant Recipients

2010–2011 Faculty Recipients

Akasha Dania
Alex D. W. Acholonu
Benedict A. Udemgba
Bobbie P. Fells
Carrie Ford
Cassandra Vaughn
David K. Addae
Eva L. Smith
Hazel L. Bell

J. Janice Coleman
John Adjaye
Judy P. Moore
Mamie Griffin
Marta A. Piva
Mary G. Harris
May Yu
Robert C. Sizemore
Steve Aazanu

2011–2012 Faculty Recipients

Aaron Anderson
Akash Dania
Alex D. W. Acholonu
Benedict A. Udemgba
Cassandra Vaughn

Danielle A. Terrell
Dickson Idusuyi
Eva L. Smith
Hazel L. Bell
John Addae

John Adjaye   Sandra Barnes
Mary Harris   William Piper
May Yu

2011–2012 Staff Recipients

Melissa Mason   Tonya Edwards
Nicole Bell

2011–2012 Student Recipients

Alex D. W. Acholonu   Jessie Hayden
Alexis Jones   Kenisha Smith
Alysha McAllister   Marcisha Johnson
Arnold Walker III   Maxwell Gidi
Arturo Tamayo   Miata Hudson
Asia Goodwin   Nick Brooks
Brandon Rook   Sabrina Smith
Carmen Campbell   Tiffany Jackson
Christopher Davis   Travis Graffree
Denzel Reed   Victoria Friday
Dominique Washington

2012–2013 Faculty Recipients

Alex Acholonu   Danielle Terrell
Hazel Bell   Benedict Udemgba
Eva Smith   Sandra Barnes
Mary Harris

2013–2014 Faculty Recipients

Akash Dania   William Piper
Cynthia Scurria   John Igwebuike
C. Diane Bunch   Dickson Idusuyi
Alex Acholonu

2013–2014 Staff Recipients

LaTasha Coleman

LeKisha Carr

Gloria Chatman

Kassie Freeman

2014–2015 Faculty Recipients

Akash Dania

Alex D. W. Acholonu

Benedict Undemgba

Cassandra Vaughn

Danielle A. Terrell

Dickson AM Idusuyi

Dorothy Idleburg

Eva L. Smith

Evelin J. Cuadra

Hazel L. Bell

John Igwebuike

Kenneth Stallings

Larry Konecky

LaWanda W. Baskins

Mary G. Harris

PJ Forest

Sandra Davis

Valtreasa Tolliver-Cook

Willie McGowan Jr.

Zulfiquar Dogar

2014–2015 Staff Recipients

Laura Drake

Melissa Mason

Wanda Arrington

William Prince

2014–2015 Student Recipients

Albert Sampana

Angel Brinner

Ari'Anna Magee

E'niya Rowry

Gail Simpson

Gerard Winters

Jhailyn Wade

Justin Knight

Rachel Granderson

Rayford Mullins

Ryshine Lucas

Shannen Price

Tyantria Leflore

Vernell McDonald

Yolanda Jackson

16. Student Organizations

Active Minds
Agriculture Business & Economics Club
Alpha Chi Sigma
Alpha Kappa Alpha Sorority, Inc.
Alpha Phi Alpha Fraternity, Inc.
Animal Science Club
ASU Bravettes
ASU Chapter NAACP
ASU Gospel Choir
ASU H.E.R.O.S. (Health Educators Reaching Other Students)
Beta Kappa Chi
Biology Club
Choir Psi Phi National Music Society
Collective Party
Collegiate Future Farmers of America
Dance Distinction
Delta Mu Delta Int'l Honor Society in Business
Delta Sigma Theta Sorority, Inc.
Dietetic Club
Ecology Club
Enactus
English Club
First Year Experience
Freshman Class
GQ Modeling Squad
Honors Student Organization
International & Multicultural Student Organization
Khem Klub
Leadership Alcorn
Louis Stokes MS Alliance for Minority Participation
Minority Association of Pre-Medical/Pre-Health Students
Mortar Board National College Senior Honor Society
The Movement
National Pan Hellenic Council
National Society of Leadership and Success
National Society of Pershing Rifles Fraternity
Omega Tau Pi
Poimne Ministries
Psychology Society
Renaissance Players
Residence Hall Association
Sigma Chi Iota
Sigma Gamma Rho Sorority, Inc.
Sigma Tau Delta National Honor Society
Student Government Association
Student National Education Association
Student Support Services
Upsilon Phi Upsilon Fraternity, Inc.
Zeta Phi Beta Sorority, Inc.

17. Quality Enhancement Plan

The Quality Enhancement Plan (QEP), "Writing Matters," is an effort by Alcorn State University to improve the writing proficiency of its undergraduate students. The central theme underlying Alcorn's QEP is that the addition of process writing as a teaching method to selected courses will increase student writing proficiency. Process writing produces a written document using techniques such as planning, drafting, revising, and editing. It is a recursive process that includes interacting with peers as well as instructors. Writing to learn and writing to models are other teaching methods used. Its desired student learning outcomes have been developed to support the university's General Education Core Curriculum Competencies. Improving the writing proficiency of students supports the university's mission of "intellectual development and lifelong learning" as well as preparing "graduates who will be well-rounded future leaders . . . who will be competitive in the global marketplace of the 21st century."

Process writing was instituted in freshman-level English composition courses by the Department of English in 2006. Alcorn's QEP builds upon these efforts by changing English 213, Introduction to Literature, to a Writing Enhanced (WE) course that will reinforce writing skills for sophomore students. This course pairs process writing with writing to learn methods, in which writing assignments are used as a method of study and retention of course content. Beginning in the QEP's second year, disciplines at the junior and senior levels will begin incorporating these techniques into existing upper-level courses. Each year, three departments will each identify at least one three-hour course at the 300 level and one at the 400 level that can become writing enhanced. Faculty teaching these courses are trained in these methods of writing instruction for improving student writing in content-intensive courses.

Alcorn State University is committed to enacting the QEP by devoting sufficient resources to it. Among these are financial resources exceeding $1 million in funds over the QEP's five years. A QEP director versed in rhetoric and composition was hired to administer the program and reports to the vice president for Academic Affairs. A QEP Oversight Committee was formed, composed of a cross section of Alcorn faculty and administration, to advise the vice president for Academic Affairs and the QEP director in the administration of the QEP throughout its tenure. The Alcorn Writing Center will be expanded to serve as a center for improvement of student writing.

The project will be assessed through the use of standardized testing using the ETS Proficiency Profile; through the use of a common rubric, Writing Matters Rubric, for assessing writing assignments; by maintaining student writing portfolios; and through the formation of an assessment team. It is expected that as students move through WE courses, scores on the Writing Matters Rubric will increase and that higher levels of proficiency as well as the ability of students to write at higher levels of complexity will be evident. The QEP director, along with the QEP Oversight Committee, monitors the implementation of the QEP on a yearly basis and evaluates whether it is meeting the goals and if activities are being carried out as articulated. In addition, the QEP director produces a report at the end of each academic year that is expected to include recommended changes for improvement of student learning outcomes.

18. *SIMPLY SHARING* PUBLICATIONS

Simply Sharing: The President's Perspective

Alcorn State University Celebrates College For Excellence & Modern Housing

Dr. Norris Allen Edney

Welcome to the first edition of *Simply Sharing*. We are delighted to communicate with you. *Simply Sharing* tells the positive stories about unprecedented progress at Alcorn State University focusing on outstanding accomplishments that leave indelible imprints. Although challenges abound, Alcorn State University forges ahead with courage and determination. As students, staff and faculty returned to Southwest Mississippi's citadel of learning this fall, several accomplishments among others, sparked excitement: remarkable successes at the College for Excellence, and students' delight at living in ultra-modern state of the art facilities that elegantly grace Alcorn State University's campus.

College For Excellence

During summer 2010, several students converged at Alcorn State University's College for Excellence, as has been the case since 1983. Under the auspices of dedicated and devoted mentors, they were initiated into university life at the College, which served as the home for all freshmen and sophomores.

The College for Excellence assisted students through proper advisement and counseling on a continuous basis. This assistance occurred throughout their degree programs from inception to graduation. Graduates expressed overflowing praise for their experiences and thanked facilitators for their help.

Over the years, the College established several departments. They helped with academic advising, First Year Experience, Counseling and Testing, Upward Bound, Student Support Services and Summer Developmental Programs.

The Summer Development program, one of the major components employed: one director, one lead teacher and five additional subject area teachers for reading, math and English. Other employees included: one survival skills coordinator, one recreation coordinator, one female dorm coordinator/evening lab and one male dorm coordinator/computer lab specialist.

Photo: Dr. Jerry Domatob

Summer Development Program 1996-2009

Program Director	Average Number of Students	Average Entering Freshmen	Average Percentage Graduating
Dr. Yinka Oredein	89	78	68%

Source: ASU 2009 College For Excellence Report

Since the College for Excellence has been eliminated, we are diligently working hard to ensure that our students continue to benefit from the services embedded in it. Alcorn State University has restructured the College and it has now become the Newtie Boyd Center for Academic Support.

Ultra Modern Housing

In another development, Alcorn State University has joined top-notch institutions in America, and indeed the world, with ultra-modern housing facilities.

Lovely and magnificent, the spacious apartment style rooms consist of: private bathrooms, lounges, study rooms, computer labs, new appliances, furniture and security cards.

Some former College for Excellence Personnel
Seated Front Row (L-R): Dr. Patricia White, Dr. Edward Vaughn,
and Deautral Davis. Standing (L-R): Ricky Coleman, Carolyn
Smith, Pearl Wilson, Harold Spencer, Roderick Martin, Nettie
King, Jiardine McDonald & Regina Rankin
(Photo: Dr. Jerry Domatob)

One of Alcorn State University's
Ultra-modern Housing Edifices
(Photo: Dr. Jerry Domatob)

Alcorn Ambulance Service Starts New Operation

Gone are the days when fear and trepidation gripped parents and visitors who foresaw gloom and doom in the event of any medical emergency. Disaster services have been upgraded tremendously.

Staff, faculty, students, parents and even community members enthusiastically smile as they welcome a revamped ambulance service on campus. Alcorn State University has now acquired additional transportation and certified, qualified and trained personnel are being hired to manage each shift.

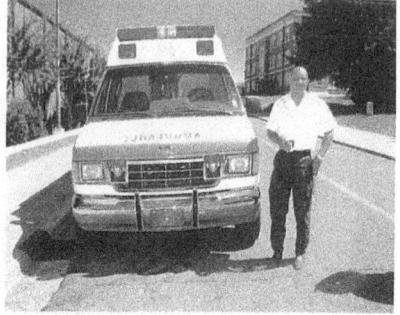

ASU Fire Chief Kelvin White standing by the newly acquired ambulance. Located at the Campus Police Department, clients are invited to consult them when they have questions. Please drop by any time.

Health is Wealth: Alcorn's New Fitness Center

Willie Malone and others relaxing at the new Fitness Center. The Center which was opened in summer 2010 is a popular spot at the Student's Union building. Visit it at your convenience.

Alcorn prides itself among other things on the adage that, "health is wealth." That explains why, university health authorities stress that students, staff and faculty eat, rest and exercise. Towards this goal, a new fitness center is now in operation at the Student Union Building. Faculty, staff and students who want to relax and exercise now have a grand spot on campus. Although the center needs more equipment, it provides basic amenities for those interested in keeping fit.

Students Embrace ASU as the University Eagerly Pursues SACS Reaffirmation

Dr. Norris Allen Edney

Though Alcorn State University grapples with the current disastrous economic crisis, the institution founded in 1871, bustles with life. The ultra-modern cafeteria, which is one of the best in the state, is always jammed to capacity at peak periods. Some classes and offices are bursting at the seams and professors, faculty and staff, smile with excitement as they teach, mentor and render valuable services to keen students.

After a period of forlorn anxiety, new optimism can be attributed to a number of factors: improved housing, new buildings, enhanced communication, customer service etc. However, one of the chief reasons, which infuse buoyancy and zeal in Alcorn State University, is the current enrollment growth.

The temporary final student count for Fall 2010 is 3682. This contrasts with the count of 3334 for Fall 2009 indicating an increase of 10.4%.

Approximate Figures For 2009/2010

Academic Year	Total No of Students
2009	3334
2010	3682
	10.4% increase

Source: Clarion Ledger 9/3/2010

ASU's SACS Reaffirmation: A Labor of Love

Alcorn State University embraces reaccreditation with unbridled zest. Although the university is addressing minor concerns raised, as the 2011 On-Sight review approaches, all hands are on deck to assure that the school does not only fulfill requirements, but soars above and beyond expectations.

In a bid to uphold the rigorous SACS standards, the entire university community has committed itself to the process with unabated fervor. Staff, students, faculty and alumni have all collaboratively involved themselves in the many facets required for the reaffirmation process. This involvement included: self-studies, updating curricula, hiring personnel, upgrading facilities and making other requirements for meeting SACS standards. Other necessary actions have also been taken to ameliorate things where needed. including giving the stadium, classrooms, dormitories and other facilities admirable face lifts.

Adequate measures are installed to rectify academic lapses with dispatch. For example, after a campus-wide survey indicated that students demanded improvements in writing, the university resolved to rectify that shortcoming by emphasizing its importance through the Quality Enhancement Plan (QEP). Small wonder, the slogan; "Writing Matters" echoes across the campus as a coveted trophy all students strive to win. Additionally, as part of the SACS core standards, a Student Support Center has been established on the Natchez campus. One will also be established in Vicksburg to address the needs of students studying at those sites.

Bravo

Alcorn State University recognizes the laudable goal and has embarked upon the process with the labor of love. As the institution diligently prepares for reaffirmation, it is with unmitigated pleasure that I extend hearty appreciation to all faculty, staff, students, alumni as well as IHL and other colleagues in the State and elsewhere, We are proud to have submitted the SACS Compliance Report for the Off-Sight review and look forward to our March 2011 On-Sight Review with success.

Simply Sharing Team

Dr. Norris Allen Edney
Mrs. Karen Shedrick
Dr. Jerry Komia Domatob
Dr. Josephine M. Posey

Simply Sharing: A University's Perspective
Celebrating Homecoming and Enrollment Bonanza
Issue 2: October—November , 2010   Dr. Norris Allen Edney

Alcorn State University Enhances Security

ASU's 2010 Police Command

At an era when security concerns traumatize students, parents, states and communities globally, Alcorn State University has taken giant strides to address the issue.

In an admirable proactive step, Alcorn hired two seasoned and experienced law enforcement officers, Mr. Melvin Maxwell and Mr. Douglas Stewart to lead the Police department.

Both bring professionalism, devotion to duty and proficiency to the unit.

Alcorn State University Celebrates 2010 Homecoming with Fervor

ASU's 2010 homecoming will go down in the annals of the school's history as memorable and uplifting. Hundreds of Alcornites and visitors zestfully converged at the gorgeous campus for the week of good cheer.

Young, old and accomplished graduates exuded overflowing love and pride for the institution with their presence and contributions. Clad in Alcorn's purple and gold, they hugged, chatted and reminisced on the past.

Reunions, music, food, fun and fanfare marked the week. A festive atmosphere gripped the campus.

2010 Miss Alcorn and SGA President

Saturday's marvelous parade, which included military cadets, clubs, associations, and area school bands, was outstanding for its pomp, panoply and pageantry. Alcorn's band, the colorful "Sounds of Dyn-o-mite", infused joy and enthusiasm in the cheerful crowd with their harmonious beat, marshal steps and dynamic moves.

The symbolic and appreciative $25,000 alumni donation to the University for scholarships, evoked a standing ovation from the capacity crowd at the stadium. Overall, it was a remarkable week of exciting celebrations. Smiles and laughter permeated Alcorn.

Sounds of Dyn-o-mites

First lady, Mrs. Lillian Edney; ASU's Interim President, Dr. Norris Allen Edney and National Alumni President, Mr. Percy Norwood

Alcornites Enjoying Homecoming 2010

1

**2010 ASU Soccer team
They won their first SWAC match
during homecoming week.**

ASU Drum Majors 2010

2

America Reads Mississippi: Alcorn's Unsung Heroes

Some educators, media practitioners and lay observers, fear the demise of the reading culture. Many argue that the era when people started their day with a cup of coffee and newspaper, relaxed over the weekend with novels and magazines, or even spent time in family and groups reading is long gone. We now live in a time when perhaps the reading culture needs a revival.

In a bid to address these concerns, some groups have taken a lead in the crusade to foster this noble culture. Standing at the cutting edge of this endeavor is America Reads Mississippi (ARMS), which has offices and facilitators throughout the state.

Alcorn's ARM Participants

America Reads-MS has 350 Ameri-Corps tutors across the state helping students during and after school as well as in the summer. Alcorn has five staff members: Dr. Helen J. Wyatt (Regional Director); Deborah Donaldson (Field Support Specialist); Janice Smith (Field Support Specialist); Sue Ann Easterling (Special Project Coordinator); Jershellia Anderson (Administrative Assistant). ASU America Reads-MS is located in 7 counties: Adams, Amite, Claiborne, Franklin, Jefferson, Lawrence, and Warren. The State Director is Ronjanett Taylor.

History

ARM started in 1998 with Delta State and Mississippi State Universities. Alcorn State University came aboard in 1999. Alcorn's America Reads Mississippi Regional Service Center is strategically located at the heart of the campus, near the gorgeous cafeteria and J.D. Boyd Library. ARM is administered by the Office of Academic and Student Affairs at the Mississippi Institutions for Higher Learning, Jackson, MS. It is funded by the Corporation of National and Community Service, through the Mississippi Commission for Volunteer Service.

The first Regional Coordinator for Alcorn State University was Dr. Shirley Reeves, who served from 1999-2000 and taught in the Education Department. Dr. Wyatt took over in 2000 and manages the program.

Dr. Edney and ASU ARM Staff

She and her staff have exemplified the highest level of commitment in ensuring that youth attain the ultimate standard of reading proficiency through Alcorn's involvement with America Reads Mississippi.

Mission

According to the Regional Director, Dr. Helen Wyatt, "America Reads Mississippi is dedicated to improving the reading skills of students, kindergarten through middle school. It also encourages public awareness and support of literacy and helps to increase the number of certified teachers in Mississippi. ARM members receive a $5350 education award to enable them go to college." To serve as members, students need 48 hours of college credits or a passing score of 4 in reading and math and 3 in writing on the ACT Work Keys Test. This test is designed for the workforce and teacher assistants in Mississippi as a job qualifier. They also have to be USA citizens or permanent residents. Additionally, they have to clear both the FBI and Child Abuse registry background checks.

Achievements

America Reads Mississippi Ameri-Corps members have increased the reading scores of elementary students. The program also encourages members to go to college and helps them become productive citizens. "Alcorn's ARM program has 94 members who graduated from Alcorn State university and 28 of those are now certified teachers," Dr. Wyatt said.

3

Alcorn Welcomes Search Committee's Listening Sessions

Although most observers often express skepticism about search committees, many welcomed the Presidential Search Listening sessions which took place at Alcorn State University.

Several Alcorn administrators, faculty, staff and students said it was a stride in the right direction, since the committee involved them in the process. During the campus visit, the committee heard from the President's Cabinet, Deans, Senior Program officers, Chairs, Unit Heads, Students, Faculty, Alumni, and Community Leaders.

The Alcorn family zealously awaits the selection of a visionary and competent President, who will valiantly lead Alcorn State University to higher heights as the school forges ahead in the 21st century.

(Sitting L-R) Dr. Stacy Davidson, Dr. Hank M. Bounds and Dr. Bettye Neely

(Standing L-R) Mr. C.D. Smith (Chair) and Mr. Ed Blakeslee.

Photo by Dr. J. Domatob

Enrollment Bonanza Uplifts Alcorn

As the good news of Alcorn's astronomical growth lift spirits across the country and the globe, a crucial question arises: what accounts for the enrollment boost?

According to Mr. Emmanuel Barnes, the Director of Admissions, "In addition to due diligence as it relates to established best practices in the admissions and recruiting; our success was fostered by a renewed spirit of enthusiasm and cooperation between the units that impact the process.

The university issued a challenge for the good of Alcorn moving forward, not looking back, which was embraced by faculty, staff, students and alumni alike. This resulted in the natural removal of barriers to progress and culminated in our record increase."

President Edney encourages students to enroll in Alcorn State University where they will earn a quality education in a safe and secure environment.

"Alcorn is a great place for studies and we invite interested students to enroll in the University's programs."

Simply Sharing Team
R-L Dr. Norris Edney
Ms. Kimberly White
Mrs. Karen Shedrick
Dr. Josephine Posey
Dr. Jerry Domatob

4

Simply Sharing: A University's Perspective
Profiles and Celebrations

Issue 3: Nov—Dec, 2010   Dr. Norris Allen Edney

Terrenell Galtney: Lorman's Wonder Boy

Student, Cook, Server and Role Model

T errenell Galtney defies negative stereotypes about youth. Yes, he challenges the misconception that several budding African American young adults face today. Rather, he admiringly showcases a responsible demeanor and attitude most parents, teachers and even his peers admire. Terrennell says "A good positive attitude will take you a long way in life. I have been in several positions where my attitude got me things that money could not buy. Keep God first."

Profile

Terrenell Galtney is an Alcorn State University student, who has served as a cook, delivery boy and cleaner since the 8th grade. At Alcorn, he was previously employed with Thompson Hospitality and currently with Sodexo. He doubles as a cashier, server, cook and performs specific assignments with gusto and enthusiasm.

Special Interests

Terrenell is a freshman Elementary Education major, who graduated from Port Gibson High School in May, 2010 with honors and aspires to be a teacher. He belongs to Spirit Filled Life Christian Church of Fayette Mississippi pastored by Rev. Larry Shannon, where he is a member of the Praise Team."

Family

Terrenell is the son of Annie Galtney and Lewis Jones. His twin brother is Trenell Galtney, who also graduated last May from Port Gibson High School. He has two older brothers: Dendrick and Christopher Galtney, as well as a ten year old sister, Angeliek Nichols. His grandparents are Henry and Lillie Patten of Lorman-MS, where he grew up.

Motivation

Terrenell says, "I love my job. I come in contact with many people, who have various personalities and backgrounds. I have time to minister to someone and brighten their day. I have several students who ask me why I always smile. They ask, 'are you always having a good day?' I realize that I face storms and trials. However, my situation could possibly be better than others. When I think about the goodness of God, I know that it is not the alarm clock that wakes me up, but it was Him."

1

ASU 2010 Picture Panorama: People, Places and Perspectives

2010 Wesley Foundation members in front of the Wesley foundation building

Professor Schaffer and her students pose for a 2010 family photo in front of Alcorn's Student Affairs Office.

The Deltas turned out in full force during the 2010 homecoming for celebrations and reunion.

2010 Alcorn State University Interfaith Gospel Choir members in front of the famous Oakland chapel .

ASU Band in a lively 2010 Homecoming display

Alcorn 2010 Football Players

Alcorn's Trilateral Committee Consolidates Campus Concord
Faculty Senate, Assembly and Staff Senate Leaders Endorse Pay Cuts before layoffs

Some university campuses operate as veritable atomistic and antagonistic war camps, with Faculty Senate, Staff Senate, Faculty Council and administration unsheathing swords as implacable enemies.

Others create panic-ridden atmospheres, where people dig their heads in sand like ostriches for fear of victimization..

Cordial Atmosphere

Alcorn State University, under the Edney administration offers a sensitive and cordial atmosphere, where meaningful discussions and dialogue reigns.

Under the initiative and tutelage of the Faculty Senate President, Dr. Dickson Idusuyi, Faculty Assembly and Staff Senate leaders met and discussed the impact of the ongoing budget cuts and strategies for solving them.

Trilateral Committee

Staff Senate President, Mrs. Donna Hayden, Faculty Assembly President and Secretary, Dr. April Owens-Rankin and Dr. Peter Malik respectively, joined the Faculty Senate for deliberations on this vital subject.

Besides the agreement on possible pay cuts, before drastic measures as layoffs, are adopted, it was resolved that a trilateral committee be formed. The body consists of three representatives from each group, who will monitor and guide the university on this issue.

(R-L) Dr. Idususyi, Dr. Obilade, Dr. Acholunu, Ms. Donna Hayden, Dr. Peter Malik, Dr. April Owen-Rankin, Dr. Shugars and extreme left Dr. Domatob

Pay Cuts

During that trilateral meeting, the three parties unanimously agreed that possible pay cuts/furloughs across the board, on a sliding scale basis, with consideration for those with minimal wages, could be the priority mode for tackling the current crisis.

Consensus

They arrived at a consensus, that although that *modus operandi* will pose excruciating pain to the Alcorn family, considering that employees earn comparatively low salaries, the campus will embrace that option before program abolitions, mergers and layoffs. They stressed the temporary nature of the measure. Observers described the meeting as an epoch-making event, since the three entities often operate separately, limiting communication with each other.

3

Fraternities and Sororities Foster Friendships and Solidarity
Alpha Phi Alpha Attracts hundreds of guests for 2010 homecoming

Alpha Phi Alpha frats celebrate 2010 homecoming

The purpose of sororities and fraternities is to serve as catalysts for growth, friendships and community building. They do not only create lasting bonds and relationships among members, but render huge community services such as health campaigns, political involvement, educational leadership, mentoring and teaching, as well as other noble volunteer services. Fraternities and sororities enhance charitable, community and international giving and sharing, internal and external to the university community. These sororities and fraternities also sponsor workshops, cookouts, dances and interact with brothers and sisters from all parts of the country.

Delta Kappa and Theta Sigma Lambda

These chapters of Alpha Phi Alpha fraternity hosted their 60th and 45th Reunions during Alcorn's 2010 homecoming. The excitement packed weekend, rich with a plethora of activities, attracted brothers who cheerfully converged at Alcorn and celebrated their vibrant legacy. The reunion assembled successful Alpha Phi Alpha Men who uphold the norms and values of the organization and continue to progress through service. The homecoming attracted 120 registered fraternity members, and approximately

375 guests. Delicious food was prepared by Rev. Morton Martin, his wife, daughter and Dr. Edward Rice.

The awesome crowds, vivacious meetings, cordial atmosphere and solidarity spirit, manifested through their activities, impressed both admirers and detractors. According to the coordinator, Mr. Tracy Cook, "the reunion was an unselfish commitment to the brotherhood to stay in touch and make an effort to reconnect in dedication to the improvement of society."

2010 Alpha Kappa Alpha sorors supports Making Strides to Survive

Fraternities and sororities, which animate campus life in many positive ways, leave indelible imprints on observers as valuable networks and associations. They marvelously link past and present members once they get inducted into the groups, and effectively assist in shaping their successful integration into campus life and future pursuits.

Simply Sharing Team

Dr. Norris A. Edney
Ms. Kimberly White
Ms. Karen Shedrick
Dr. Josephine Posey
Dr. Jerry Komia Domatob

4

Simply Sharing: A University's Perspective
Welcome and May Success Crown Your Tenure
Issue 4 : Dec. 2010—Jan. 2011   Dr. Norris Allen Edney

Alcorn Welcomes President Dr. M. Christopher Brown

Dr. M. Christopher Brown

As the new academic semester begins with unbridled enthusiasm, Alcornites warmly welcome Dr. M. Christopher Brown as the schools 18th president.

Distinguished

Dr. Brown, a seasoned academician, professor, author and researcher, brings the zest for scholarship, governance and youthful élan to Alcorn. He enters the school's historical annals at a crucial turning point when continuity and change are the watchwords. Like most institutions globally, Alcorn while charting new paths, still cherishes its founding mission, tradition and history.

Herculean Task

Tottering at a tough juncture, when schools and universities globally grapple with issues of inadequate funding; competition, recruitment, retention, salary caps and job insecurity, the new chief executive has his job carved out for him.

Impressive

It is therefore impressive for a young scholar as Dr. Brown, to assume the leadership position as president of this elite four year institution. It depicts his bravery and readiness for the tasks ahead. This is a remarkable stride in the right direction worthy of relentless commendation.

The Simply Sharing team welcomes President Brown and wishes him a smashing success during his tenure as the historic institution's leader.

Faith, devotion and dedication

With faith, confidence, devotion, dedication and effective decision-making based on valid facts, nothing but resounding accomplishments will grace his tenure. Alcorn's faculty, staff, students, and the university community, hail his arrival and wish him the very best.

IHL Board Members & Dr. Brown
Mr. Ed Blakeslee, C.D. Smith, Dr. Hank Bounds, Dr. Brown, Dr. Bettye Neely, Dr. Doug Rouse, Dr. Stacy Davidson

1

Picture Panorama: Alumni, Administrators & Students

Dr. Brown with Student leaders

Eight 2010 Golden Girls

Dr Brown & ASU Search Team

State Officials at 2010 Homecoming

Dr. Brown Greets Senior Campus Administrators

Police Chief Melvin Maxwell

NCAA Accreditation Members

Dr. Brown & Alcorn Students

Dr. Norris Allen Edney's Reflections on Alcorn

Dr. Norris Allen Edney

Barely two years after Alcorn's 17th president, Dr. George E. Ross took office, news trickled out that he was leaving for Central Michigan. Apprehension gripped the campus and even the state. The question arose as to who would serve as Interim President.

That speculation was dispelled when a retired dean of Arts and Sciences, the tall, charismatic and eloquent, Dr. Norris A. Edney emerged as the Interim President. For almost one year, he has led Alcorn State University as the chief executive with dignity and respect. Dr. Edney reflects on his tenure.

Simply Sharing: *What was your impressions after the appointment as Interim President?*
Dr. Edney

At the time, I wondered about the timing of the opportunity. I wanted to make a difference in a positive way or there was no need for me to accept the challenge. I wanted to focus strongly on what the university truly needed.

What was your mission as you took office?
Dr. Edney

This is a great historical institution and my mission was to make Alcorn better than I found it. I wanted to leave it in a much improved mode.

What are some of the challenges the University faces?
Dr. Edney

The greatest challenge is to motivate the entire university community to move in the same direction. All forces must pull together in order to accomplish the university's mission. There should only be one chief executive officer and others should support him following the pathway he sets as president.

The agenda should be that of the president. You can only have one president and others should follow his lead.

What is your counsel to the New President?
Dr. Edney

Firing is never the first solution to a problem. One must first find out the root of the problem, analyze what happened and try to resolve it in the most effective manner.

Let the data speak for itself. The president needs to rely on data for decision-making and learn personnel to the point where each is understood. Each one brings uniqueness to the table and the goal should be to get the best results by listening to and showing them respect. They also need to earn the proper accolades at the right time. In my opinion, there are no complicated problems at Alcorn. All problems are simple and can be solved if all minds work together.

Dr. Edney Reflecting

Dr. Norris A. Edney's Parting Thoughts

Extend Cooperation & Support To President Dr. M. Christopher Brown

Dr. Posey Thanks Dr. Edney for His Leadership

After almost a year as Alcorn State University's Interim President, permit me to thank you for all encouragement and support. During this period, we witnessed a phenomenal growth in enrollment, successful accreditation efforts, the completion of student housing development and other worthwhile projects on campus.

Accomplishments

We also revamped the Police Department, hired two experienced officers and bought vehicles at reasonable costs to replace those damaged by unanticipated and vicious torrential storms. Additionally, we acquired a full-fledged ambulance service with qualified staff who assists campus and community residents in times of medical emergencies.

Dedication

These accomplishments would have been impossible without Alcorn's true commitment and dedication to success. With your help and guidance, Alcorn was able to achieve these modest but significant goals. Our gratitude is boundless.

Excellence

Although major challenges remain, there is no shred of doubt in my mind that Alcorn will weather the storms that lie ahead as it has done in the past. With documented accomplishments during my term as Interim President, evidence abounds that Alcorn will continue to excel towards higher heights.

Support 18th President

Please extend the same cooperation and support to the new President, Dr. M. Christopher Brown as he takes on the leadership helm at this great institution.

Simply Sharing Team

Dr. Norris A. Edney
Ms. Karen Shedrick
Ms. Kimberly White
Dr. Josephine Posey
Dr. Jerry Domatob

4

Simply Sharing: Ride On President Brown

Issue 5: April 2011   Simply Sharing Team

IHL Board Members: L-R
Mr. Ed Blakeslee, Mr. C.D. Smith, Dr. Hank Bounds (Commissioner), President Brown, Dr. Bettye Neely, Dr. Doug Rouse and Dr. Stacy Davidson

As Dr. M. Christopher Brown II accepts the mantle of office as Alcorn State University's 18th President, we extend our hearty congratulations to him. He follows Hiram Revels, the first president and other distinguished leaders.

A dynamic, dedicated, devoted and driven achiever, Dr. Brown brings zeal, zest and zing to the institution. He takes office at a critical time in human history, when harsh,

Dr. Brown, with immediate Past Interim President Dr Norris A. Edney, as Jefferson County District 4 Supervisor, Larry McKnight approaches.

socio-economic and other cultural traumas and globalization challenges, dominate human affairs. However, the emergence of an urbane, approachable, God fearing and dashing youth as Alcorn's president, is an inspiring stride in the right direction.

Alcorn State University, founded in 1871, now charts new paths, while keeping to the school's cherished traditions. In an era when resources are limited, Dr. Brown's intellectual prowess, negotiating acumen and outstanding communication skills are assets.

President M. Christopher Brown II

The leadership smoothly transitioned from Interim President, Dr. Norris E. Edney to Dr. M. Christopher Brown II. Dr. Edney's commitment, passion and immense contributions shine like mountain lights.

Happily, Dr Brown grandly supports the splendid benchmarks Dr. Edney set for Alcorn State University.

May God, the omniscient, omnipotent and omnipresent, guide him as he makes momentous decisions that will shape Alcorn's future.

Ride on Dr. M. Christopher Brown II. We commend, salute, and wish you a smashing success in all pursuits.

1

Dr. M. Christopher Brown II Displays Leadership "Cs"

Great leaders exude certain qualities. While there is no universal fix for all of the traits, some managers who attain the summit of success, manifest a series of them. They range from community relations, through communication to compassion. How is Alcorn State University's 18th president faring, based on the above mentioned criteria?

Community Relations

At the heart of leadership is relationship building with various communities. Since Dr. Brown's arrival, he has not only created relations with students, faculty and employees, but has also extended a hand of fellowship to the community, political, economic, social leaders and other people.

Connection

Great leaders are those who connect with their followers. They monitor, react to and above all, take proactive steps not only to solve problems but also to initiate projects, evaluate them and ensure that they are executed. Dr. Brown displays that characteristic.

Communication

Outstanding leaders communicate effectively. They have a message for their people and they transmit it clearly, lucidly and persuasively. Dr. Brown possesses that ability. A remarkable communicator, he speaks with the tone, pitch, rate and diction that appeal to his audience. When he discusses, he responds with the appropriate enunciation, body language and skills. While on the pulpit, podium, radio or television, Dr. Brown adapts to the needs of the specific media.

Cooperation

Accomplished leaders are not only head persons but team players as well. They recognize their role as "primus inter pares" first among equals.

Dr. Brown

Dr. Brown is a masterful team player who consults and collaborates with his staff, managers, department heads, deans, community leaders, IHL authorities and legislators. This explains why he has been successful in his first one hundred days as president. He demonstrates, through words and deeds, that no man is an island.

Conflict Resolution

Leaders by dint of their elevated status; perceived, imagined or real, resolve conflicts. Indeed, disagreements erupt over big and little things. People in all organizations, including schools and universities, grapple with different goals and objectives that cry for alignment.

Although Dr. Brown has not yet tackled a major crisis, as an effective leader, he is putting mechanisms in place to nip disasters in the bud before they expand into conflagrations. In that regard, he demonstrates proaction rather than reaction.

Compassion

Famous leaders show compassion. Dr. Brown demonstrates this aptitude daily as he intermingles with Alcorn's administrators, faculty, staff, students and the general university community.

2

Alcorn's 18th President Welcomes SACS Accreditation Team

Faculty, Staff and Senate Leaders support SACS

Alcorn State University recently hosted evaluators for its On-Site Southern Association of Colleges and Schools (SACS) Reaffirmation visit. Alcorn State University's President and the entire community warmly welcomed the team to the campus.

The ten-member SACS Accreditation team visited Alcorn State University on March 29-30th, 2011. The Commission on Colleges will announce the final decision in December 2011, indicating whether Alcorn is charting the right path.

Chaired by Dr. Stephen Hulbert, the President of Nicholls State University, Thiboeaux, Louisiana; the team consisted of seasoned administrators and faculty from various institutions across the region.

Dr. Josephine Posey, former Interim Vice President for Academic Affairs, recommended Dr. Donzell Lee as SACS chair and he accepted to serve. Dr. Posey knew that he was the person for the task after having served as one of his co-chairs during the last two SACS reaffirmation processes. Dr. Lee and Ms. Patricia Keys, Alcorn's SACS Administrative Assistant for the third time, took on the assignment with enthusiasm.

Success did not occur without challenges. When Dr. Norris Allen Edney was selected as Interim President in January 2010, he made SACS, which embedded the Quality Enhancement Plan (QEP), his major priority. Through his leadership and proficiency in getting the job done, the university family, collectively worked as a team on SACS accreditation requirements.

When Alcorn's 18th President, Dr. M. Christopher Brown II, came aboard on January 2011, he immediately threw his support behind the existing SACS accreditation process to the fullest. His contributions are invaluable.

Alcorn's 18th President, Dr. Brown; past Interim President, Dr. Edney; Accreditation Liaison, Dr. Lee; and the SACS Leadership Team, including members of the QEP committee, participated in the exit meeting on March 29, 2011 where the evaluators shared their findings.

Accreditation Liaison, Dr. Donzell Lee said, "The reaffirmation of accreditation by SACS is a formidable challenge for most institutions. With the highest level of administrative support, Alcorn received very favorable feedback from the off-site and the on-site reviews. The on-site team was very complementary of Alcorn's Quality Enhancement Plan (QEP), which focuses on improving the writing abilities of our students. We anticipate a favorable decision by the Commission on Colleges at its December 2011, meeting in Orlando, Florida."

Dr. Donzell Lee, Accreditation Liaison

3

Poetic Salutes To Alcorn's 18th President

18th ASU President's Investiture

By Dr. Jerry Komia Domatob

As Dr. M. Christopher Brown II
Earns Alcorn's cherished crown
Rising as 18th President
Joy thrills, like a glorious incident

Rebirth, revival and renewal
Uplift Alcorn State University
Like a breadth of fresh air
That empowers and energizes

Splendidly welcoming the leader
Wise as an astute manager
Fans celebrate with cheers
As optimism wipes tears

Ace and seasoned educator
Inspiring as a star mentor
Dr. Brown ushers enthusiasm
Translating into positive activism

Youthful scholar of dynamism
His deeds sack cynicism
Like historic conquerors
Dr. Brown works as victors

Though inevitable obstacles ring
Like challenges that sing
Dr. Brown's skillful drive
Stimulates staff and students strive

Alcorn State University
Like a celebrity entity
Enters a fresh phase
Like players in a novel arena

Prayers, praises and entertainment
Mount motivation's merriment
As friends and families affection
Spur Dr. Brown to pilot in God's direction

Welcome President Brown
May resounding success grace your path.

Author

President Brown Receives Alcorn's Leadership

By Dr. Jerry Komia Domatob

On this great day, April 17th 2011, bells toll
Like melodious fall
Ushering Dr. M. Christopher Brown II
As Alcorn State University's 18th Executive

Amidst profuse prayers and praises
Gracing joyful faces
Admirers and fans, grandly salute
Like enthusiasts, who eagerly elevate

Acceding to his spot in Alcorn's history
Like 17 previous educators, with star stories
Dr. Brown, brings brilliance
Consolidating resort's excellence

As admirers welcome milestone
Planting another cornerstone
Glory, honor and praise to Almighty God
For a pilot, who will lead Alcorn through fog

As his task formally begins
Like most human pursuits
Doubts, uncertainties and expectations
Yearn for positive direction

Yes, challenges haunt like storms
Defying easy policy forms
Overwhelming best and brightest
Unnerving champions who beat test

But with Dr. Brown
Who battles odds without frown
A new era of progress and development
Shines Alcorn's arena as ointment

Take your tiara, President Brown
Lead like managers with a crown
Pave paths with a positive attitude
Steer Alcorn to a new altitude
Bravo! Bravo! Bravo!

Simply Sharing Team
Dr. Norris Edney, Dr. Josephine Posey,
Dr. Jerry Domatob, Mrs. Karen Shedrick,
Ms. Kimberly White

4

19. MID-WINTER CONFERENCES

1978	February 17–19	Chicago, Ill.
Host: Chicago Chapter Alumni		
1979	March 2–4	New Orleans, La.
Host: Alcorn State Alumni Chapter of New Orleans		
1980	February 1–3	Vicksburg, Miss.
Host: Vicksburg Alcorn Alumni Chapter		
1981	March 5–7	Washington, D.C.
Host: Washington, D.C., Metropolitan Area Chapter		
1982	February 26–28	Cleveland, Ohio
Host: Cleveland, Ohio Alumni Chapter		
1983	March 11–13	Dallas, Tex.
Host: Dallas/Ft. Worth Alcorn Alumni Chapter		
1984	February 24–26	Jackson, Miss.
Host: Jackson Alcorn Alumni Chapter		
1985	February 22–24	Detroit, Mich.
Host: Detroit Chapter		
1986	February 21–23	New Orleans, La.
Host: Alcorn State Alumni Chapter of New Orleans		
1987	February 27–March 1	Los Angeles, Calif.
Host: Los Angeles Alcorn Alumni Chapter		
1988	February 26–28	Laurel, Miss.
Host: Jones County Chapter		
1989	February 24–26	Chicago, Ill.
Host: Chicago Chapter Alumni		
1990	February 23–25	Washington, D.C.
Host: Washington, D.C., Metropolitan Area Chapter		
1991	February 22–24	Greenville, Miss.
Host: Washington County Alumni Chapter		
1992	February 28–March 1	San Francisco, Calif.
Host: San Francisco Alumni Chapter		
1993	February 19–21	Detroit, Mich.
Host: Detroit Chapter		
1994	February 25–27	Biloxi, Miss.
Host: Gulf Coast Alcorn Alumni Chapter		

1995	February 23–26	Houston, Tex.
Host: Houston Alcorn Alumni Chapter		
1996	February 22–25	Los Angeles, Calif.
Host: Los Angeles Alcorn Alumni Chapter		
1997	February 20–23	Jackson, Miss.
Host: Metro Jackson Alcorn Alumni Chapter		
1998	February 26–March 1	Atlanta, Ga.
Host: Atlanta Alcorn Alumni Chapter		
1999	February 25–28	Memphis, Tenn.
Host: Memphis Alcorn Alumni Chapter		
2000	February 24–27	Vicksburg, Miss.
Host: Vicksburg Alcorn Alumni Chapter		
2001	February 28–March 4	Dallas, Tex.
Host: Dallas/Ft. Worth Alcorn Alumni Chapter		
2002	February 28–March 3	New Orleans, La.
Host: New Orleans Alcorn Alumni Chapter		
2003	February 20–23	Hattiesburg, Miss.
Host: Hattiesburg/Forrest County/ Pine Belt Area Alcorn Alumni Chapter		
2004	February 26– 29	Tupelo, Miss.
Host: Northeast Alcorn Alumni Chapter		
2005	February 24–27	Arlington, Va.
Host: Washington, D.C., Metropolitan Alcorn Alumni Chapter		
2006	February 23–26	Birmingham, Ala.
Host: Birmingham Alumni Chapter		
2007	February 22–25	Jackson, Miss.
Host: Metro-Jackson Alumni Chapter		
2008	February 21–24	Detroit, Mich.
Host: Metro-Detroit Alumni Chapter		
2009	February 26–March 1	Houston, Tex.
Host: Greater Houston Alumni		
2010	February 25–28	Tunica, Miss.
Host: Panola County Alumni		
2011	February 24–27	Oak Brook, Ill.
Host: Chicago Chapter Alumni		
2012	February 23–26	Vicksburg, Miss.
Host: Vicksburg Warren Alumni		
2013	February 21–24	Atlanta, Ga.
Host: Metro-Atlanta Chapter		

2014	February 13–16	Washington, D.C.
Host: Metro Washington, D.C., Chapter		
2015	February 26–March 1	Biloxi, Miss.
Host: Mississippi Gulf Coast Alumni Chapters		

20. 1928 Commencement Day Program

CENTENNIAL
1928

COMMENCEMENT DAY

Wednesday, May 23, 1928—10:30 A. M.

PROGRAM

THE COMMENCEMENT PROCESSION:

President's Home to Chapel—The President, Commencement Speaker, Faculty Members, the Alumni, and the Graduating Classes, led by the College Band.

MUSIC ....College Band

INVOCATION

"Daybreak" .... Eaton-Fanning

REMARKS

LADIES' CHORUS—Gypsies .... Brahms

SALUTATORY ADDRESS—"American Ideals"
Meredith J. Lyells, Hazlehurst, Mississippi

SOLO .... Ernestine Mason

THE VALEDICTORY—"Our Heritage"—
James Thomas Hall Bolden, Gulfport, Mississippi

TRIO and CHORUS—"The Lord is Great".........................Haydn

THE COMMENCEMENT ADDRESS—
Dr. John Hope, President of Morehouse College

"Deep River" ....Harry T. Burleigh

CONFERRING DEGREES AND PRESENTING CERTIFICATES

HALLELUJAH CHORUS .... Handel

ANNOUNCEMENTS

BENEDICTION

Page fifty-two

21. AWARD OF EXCELLENCE RECIPIENTS

1982	Linda R. Smith	Agriculture	Coila, Miss.
1983	Pamela A. Davis	Biology	Jayess, Miss.
1984	Donita G. Morgan	Chemistry	Carthage, Miss.
1985	Clyde E. Glenn	Biology	Cleveland, Miss.
1986	Imogene McGriggs	English	Port Gibson, Miss.
1987	Charmaine Edwards	Chemistry/Pre-Med	St. Catherine, Jamaica
1988	Robert R. Norvel Jr.	Biology	Moss Point, Miss.
1989	Sharon Patterson	Animal Science	Kingston, Jamaica
1990	Robert Tatum	Chemistry	Oxford, Miss.
1991	Nancy R. Palmer	Pre-Med/Chemistry	Crystal Springs, Miss.
1992	Marcus Reeves	Biology/Pre-Med	Jonestown, Miss.
1993	Trena L. Brown	Elementary Education	Leland, Miss.
1994	Jeffrey Walker	Biology/Pre-Med, Chemistry	St. Louis
1995	Myra A. Hoskin	Accounting	Natchez, Miss.
1996	Angela Waller	Nursing	Natchez, Miss.
1997	Ramel Cotton	Political Science/Pre-Law	Vicksburg, Miss.
1998	April Smith	Biology	Ocean Springs, Miss.
1999	Sabrina Rene' Palmer	Biology	Bolton, Miss.
2000	Bernita Finley	Chemistry	Jackson, Miss.
2001	Cassandra Ford	Nursing	Starkville, Miss.
2002	Natalie Ballard	Chemistry	Fayette, Miss.
2003	Alfred Galtney	Political Science (Pre-Law)	Lorman, Miss.
2004	Deidre Jones	Biochemistry & Biology	Port Gibson, Miss.
2005	Marie Winston	Chemistry	Vicksburg, Miss.
2006	Wesleyne Whittaker	Chemistry (Biochemistry)	Vicksburg, Miss.
2007	Brittany Green	Chemistry	Morton, Miss.
2008	Morgan Rainey	Chemistry & Physics	St. Joliet, Ill.
2009	Joshlean Fair	Biochemistry	Chicago, Ill.
2010	Luella Jones	Chemistry (Biochemistry)	Lorman, Miss.
2011	Justin Nash	Pre-Medicine	Vicksburg, Miss.
2012	Kimber Thomas	English	Jackson, Miss.
2013	Casey Mock	Business Administration	Natchez, Miss.
2014	Anastacia Tuset	Business Administration	Fayetteville, N.C.
2015	Rachelle Abram	Business Administration	Fishkill, N.Y.

22. COMMENCEMENT SPEAKERS

Honorable W. E. Molleson	1887	Dr. C. V. Troup	1949
Dr. Robert T. Brown	1909	Jacob L. Reddix	1950
Honorable L. K. Atwood	1912	Rev. Blair T. Hunt	1951
Dr. W. T. Vernon	1913	Dr. Laurence C. Jones	1952
J. H. Burrus	1914	Dr. Benjamin E. Mays	1953
Bishop R. A. Carter	1915	Dr. Ira D. Reed	1954
Major Jno. R. Lynch	1916	Mr. Haien	1955
Dr. C. V. Romans	1917	Dr. Lawrence A. Davis	1956
Professor J. C. Whitaker	1918	Dr. Robert Hatch	1957
Dr. M. S. Davage	1919	Dr. Dorothy L. Branch	1958
Judge William Harrison	1920	Dr. C. V. Troup	1959
Dr. Kelley Miller	1921	Mr. J. M Tubb	1961
Dr. J. A. Gregg	1922	Dr. Helen G. Edmonds	1962
Isaac Fisher	1924	Dr. Samuel Proctor	1963
Dr. P. James Bryant	1925	S. Edward Peal	1965
Dr. Lorenzo H. King	1926	Dr. Felton G. Clark	1966
Bishop A. J. Carey	1927	Dr. Lewis C. Dowdy	1967
Dr. John M. Gandy	1929	Dr. Herman R. Branson	1968
Dr. Carter G. Woodson	1930	Dr. A. P. Torrence	1969
Dr. Kelley Miller	1931	Dr. Robert Hunter	1970
Professor William A. Bell	1932	William S. Demby	1971
Bishop William Mercer Green	1933	Honorable Earl L. Butz	1972
Excellency Sennett Connor	1934	Honorable Melvin H. Evans	1973
Dr. M. S. Davage	1935	Malvin R. Goode	1974
Dr. James R. Reynolds	1936	Dr. Preston Valien	1975
Dr. Benjamin E. Mays	1937	Honorable Evelyn Gandy	1976
Dr. Felton G. Clark	1938	Dr. George A. Owens	1977
Dr. Charlotte Hawkins Brown	1939	Dr. Milton K. Curry Jr.	1978
Dr. J. E. Walker	1940	Honorable Ernest N. Morial	1979
Dr. F. D. Patterson	1941	Dr. Jan S. Wallace	1980
Dr. Bertram W. Doyle	1942	Herman Coleman	1981
Honorable Arthur W. Mitchell	1943	Dr. Cleopatra D. Thompson	1982
Dr. J. S. Clark	1944	Dr. Samuel D. Proctor	1983
George W. Cox	1945	Dr. Wright L. Lassiter Jr.	1984
Dr. P. H. Easom	1947	Dr. C. Ronald Kimberling	1985
Honorable Hodding Carter	1948	Honorable William F. Winter	1986

Edwin Lupberger	1987	Katina Rankin	2002
E. B. Robinson Jr.	1988	Honorable Henry T. Wingate	2003
Honorable George Bush	1989	Earl G. Graves Sr.	2004
Honorable Mike Espy	1990	Honorable Ray Mabus	2005
Dr. Joe A. Haynes	1991	Honorable Percy W. Watson	2006
Dr. Samuel Dubois Cook	1992	Honorable Bennie G. Thompson	2007
Dr. Rudolph E. Waters	1993	Honorable John R. Lewis	2008
Honorable Maxine Aldridge White	1994	Dr. Charles H. Bridges	2009
Dr. H. Beecher Hicks Jr.	1995	Honorable Lillie Blackman Sanders	2010
Dr. Thomas D. Layzell	1996	Honorable William H. Gray III	2011
Ray Johnson	1997	Xerona Clayton	2012
Honorable Robert Major Walker	1998	Dr. Randal Pinkett	
Honorable Willie Simmons	1999	Marc. H. Morial	2013
Honorable Thad Cochran		Myrlie Evers	2014
Honorable Trent Lott	2000	Dr. Jacqueline Walters	2015
Honorable Robert G. Clark	2001		

23. 1952 SUMMER COMMENCEMENT PROGRAM

ALCORN AGRICULTURAL AND MECHANICAL COLLEGE

ALCORN, MISSISSIPPI

SUMMER

COMMENCEMENT

AUGUST THE FIFTEENTH

NINETEEN HUNDRED AND FIFTY-TWO

4:00 P.M.

OAKLAND MEMORIAL CHAPEL

ORDER OF EXERCISE

PRELUDE

PROCESSIONAL: THE MARCH OF THE PRIESTS -------- MENDELSOHN

MUSIC: THE NATIONAL ANTHEM ----------------------------- KEY

INVOCATION

> THE REVEREND M. L. UPTON
> COLLEGE CHAPLAIN

MUSIC: BLESS THIS HOUSE ------------------------------ BRAHAL
> MYRTIS HAYES

PRESENTATION OF SPEAKER

THE COMMENCEMENT ADDRESS

> MISS FLORENCE O. ALEXANDER
> STATE SUPERVISOR OF JEANES TEACHERS
> JACKSON, MISSISSIPPI

MUSIC: BEAUTIFUL SAVIOR --------------------------- RIEGGER
> WOMEN'S GLEE CLUB

CONFERRING OF DEGREES

> DR. J. R. OTIS, PRESIDENT
> ALCORN A. & M. COLLEGE

PRESENTATION OF AWARDS

INDUCTION OF GRADUATING CLASS INTO ALUMNI ASSOCIATION

ANNOUNCEMENTS

ALMA MATER

RECESSIONAL: THE MARCH OF THE PRIESTS --------- MENDELSOHN

-00-00-

24. PRESIDENTIAL AWARD OF EXCELLENCE RECIPIENTS

2012

Charles Wesley

John Igwebuike

Yufeng Zheng

Bettaiya Rajanna

Johnnie Dorris

Isiah Starks

Charles C. Teamer Sr.

2013

Marta A. Piva

Wesley Lloyd Whittaker

Mary Marie Trimble

Belinda Benjamin

Samuel Griffin

25. LETTER FROM COMMISSIONER HANK BOUNDS

MISSISSIPPI

INSTITUTIONS OF HIGHER LEARNING

Office of Commissioner

October 23, 2009

Mrs. Karen Shedrick
Executive Secretary
Alcorn State University
1000 ASU Drive 359
Alcorn State, MS 39096

Dear Mrs. Shedrick:

I enjoyed visiting the Alcorn campus last week. As the Executive Secretary to the President, I know that a lot of the preparation for the Board meeting fell on your shoulders. You and the rest of the committee did an excellent job in preparing for our visit. Thank you for all of your hard work.

Sincerely,

Hank M. Bounds
Commissioner of Higher Education

HMB/bb

3825 Ridgewood Road • Jackson, Mississippi 39211-6453 • (601) 432-6623 • FAX (601) 432-6972

---

26. ACADEMIC SCHOOLS AND
MAJOR SUPPORT DIVISIONS AS OF 2015

ACADEMIC AFFAIRS

Donzell Lee, Provost and Executive Vice President

John Igwebuike, Associate Provost

Patricia Keys, SACS Coordinator and Administrative Assistant to the Provost

LeKita Carr, Special Assistant to the Provost

Belinda Benjamin, Administrative and Student Support Services

LaToya Hart, Institutional Effectiveness and Assessment

Ramesh Maddali, Institutional Research and Assessment

Thomas Sturgis, Pre-Professional Programs

Wandra Arrington, Honors Curriculum Program

Jimmy Smith, Registrar's Office

Ivan Banks, Vicksburg Expansion Program

Lola Brown, Title III Coordinator

Coretta Jackson, Associate Title III Coordinator

Alfred Galtney, Director, Research and Sponsored Programs

SCHOOL OF AGRICULTURE, RESEARCH EXTENSION
AND APPLIED SCIENCES

Ivory Lyles, Dean

Daniel Collins, Chairperson, Agriculture

Carrie Ford, Chairperson, Human Sciences

Magid Dagher, Agriculture Small Farm Development

Gregory Reed, Extension Program

Keith McGee, Biotechnology

Kwabena Agyepong, Advanced Technologies

Patrick Igbokwe, Alcorn Experiment Station

Dovi Alipoe, Global Programs

Donald Smith, Office of Development

School of Arts and Sciences

Babu Patlolla, Dean
Bettaiya Rajanna, Chairperson, Biological Sciences
Sandra Barnes, Chairperson, Chemistry and Physics
Cynthia Scurria, Chairperson, English and Foreign Languages
Jerry Domatob, Interim Chairperson, Mass Communications
Larry Konecky, Chairperson, Fine Arts
Lixin Yu, Chairperson, Mathematics and Computer Science
Andrell Hardy, Chairperson, Military Science
Dickson Idusuyi, Chairperson, Social Sciences
Dorothy Idleburg, Chairperson, Social Work

School of Business

John Igwebuike, Interim Dean
Donna Williams, Chairperson, Undergraduate Business Programs
Akash Dania, Graduate Business Programs
Beverly Adams, Student Services

School of Education and Psychology

Robert Carr, Dean
Malinda Butler, Associate Dean
Helen Wyatt, Chairperson, Education and Psychology
Johnny Thomas, Chairperson, Health, Physical Education, and Recreation
LaShundia Carson, Field Experiences and Student Teaching
Tabitha Smith, Master of Arts in Teaching Program

School of Nursing

Yolanda Powell-Young, Dean
Janelle Baker, Associate Dean and Associate Professor

University College

Valerie Thompson, Dean
Rickey Coleman, Academic Advising, Summer Developmental Program
Patricia White, First Year Experience
Abegayle Goldblatt, Retention Specialist
Mary Coleman, Student Support Services
Lucille Donaldson, Upward Bound

University Libraries

Blanche Sanders, Dean
Clarence Love, Natchez Campus Learning Resource Center
Darlene Jones, Natchez Student Service Center

Student Affairs

Emanuel Barnes, Vice President
Katangela Tenner, Admissions and Recruiting
Joey Mitchell, Career Services
Dyann Moses, Counseling and Testing
Juanita McKenzie Edwards, Financial Aid
Devina Hogan, Student Engagement
Dorothy Jackson Davis, Health and Disability Services
Willie Moses, James L. Bolden Campus Union
Ella Hudson, Judicial Affairs
Jessica Foxworth, Resident Life

Athletics

Derek Horne, Intercollegiate Athletics Director
Jason Cable, Associate Athletics Director for Compliance
John Igwebuike, Faculty Athletic Representative

FINANCE AND ADMINISTRATIVE SERVICES

Carolyn Dupre, Vice President
Brenda Square, Auxiliary Services
Donna Hayden, Center for Information Technology and Services
Douglas Stewart, Campus Police
Carla Williams, Human Resources
Shundera Stallings, Parking Services
Marlin King, Facilities Management
Ray White, Environmental Health and Safety
Donna Horton, Printing and Duplicating
Natalie Green, UPS Printing and Shipping

INSTITUTIONAL ADVANCEMENT

Marcus Ward, Vice President, Executive Director for ASU Foundation, Inc.
Janice Gibson, Director of Development and Alumni Affairs
Larry Smith, Director, Athletic Development

MARKETING AND COMMUNICATION

Clara Ross Stamps, Vice President
Tanya Carr, Office Manager
Christopher Davis, Communication Assistant
Justus Reed, Staff Writer
Stacey Springfield, Senior Graphic Designer

UNIVERSITY INTERNAL AUDITOR

Permy Thuha, Internal Auditor

EDUCATIONAL EQUITY AND INCLUSION

Lljuna Weir

27. LEADERSHIP OF PERMANENT, INTERIM, AND ACTING PRESIDENTS FROM 1994 TO 2015

ALFRED RANKINS JR.
Nineteenth President

- Karen Shedrick, Executive Assistant to the President
- Donzell Lee, Provost and Vice President for Academic Affairs
- Carolyn DuPre, Vice President for Finance and Administrative Services
- Marcus Ward, Vice President for Institutional Advancement
- Clara Ross Stamps, Vice President for Marketing and Communication
- Emanuel Barnes, Vice President for Student Affairs
- Ruth Nichols, Special Assistant to the President for Community and Economic Development
- Derek Horne, Intercollegiate Athletics Director
- Jason Cable, Associate Athletics Director for Compliance
- LLJuna Weir, Director of Educational Equity and Inclusion

NORRIS ALLEN EDNEY SR.
December 2013–March 2014 Acting

(There were no changes in leadership.)

M. CHRISTOPHER BROWN II
Eighteenth President

- Karen Shedrick, Executive Assistant to the President
- Samuel L. White, Executive Vice President and Provost
- Betty J. Roberts, Senior Vice President for University Operations and Chief Operating Officer
- E. Cheryl Ponder, Vice President for Student Affairs
- Marcus D. Ward, Vice President for Institutional Advancement
- Clara Ross Stamps, Vice President for Media Relations
- Derek Greenfield, Director of Educational Equity and Inclusion
- Ramesh Maddali, Director of Institutional Research and Assessment
- Kassie Freeman, Director of Strategic Innovation
- Dwayne White, Interim Director of Intercollegiate Athletics
- Jeremy Mason, Special Assistant for University Initiatives

NORRIS ALLEN EDNEY SR.
2010–2011 Interim

- Karen Shedrick, Administrative Assistant/Executive Secretary to the President
- Josephine Posey, Special Assistant to the President
- Kevin Appleton, Vice President for Finance and Administrative Services
- Richard Green, Provost and Vice President for Academic Affairs
- Stephen L. McDaniel, CFRE, Vice President for Development and Marketing, Executive Director ASU Foundation
- Gerald Peoples, Vice President for Student Affairs

GEORGE E. ROSS
Seventeenth President

- Brenda T. Square, Chief of Staff/Executive Assistant to the President
- Karen Shedrick, Administrative Assistant/Executive Secretary to the President
- Josephine M. Posey, Vice President for Academic Affairs
- Elvin Parker, Vice President for Business Affairs
- Stephen L. McDaniel, Vice President for Development and Marketing, Executive Director, Alcorn State University Foundation, Inc.
- Gerald C. Peoples, Vice President for Student Affairs

MALVIN A. WILLIAMS SR.
2006–2008 Interim

- Cheryl Kariuki, Chief of Staff
- Karen Shedrick, Administrative Assistant/Executive Secretary to the President
- Napoleon Moses, Vice President for Academic Affairs
- Claudine Gee, Vice President for Business Affairs
- LaPlose Jackson, Vice President for Student Affairs
- Franklin Jackson, Vice President for Institutional Advancement, Planning and Research

CLINTON BRISTOW JR.
Sixteenth President

- Karen Shedrick, Administrative Assistant/Executive Secretary to the President
- Rudolph E. Waters Sr., Executive Vice President
- Franklin D. Jackson, Vice President for Institutional Advancement, Planning and Research

- LaPlose T. Jackson, Vice President for Student Affairs
- Wiley F. Jones, Vice President for Business Affairs
- Malvin A. Williams Sr., Vice President for Academic Affairs

RUDOLPH E. WATERS SR.
1994–1995 Interim

- Karen Shedrick, Administrative Assistant/Executive Secretary to the President
- Franklin Jackson, Vice President for Institutional Advancement and Planning
- LaPlose Jackson, Acting Vice President for Student Affairs
- Wiley Jones, Vice President for Business Affairs
- Malvin Williams Sr., Vice President for Academic Affairs

WALTER WASHINGTON
Fifteenth President

- Karen Shedrick, Administrative Assistant/Executive Secretary to the President
- J. I. Hendricks Jr., Director of Public Relations
- O. W. Moses, Business Manager
- Marino H. Casem, Athletic Director and Head Football Coach
- Oliver G. Taylor Jr., Director of Development
- James L. Bolden, Director of Student Personnel
- Calvin White, Dean of Instruction
- Robert W. Bowles, Director of Alumni Affairs
- Rudolph E. Waters, Vice President

Leadership during Dr. Washington's administration at some point also included:

- Rudolph E. Waters, Vice President
- Malvin Williams, Dean of Academic Affairs
- Samuel Donald, Director of Agriculture, Research, Extension, and Applied Sciences
- Wiley Jones, Business Manager
- Emanuel Barnes, Dean of Student Affairs
- Franklin Jackson, Director of Institutional Advancement
- Francis Henderson, Director of the School of Nursing
- Norris Allen Edney Sr., Director of the Graduate School

28. 2014–2015 FOUR-YEAR CAREER PLAN

Office of Career Services F

Four-Year Career Plan 2014-2015

Freshman Year

- Visit the Center for Career Services, James L. Bolden Campus Union, 2nd floor and meet the staff.
- Research careers and majors using our website and FOCUS 2.
- Attend one of the Career Services Seminars.
- Take a variety of classes to get an idea of different academic fields.
- Complete FOCUS 2, a self-paced online program that will help you explore and make decisions about your major area of study and your career goals.
- Meet with professional staff to explore possible majors and careers that fit your interests, skills, and values.
- Attend Career Services workshops and programs including Career Fairs.

Sophomore Year

- Research career options using our website and FOCUS 2 to utilize related links and JOBS4Braves: *Job Opportunities Benefiting Alcorn State University students.*
- Continue to study hard and remain focused. Participate in on-campus organizations to gain valuable work-related skills.
- Explore co-ops, internships, and part-time career related employment using JOBS4Braves, Career Services online Students link.
- Complete FOCUS 2, a self-paced online program that will help you explore and make decisions about your major area of study and your career goals.

Junior Year

- Register with JOBS4Braves and create a profile if you haven't done so already.
- Participate in co-ops, internships or career related employment.
- Maximize involvement with campus clubs and organizations to further develop leadership skills.
- Continue informational interviewing – expanding your network.
- Identify professional associations related to career interests.
- Participate in job shadowing and/or volunteer and community service opportunities.
- Attend Career Services workshops and programs including Career Fairs.

Senior Year

- Make an appointment with Career Services to help plan your job search.
- Develop a refined resume, cover letter, and list of references.
- Practice interviewing skills via a mock interview with a career counselor and review professional dress guidelines.
- Begin developing a professional wardrobe for future job interviews.
- Sign up with Career Services for the on-campus interview program.
- Continue developing your network. Remember social (Facebook and Twitter) and professional (LinkedIn) networking sites can help or hinder your job search.

Office of Career Services
1000 ASU Drive, #540
Alcorn State, MS 39096-7500
Office: 601·877·6324
Fax: 601·877·6279

29. ALCORN ENROLLMENT BY ETHNICITY, GENDER, RESIDENCY, LEVEL, AGE, AND FULL-TIME EQUIVALENT

ALCORN STATE UNIVERSITY ENROLLMENT BY ETHNICITY, GENDER, RESIDENCY, LEVEL, AGE AND FTE

Fall Session	White	Black	Other	Men	Women	Resident	Non-Resident	Under-graduate	Graduate	Under 25	25 and Over	Age Unknown	Total FTE	Total Headcount
1999	134	2,706	31	1,088	1,783	2,465	406	2,405	466	2,213	649	9	2,678.0	2,871
2000	207	2,691	38	1,125	1,811	2,523	413	2,398	538	2,130	806	0	2,691.9	2,936
2001	219	2,841	36	1,180	1,916	2,652	444	2,543	553	2,197	899	0	2,777.3	3,096
2002	261	2,858	31	1,192	1,958	2,702	448	2,522	628	2,133	1,017	0	2,753.2	3,150
2003	327	2,955	27	1,209	2,100	2,777	532	2,662	647	2,204	1,105	0	2,836.3	3,309
2004	325	3,080	38	1,206	2,237	2,924	519	2,832	611	2,236	1,207	0	3,024.1	3,443
2005	275	3,228	41	1,255	2,289	2,999	545	2,962	582	2,315	1,229	0	3,166.2	3,544
2006	301	3,240	42	1,223	2,360	3,049	534	3,014	569	2,361	1,222	0	3,222.6	3,583
2007	312	3,315	41	1,198	2,470	3,186	482	3,004	664	2,295	1,373	0	3,259.2	3,668
2008	238	2,967	47	1,036	2,216	2,866	386	2,626	626	2,053	1,199	0	2,891.9	3,252
2009	214	3,066	54	1,055	2,279	2,933	401	2,700	634	2,046	1,288	0	2,913.3	3,334
%Change 1999 to 2004	142.5%	13.8%	22.6%	10.8%	25.5%	18.6%	27.8%	17.8%	31.1%	1.0%	86.0%	-100.0%	12.9%	19.9%
%Change 2004 to 2009	-34.2%	-0.5%	42.1%	-12.5%	1.9%	0.3%	-22.7%	-4.7%	3.8%	-8.5%	6.7%	0.0%	-3.7%	-3.2%
%Change 1999 to 2009	59.7%	13.3%	74.2%	-3.0%	27.8%	19.0%	-1.2%	12.3%	36.1%	-7.5%	98.5%	-100.0%	8.8%	16.1%

Percent of Total

Fall Session	White	Black	Other	Men	Women	Resident	Non-Resident	Under-graduate	Graduate	Under 25	25 and Over	Total FTE
1999	4.7%	94.3%	1.1%	37.9%	62.1%	85.9%	14.1%	83.8%	16.2%	77.1%	22.6%	93.3%
2000	7.1%	91.7%	1.3%	38.3%	61.7%	85.9%	14.1%	81.7%	18.3%	72.5%	27.5%	91.7%
2001	7.1%	91.8%	1.2%	38.1%	61.9%	85.7%	14.3%	82.1%	17.9%	71.0%	29.0%	89.7%
2002	8.3%	90.7%	1.0%	37.8%	62.2%	85.8%	14.2%	80.1%	19.9%	67.7%	32.3%	87.4%
2003	9.9%	89.3%	0.8%	36.5%	63.5%	83.9%	16.1%	80.4%	19.6%	66.6%	33.4%	85.7%
2004	9.4%	89.5%	1.1%	35.0%	65.0%	84.9%	15.1%	82.3%	17.7%	64.9%	35.1%	87.8%
2005	7.8%	91.1%	1.2%	35.4%	64.6%	84.6%	15.4%	83.6%	16.4%	65.3%	34.7%	89.3%
2006	8.4%	90.4%	1.2%	34.1%	65.9%	85.1%	14.9%	84.1%	15.9%	65.9%	34.1%	89.9%
2007	8.5%	90.4%	1.1%	32.7%	67.3%	86.9%	13.1%	81.9%	18.1%	62.6%	37.4%	88.9%
2008	7.3%	91.2%	1.4%	31.9%	68.1%	88.1%	11.9%	80.8%	19.2%	63.1%	36.9%	88.9%
2009	6.4%	92.0%	1.6%	31.6%	68.4%	88.0%	12.0%	81.0%	19.0%	61.4%	38.6%	87.4%

Notes: Percents may not add to 100% due to rounding.
Enrollment figures are unduplicated.

ALCORN STATE UNIVERSITY ENROLLMENT BY ETHNICITY, GENDER, RESIDENCY, LEVEL, AGE AND FTE

Fall Session	White	Black	Other	Men	Women	Resident	Non-Resident	Under-graduate	Graduate	Under 25	25 and Over	Age Unknown	Total FTE	Total Headcount
2005	275	3,228	41	1,255	2,289	2,999	545	2,962	582	2,315	1,229	0	3,166.2	3,544
2006	301	3,240	42	1,223	2,360	3,049	534	3,014	569	2,361	1,222	0	3,222.6	3,583
2007	312	3,315	41	1,198	2,470	3,186	482	3,004	664	2,295	1,373	0	3,259.2	3,668
2008	238	2,967	47	1,036	2,216	2,866	386	2,626	626	2,053	1,199	0	2,891.9	3,252
2009	214	3,066	54	1,055	2,279	2,933	401	2,700	634	2,046	1,288	0	2,913.3	3,334
2010	240	3,378	64	1,172	2,510	3,217	465	2,980	702	2,255	1,427	0	3,240.4	3,682
2011	212	3,741	65	1,288	2,730	3,535	483	3,296	722	2,485	1,533	0	3,463.5	4,018
2012	193	3,694	63	1,302	2,648	3,451	499	3,208	742	2,466	1,484	0	3,454.9	3,950
2013	173	3,621	54	1,285	2,563	3,368	480	3,157	691	2,397	1,451	0	3,332.0	3,848
2014	132	3,445	62	1,244	2,395	3,169	470	3,006	633	2,358	1,281	0	3,154.0	3,639
2015	130	3,229	159	1,226	2,292	2,838	680	2,911	607	2,423	1,095	0	3,138.6	3,518
2005 to 2010 %Change	-12.7%	4.6%	56.1%	-6.6%	9.7%	7.3%	-14.7%	0.6%	20.6%	-2.6%	16.1%	N/A	2.3%	3.9%
2010 to 2015 %Change	-45.8%	-4.4%	148.4%	4.6%	-8.7%	-11.8%	46.2%	-2.3%	-13.5%	7.5%	-23.3%	N/A	-3.1%	-4.5%
2005 to 2015 %Change	-52.7%	0.0%	287.8%	-2.3%	0.1%	-5.4%	24.8%	-1.7%	4.3%	4.7%	-10.9%	N/A	-0.9%	-0.7%

Percent of Total

Fall Session	White	Black	Other	Men	Women	Resident	Non-Resident	Under-graduate	Graduate	Under 25	25 and Over	Total FTE
2005	7.8%	91.1%	1.2%	35.4%	64.6%	84.6%	15.4%	83.6%	16.4%	65.3%	34.7%	89.3%
2006	8.4%	90.4%	1.2%	34.1%	65.9%	85.1%	14.9%	84.1%	15.9%	65.9%	34.1%	89.9%
2007	8.5%	90.4%	1.1%	32.7%	67.3%	86.9%	13.1%	81.9%	18.1%	62.6%	37.4%	88.9%
2008	7.3%	91.2%	1.4%	31.9%	68.1%	88.1%	11.9%	80.8%	19.2%	63.1%	36.9%	88.9%
2009	6.4%	92.0%	1.6%	31.6%	68.4%	88.0%	12.0%	81.0%	19.0%	61.4%	38.6%	87.4%
2010	6.5%	91.7%	1.7%	31.8%	68.2%	87.4%	12.6%	80.9%	19.1%	61.2%	38.8%	88.0%
2011	5.3%	93.1%	1.6%	32.1%	67.9%	88.0%	12.0%	82.0%	18.0%	61.8%	38.2%	86.2%
2012	4.9%	93.5%	1.6%	33.0%	67.0%	87.4%	12.6%	81.2%	18.8%	62.4%	37.6%	87.5%
2013	4.5%	94.1%	1.4%	33.4%	66.6%	87.5%	12.5%	82.0%	18.0%	62.3%	37.7%	86.6%
2014	3.6%	94.7%	1.7%	34.2%	65.8%	87.1%	12.9%	82.6%	17.4%	64.8%	35.2%	86.7%
2015	3.7%	91.8%	4.5%	34.8%	65.2%	80.7%	19.3%	82.7%	17.3%	68.9%	31.1%	89.2%

Notes: Percents may not add to 100% due to rounding.
Enrollment figures are unduplicated.

Fall Enrollment Book

27

30. ACADEMIC DEGREE PROGRAMS AS OF 2015

ALCORN STATE UNIVERSITY
ACADEMIC DEGREE PROGRAMS
ACADEMIC YEAR 2015

Degree Programs	Types of Degrees			
	Associate	Bachelor	Master's	Specialist
Accounting		BS		
Agribusiness Management		BS		
Agricultural Economics		BS		
Agricultural Science		BS		
Applied Science		BS		
Applied Science and Technology			MS	
Biology		BS	MS	
Biotechnology			MS	
Business Administration		BBA		
Chemistry		BS		
Child Development		BS		
Computer and Information Science			MS	
Computer Networking and Information Technology		BS		
Computer Science		BS		
Criminal Justice		BA		
Elementary Education		BS	MSED	EDS
English		BA		
General Agriculture			MS	
General Business Administration			MBA	
General Studies		BA		
History		BA		
Mass Communications		BA		
Mathematics		BS		
Music		BA/BM		
Nursing	ASN	BSN	MSN	
Nutrition and Dietetics		BS		
Political Science		BA		
Psychology		BS		
Recreation		BS		
Robotics and Automation Technology		BS		
Secondary Education			MSED	
Social Work		BSW		
Sociology		BA		
Sport Management		BS		
Teaching (Alternate Route)			MAT	
Workforce Education Leadership			MS	

Source: ASU Academic Program Inventory

31. 2015 UNIVERSITY CALENDAR FOR JUNE

Home > Calendars

Calendars

EVENTS

THU JUN 04 Faculty Report for Non-Attendance - UW **(Unofficial Withdrawal)**

FRI JUN 05 Classes Dropped for Non-Attendance UW (Unofficial Withdrawal)

MON JUN 08 Freeze Date/Authorize Disbursement of Financial Aid/Last Day to Apply for Student Loans

MON JUN 08 Last Day for Attendance Verification Forms

FRI JUN 12 Last Day for Official Withdrawal

FRI JUN 12 Last Day to Drop a Class by Any Means

MON JUN 15 **ACT Residual (8:30 a.m.)**
Thru: Friday, June 19, 2015

MON JUN 15 **Placement Test (Over 21 - 8:30 a.m.)**
Thru: Friday, June 19, 2015

TUE JUN 30 **Final Examinations**

SHARE

June 2015

| Prev | | | | | | Next |

SUN	MON	TUE	WED	THU	FRI	SAT
31	1	2	3	4	5	6
7	8	9	10	11	12	13
14	15	16	17	18	19	20
21	22	23	24	25	26	27
28	29	30	1	2	3	4

| June 2015 | ▼ |

| Month | Week | Print |

Subscribe & Download

📅 Visit the iCalendar Feeds page

Customize:

☑ Academic Calendar
☐ Alumni
☐ Events Calendar
☐ Student Affairs
☐ Vicksburg Office
☐ AREAS Calendar
☐ Arts and Entertainment
☐ Career Services
☑ Workshops
☐ Natchez Campus
☐ Professional Development
☐ Special Events

32. 1888 UNIVERSITY CALENDAR

CALENDAR.

1888.

Monday, January 2d—Second Term begins.
Thursday, March 22nd—Public Rhetoricals at 7:30 P. M.

COMMENCEMENT WEEK.

June 8th, 11th and 12th—Examination of Classes.

Sunday, 10th.
⎱ Sabbath School Exercises at 10 A. M.
⎰ Baccalaureate Sermon at 2:30 P. M.
⎱ Y. M. C. A. Anniversary at 7:30 P. M.

Tuesday 12th—Annual Meeting of Trustees at 10 A. M.
Wednesday, June 13th—Commencement Exercises at 10 A. M.

SUMMER VACATION.

Thursday, September 13th.
⎱ Fall Term begins.
⎰ The Boarding Hall opens.

13th and 14th—Examination for Assignment to Classes.
Thursday, December 20th.—Public Rhetorical Exercises by the
Literary Societies, at 7:30 P. M.
Monday, December 31st—Second Term begins.

1889.

Thursday, March   .—Public Rhetoricals at 7:30 P. M.

COMMENCEMENT WEEK.

June 7th, 10th and 11th—Examination of Classes.

Sunday, 9th.
⎱ Sabbath School Exercises at 10 A. M.
⎰ Baccalaureate Sermon at 2:30 P. M.
⎱ Y. M. C. A. Anniversary at 7:30 P. M.

Tuesday, 11th—Annual Meeting of Trustees at 10 A. M.
Wednesday, 12th—Commencement Exercises at 10 A. M.

OFFICE HOURS FOR STUDENTS.

General office hours for students are Saturday mornings from
7 to 8, and from 6 to 7 o'clock every evening except Sundays
and Wednesdays. Books may be had at noon, before the bell
for the afternoon classes. Students from the neighborhood
may also transact other business at the office during the noon
recess.

33. 2012 J. D. BOYD LIBRARY ANNUAL STATISTICS

Annual Statistics 2012
J. D. Boyd Library

Collections

Volumes held 2012:	380,876
Volumes added during year:	1,400
Volumes withdrawn during year	14
Volumes added during year(Net)	1,386
Volumes held June 30, 2012	**382,262**

Serials

# of current serial, including periodicals, purchased:	12,386
# of current serial, including periodicals, received:	6,190
Total # of current serials received:	**18,576**

Other Library Material

Microform units:385,629
Government documents not counted elsewhere:0
Computer files: 0
Manuscripts and archives (linear feet):12,111

Audiovisual Materials

Cartographic	385,629
Audio	2,848
Graphic	0
Film and video	1938
Total Titles	**390,415**

Expenditures

Library Material

Monographs	32,850.63
Current serials including periodicals	200,338.83
Other library materials (e.g., microforms, a/v, etc.)	14,170.34
Miscellaneous (all materials not included above)	50,000.00
Total library materials	**297,359.39**

Contract Binding
Salaries and Wages

Professional & Support Staff	731,897
Student assistants (including federal w/s funds)	21,648
Total salaries and wages	753,545
Fringe benefits	39,646
Total Expenditures	**2,038,221.39**

PERSONNEL

Professional staff, FTE	07
Support staff, FTE	17
Student assistants, FTE	11
Total **FTE** staff	**35**

INSTRUCTION

Number of library presentations to groups	10
Number of total participants in group presentations	249

REFERENCE

Number of reference transactions	649

CIRCULATION

Number of initial circulations (excluding reserves)	816
Total circulations (initial and renewals, excluding reserves)	**1808**

34. ANALYSIS OF OPERATING BUDGET SUMMARY OF IHL APPROPRIATIONS

Analysis of Operating Budgets
Summary of IHL Appropriations

	Original Appropriation FY 2010	Original Appropriation FY 2011		
Alcorn State University E&G				
General Fund	16,282,836	13,209,008	-3,073,828	-18.9%
Washington Scholarship	6,250	6,250	0	0.0%
Interest	12,592	12,592	0	0.0%
Total General Fund	16,301,678	13,227,850	-3,073,828	-18.9%
Education Enhancement Fund	2,514,594	2,215,140	-299,454	-11.9%
Budget Contingency Fund	0	0	0	
ARRA Funds	1,651,501	2,308,093	656,592	39.8%
Total E&G	20,467,773	17,751,083	-2,716,690	-13.3%
ASU Agricultural Units				
General Fund	5,586,114	5,194,352	-391,762	-7.0%
Education Enhancement Fund	21,004	19,322	-1,682	-8.0%
Budget Contingency Fund	0	0	0	
Total AG	5,607,118	5,213,674	-393,444	-7.0%
AYERS:				
General Funds: ASU Programs	4,350,000	4,350,000	0	0.0%
GRAND TOTAL ASU	30,424,891	27,314,757	-3,110,134	-10.2%

35. FALL 2013–SPRING 2014 TUITION

ALCORN STATE UNIVERSITY
Fall 2013 - Spring 2014

Tuition
(Rates for New, Honors and Renovated Dorms)

UNDERGRADUATE

Hours	Commuting Students In-State	Out-of-State	Hiram Revels In-State	Out-of-State	Honors Dorm In-State	Out-of-State	New Dorms A B C D In-State	Out-of-State
12	$3,048	$7,548	$6,513	$11,013	$6,576	$11,076	$7,263	$11,763
11	$2,794	$6,919	$6,259	$10,384	$6,322	$10,447	$7,009	$11,134
10	$2,540	$6,290	$6,005	$9,755	$6,068	$9,818	$6,755	$10,505
9	$2,286	$5,661	$5,751	$9,126	$5,814	$9,189	$6,501	$9,876
8	$2,032	$5,032	$5,497	$8,497	$5,560	$8,560	$6,247	$9,247
7	$1,778	$4,403	$5,243	$7,868	$5,306	$7,931	$5,993	$8,618
6	$1,524	$3,774	$4,989	$7,239	$5,052	$7,302	$5,739	$7,989
5	$1,270	$3,145	$4,735	$6,610	$4,798	$6,673	$5,485	$7,360
4	$1,016	$2,516	$4,481	$5,981	$4,544	$6,044	$5,231	$6,731
3	$762	$1,887	$4,227	$5,352	$4,290	$5,415	$4,977	$6,102
2	$508	$1,258	$3,973	$4,723	$4,036	$4,786	$4,723	$5,473
1	$254	$629	$3,719	$4,094	$3,782	$4,157	$4,469	$4,844

GRADUATE

Hours	Commuting Students In-State	Out-of-State	Hiram Revels In-State	Out-of-State	Honors Dorm In-State	Out-of-State	New Dorms A B C D In-State	Out-of-State
9	$3,051	$7,548	$6,516	$11,016	$6,579	$11,079	$7,266	$11,766
8	$2,712	$6,712	$6,177	$10,177	$6,240	$10,240	$6,927	$10,927
7	$2,373	$5,873	$5,838	$9,338	$5,901	$9,401	$6,588	$10,088
6	$2,034	$5,034	$5,499	$8,499	$5,562	$8,562	$6,249	$9,249
5	$1,695	$4,195	$5,160	$7,660	$5,223	$7,723	$5,910	$8,410
4	$1,356	$3,356	$4,821	$6,821	$4,884	$6,884	$5,571	$7,571
3	$1,017	$2,517	$4,482	$5,982	$4,545	$6,045	$5,232	$6,732
2	$678	$1,678	$4,143	$5,143	$4,206	$5,206	$4,893	$5,893
1	$339	$839	$3,804	$4,304	$3,867	$4,367	$4,554	$5,054

Meal Plan: Commuting students have the option of purchasing a meal plan for $1,321 per semester.

Approved: _____
Vice President for Fiscal Affairs

Fees are subject to change without notice

Revised: May 3, 2013

36. Alcorn State University National Alumni Association History

The Alcorn State University National Alumni Association was organized in 1890 and later incorporated in 1952. The association supports programs and projects that enhance the vision and mission of the university. Dr. A. D. Snodgrass, class of 1952, founded the association and became its first president and has been followed by many committed presidents throughout its history who have shown the determination to carry out Snodgrass's vision.

The national officers who serve two-year terms are the president, first vice president, second vice president, executive secretary, treasurer, recording secretary, assistant recording secretary, historian, and parliamentarian. These officers constitute the executive board of the association, which meets four times annually—August and December executive board meetings, Mid-Winter Conference, and Alumni Weekend. The board also includes the director of Alumni Affairs, today known as the director for Development and Alumni Affairs, and the immediate past president.

The association includes many chapters throughout the nation. If there are five or more individuals interested in organizing a chapter in an area where there is no chapter, they may petition to organize one and receive the proper documents needed from the executive secretary. Dues have increased through the years from $1.00 to the current $50.00.

More than 25,000 degrees have been conferred in many professional areas, including agriculture, business, education, nursing, and other areas of industry, government, and public and foreign services since Alcorn was founded in 1871.

Through the National Alumni Association and its affiliated chapters, recruitment of students is a priority. Students are encouraged to attend Alcorn and to seek admission and financial support through the appropriate university means, including grants and/or other financial incentives. The association is committed to fund-raising projects to support the university and students through sponsoring activities toward this end enabling scholarship availability and the meeting of other critical needs.

Other major focus areas of the National Alumni Association include support of Purple and Gold Day at the State Capitol; selection and support of the Alcornite of the Year; and Hall of Honors, Hall of Fame, and the Chapter Service Awards recipients. Donations are also made to the Alcorn State University Alumni Foundation and the University Foundation. The association is governed by its constitution and by-laws and standard operating procedure manual.

The Alcorn State University National Alumni Association is totally committed to the upward growth of Alcorn State University and will continue to enhance the university's history by never giving up, never envisioning a day of doom, and always looking forward to the best yet to come!

A total of nineteen presidents have served the National Alumni Association.

37. Alcorn State University National Alumni Association Chapter Presidents as of 2015

Augustus Russ .... Amite County Chapter

Ronnie Hampton .... Arkansas Chapter

Doris McGowan ....ASU Campus Chapter

Alvin Moore ....Birmingham, Ala., Chapter

Bettye Mosley...Bolivar County Chapter

Bobby E. Boone..Carthage Leake County Chapter

Grady Jordan..Chicago Alumni Chapter

Derrick V. Beasley..Covington County Chapter

Joe Williams ....Dallas/Ft. Worth, Tex., Chapter

Anthony Neal ....Detroit, Mich., Chapter

Sarah Hunter-Tucker ....Flint/Saginaw, Mich., Chapter

W. C. Johnson ....Golden Triangle Chapter

Lecrease Hicks .... Gulf Coast Chapter

James Stubbs .... Hancock/Harrison County Chapter

Marylan Carter .... Hattiesburg/Pine Belt Area Chapter

Shintri Hathorn..Holmes County Chapter

Kristy Love .... Houston, Tex., Chapter

Tommie James.. Humphreys County Chapter

Annie Marie Moffet..Jasper/Smith County Chapter

Jesse Harness..Jefferson County Chapter

Spencenia Hinton..Jefferson Davis Chapter

Andrea M. Martin ....Jones County Chapter

Barbra Esters.. Kosciusko/Attala County Chapter

Kenneth Beal..Leflore County Chapter

Pearline Y. McReynolds..Louisville/Winston County Chapter

George S. Cole..Madison County Chapter

Charles Marshall .... Marion County Chapter

Adrienne Allen .... Memphis, Tenn., Chapter

Wilbert Jones .... Meridian/Lauderdale Chapter

Terry Sadler ....Metro Atlanta Chapter

Robert Cole Sr. ....Metro Columbus, Ohio, Chapter

Victoria Mumford .... Metro Jackson Chapter

Evelyn Johnson ....Metro Washington, D.C., Area Chapter

Anthony Tuggle .... Middle Tennessee Chapter

DeWonda McComb .... Midwest Chapter

Eddie Murphy .... Milwaukee, Wis., Chapter
Percy Norwood .... Montgomery-Carroll-Grenada County Chapter
James Hill Jr. .... Monticello Chapter
Henry Houze .... Natchez–Adams County Chapter
Cassandra Scott .... New Orleans Chapter
John Prentiss .... North Delta Chapter
Gloria McKinney .... Northeast Miss. Chapter
LaSandra Watkins .... Northeast Regional (US) Chapter
Dorothy K. Wilbourn .... Panola County Chapter
Grady McMillon .... Pascagoula/Moss Point Chapter
Henry Tucker .... Pike County Chapter
Rico J. Buckhalter .... Rankin County Chapter
Brenda Jones .... San Antonio, Tex., Chapter
Daniel Walton .... San Francisco Bay Chapter
Johnny Qualls .... Scott County Chapter
John W. Evans .... Sharkey/Isaquenna County Chapter
Evelyn Dawson .... Shreveport/Bossier Chapter
Tonya Ball .... Sunflower County Chapter
Samuel King .... Tennessee Valley Chapter
Lakesha Batty .... Vicksburg Warren Chapter
Eric Steel .... Walthall County Chapter
Donald Atley .... Washington County Chapter

---

38. ALCORN STATE UNIVERSITY NATIONAL ALUMNI ASSOCIATION PRESIDENTS

A. D. Snodgrass 1890–1929
J. H. Moseley 1929–1950
William S. Demby 1950–1957
Ruby S. Lyells 1957–1959
E. T. Hawkins 1959–1970
Thomas Moman II 1970–1972
Frank Dobbins 1972–1974
James E. Stirgus Sr. 1974–1978
Luther Alexander 1978–1986
Matthew Thomas 1986–1990
John Rigsby 1990–1992
John E. Walls Jr. 1992–1996

Robert W. Bowles 1996–2000

James A. Minor Sr. 2000–2002

John E. Walls Jr. 2002–2006

Freddie Owens 2006–2007

James McDonald .... 2007 (Completed Owens's term after death)

James McDonald 2008–2010

Percy Norwood 2010–2012

James Stubbs 2012–present

---

39. ALCORN STATE UNIVERSITY NATIONAL ALUMNI ASSOCIATION NATIONAL OFFICERS FROM 2008 TO 2015

2008–2010

James McDonald, President (Past)

Freddie Owens, Immediate Past President

James Stubbs, First Vice President

James Hill Sr., Second Vice President

Josephine Posey, Executive Secretary

Dorothy Wilborn, Corresponding Secretary

Victory Mumford, Recording Secretary

Alpha Morris, Treasurer

Joseph Bartee, Chaplain

Zelmarine Murphy, Historian

Beulah Walker, Parliamentarian

Janice Gibson, Director of Alumni Affairs

2010–2012

Percy Norwood, President

James McDonald, Immediate Past President

James Stubbs, First Vice President

Charles Davis, Second Vice President

Alpha Morris, Executive Secretary

Melissa Norman, Recording Secretary

Beulah Walker, Assistant Recording Secretary
Zelmarine Murphy, Treasurer
Joseph Bartee, Chaplain
Josephine Posey, Historian
Cedric Bush, Parliamentarian
Janice Gibson, Director of Development and Alumni Affairs

2012–2014

James Stubbs, President (Current)
Percy Norwwood, Immediate Past President
Charles Davis, First Vice President
Ivory Lyles, Second Vice President
Alpha Morris, Executive Secretary
Melissa Norman, Recording Secretary
Beulah Walker, Assistant Recording Secretary
Zelmarine Anderson Murphy, Treasurer
Neddie Winters, Chaplain
Josephine Posey, Historian
Judge Cedric Bush, Parliamentarian
Janice Gibson, Director of Development and Alumni Affairs

2014–2016

James Stubbs, President (Current)
James Stubbs, Immediate Past President
Charles Davis, First Vice President
Ivory Lyles, Second Vice President
Mildred Holland, Executive Secretary
Jo Ella Walls, Recording Secretary
Vickie Mumford, Assistant Recording Secretary
Mack Tuggle, Treasurer
Neddie Winters, Chaplain
Zelmarine Murphy, Historian
Cynthia Bell, Parliamentarian
Janice Gibson, Director of Development and Alumni Affairs

40. Hall of Honor Inductees

1990

Alumni
Luther Alexander
George John Bacon Jr.
William Smith Demby
Cleveland J. Duckworth
Medgar Evers
Andrew Graves
Leon Griffith
T. L. Jordan
Lillian Cade Lane
Jewell C. Lockhart Sr.
Grady McMillion Jr.
Alpha L. Morris
Arthur Bennett Peyton Sr.
Willie Mimms Powell
Calvin Rhodes
David Eugene Thomas Sr.
Cleopatra D. Thompson
David Wilson Wilburn

Athletics
Clifton Osborne Davis
Felix H. Dunn
James Ford
William Foster
Glover Clarence Gardner
John A. Jackson
Robert Pickett
Johnny Spinks
Claude E. Watson

1991

Alumni
Barbara D. Bacon
Robert Bowles
George Hull Jr.
Carl E. Jones
Thomas Moman II
Gertrude Payton
Mack Payton
John Rigsby
Kenneth Simmons Sr.
Ann Johnson Stepney

Service
Walter Downs
Leander T. Ellis Sr.
George Jones Sr.
James D. Martin
William Nelson
Sidney L. Richmond
Emmett J. Stringer

Athletics
Lonnie Moore

1992

Alumni
William C. Boykin Sr.
Willie Burton
LaPose T. Jackson
James E. Miller
James A. Minor
Clementine A. Williams
Jesse A. Morris Sr.

Esther M. Rigsby
Henry R. Smith
Issac Thomas
Shelby R. Wilkes

Service
James E. Brown
Melissa L. Demby
Benjamin F. Harper Jr.
Laura H. Hearn
Waldo James
Leon L. Knowles
Aretta E. Moore
Patricia A. Segrest
Christine L. Simmons
Lutille Stepney
Mabel Thomas
Rosa B. Wynn

Athletics
Harry G. Brown
David Weathersby

1993

Alumni
James "Bo" Clark
Warren Cox
Ella Watson Robinson
Joseph W. Reese
Albert Lott

Service
Alma Brent Edwards
Johnny Greenwood
Walter Washington

Athletics
Marino Casem
Davey Whitney Sr.
E. T. Hawkins
Charles R. Humphrey

1994

Alumni
Maggie Terry-Harper
Irma R. Walton
Jewell Moore Hull
Odessa H. Graves
Robert L. Prater
Matthew W. Thomas

Service
Gladys Noel Bates
Alyce Griffin Clarke
E. Albert Dumas
William "Doc" Chambers
Henry Houze
Frankie Peyton

Athletics
Samuel Crump
Richard Polk

1995

Alumni
Joseph Bartee
Ada Bynum Brown
Jewel Wendell Forten-
berry Sr.
Willie F. Jackson
Zelmarine Anderson
Murphy
Freddie L. Owens

Patricia Bufkin Vardaman

Service
Reginald M. Head
James W. Hill Sr.
Samuel S. Jackson Sr.
Lorine Purnell Minor
Jessie R. Nichols Sr.
Robert L. Seabron

Athletics
Alphonse Marks

1996

Athletics
Charles Boston
Elijah Moore
Richard H. Smith

Alumni
Lawrence M. Lawson
Walter Martin
Angeline Roberson
Raymond Trass

Service
James L. Bolden
Ann R. Holland
Frankye B. Jordan
Tommie Ratcliff
Eugene Spencer Jr.
Oliver G. Taylor
Rudolph E. Waters

1997

Alumni
Mildred Neal

Georgia Williams
Thelma Atkins Giles

Service
Virginia Caples
Clifford E. Jones
Roscoe S. Pickett
Howard H. Robinson
Charles J. D. Tillman

Athletics
Willie McGowan Sr.

1998

Alumni
Bennye Morris Hayes
Henry C. Purnell

Service
Shelby Buford
George Hicks
Ruth S. Lockhart
Marshall Longmire
Josephine M. Posey

Athletics
Orsmond Jordan Jr.

1999

Alumni
Harry Crockett
Mary Martin
Eunice McGee
Evelyn Palmer
John E. Walls Jr.

Service
Bennie L. Rayford
Hilda Debro Rayford
Mary Thompson Samuels

2000

Alumni
Fred Prater
Ernestine Page Strong
Exie T. Williamson
Delphine Williams Coleman
Roy P. Huddleston
Sidney J. James

2002

Alumni
Mary P. Demby
John A. Wicks Sr.
Johnnie R. Jordan Keys
Emma R. H. Moore

2003

Alumni
Thelma C. Smith Johnson
Joseph C. Risby
Quitman C. Walker
Jessica Hayes Williams

Athletics
William Smith Demby Jr.
Willie Neal Simpson

Service
Katie Grays Dorsett
Virginia Foster Henderson

Annie Marie Moffett
Joe E. Smith

2004

Alumni
Charles H. Bridges

Athletics
Robert Calvin Bell
Peter Boston

Service
Douglas Fitzgerald
Mary Lee Dunbar Jackson
Jacqueline M. Shorter
Dorothy Kerney Wilbourn

2006

Alumni
James F. McDonald

Service
Percy Norwood

2008

Alumni
Levernis F. Eiland Crosby
Audrey Wayne Jones
Jesse J. Lucas
Jesse Edward McGee
Charles Marshall
Archie Parnell
Mary R. Wiley

Athletics
Charles F. McClelland

Service
Arthur James Anderson
Charles Victor McTeer
Malvin A. Williams Sr.

2009

Alumni
Emma J. Allen
Robert Collier
Pastella T. Hampton

Service
Lemore Allen
Ethel S. Boyd
Barbara B. Kennedy
Johnny Robinson

2010

Alumni
James Stubbs
Pearline McReynolds
Martha Bell
Madeline Robinson

Service
Charles Davis

2011

Alumni
Jesse Harness
Samuel E. King
Bernice Wayne Maxwell

Jean A. Pittman
Robert E. Simmons

2012

Alumni
Jessie W. Rushing

Athletics
Kalvin D. Robinson

Service
Donald Ray Atley
Clarence Edward McGee
Neddie R. Winters

2013

Alumni
LaKesha Batty
Marilyn Lynn
Alvin Moore
Theresa Prater
Veronica Richardson
Walter Sheriff
Henry Tucker
Randolph Walker

Service
Marian Mixon
Shirley Tinner

2014

Alumni
Mildred Crockett
Jamelda F. Fulton

Ivory W. Lyles
Victory D. Mumford
Jerry Paige
Harper Wilson

Service
Carnell Lewis
Dorothy Smith Nelson
Macelle R. Turner

2015

Alumni
Lettie Brox
Grace Brown
Samuel Washington Jr.
Andrew Wilson
Patricia Yates

Service
Charles Johnson

41. Alcornite of the Year Recipients

1948	George Cox	1984	Issac L. Thomas
1949	Richard Sylvester Grossley	1985	Kenneth L. Simmons
1950	Milan W. Davis	1986	Lottie H. Powell
1951	Daniel W. Ambrose	1987	Alyce G. Clark
1952	George W. Lee	1988	Alpha L. Morris
1953	Robert Hunter	1989	Mack Willie Payton
1954	Ruby Elizabeth Cowan Stutts Lyells	1990	Mary P. Demby
1955	Hampton P. Wilburn	1991	Matthew W. Thomas Jr.
1957	John D. Boyd	1992	George Jones Jr.
1959	W. S. Demby	1993	Robert Wayne Bowles
1961	Cleopatra D. Thompson	1994	Thomas Madison Moman II
1962	Chester L. Marcus	1995	Laplose Turner Jackson Sr.
1963	Jessie A. Morris	1996	Davis "Redskin" Weathersby
1964	Delors E. Magee	1997	John E. Walls Jr.
1965	Benjamin Franklin McLaurin	1998	Arthur Bennett Peyton
1966	Rube Harrington Jr.	1999	Laura Hart Hearn
1967	George J. Bacon	2000	Lonnie Edward Moore Sr.
1968	Evans T. Hawkins	2001	James Walter Hill Sr.
1969	William Earthy Ammons	2002	Allene Demby Gayles
1970	James Charles Evers	2003	James "Bo" Clark
1971	James C. Gilliam	2004	Irma R. Smith Walton
1972	Charles Humphrey	2005	Robert L. Prater
1973	James E. Miller	2006	Barbara Darris Bacon
1974	Calvin Rhodes	2007	Zelmarine Murphy
1975	David Wilson Wilburn	2008	Percy O. Norwood Jr.
1976	Luther Alexander	2009	Jo Ella (Harrison) Walls
1977	Robert Jordan	2010	Willie C. Harper
1978	Henry R. Smith	2011	Exie Ola Griggs Williamson
1979	Andrew Graves	2012	Charles Franklin McClelland Sr.
1980	E. A. Dumas	2013	Ella Robinson
1981	Fred Cunningham	2014	Clarence E. Magee
1982	Jewell C. Lockhart	2015	Charles E. Davis
1983	Vera H. Bryant		

42. Golden Classes

1933

Roscoe E. Alexander
Thelma Bailey
Annie Barron
Newton Billups
Geraldine Brown
Wayne Calbert
Albert Clark
Clarence Cooper
Josephine Davis
Susetta Gibson
Estelle Green
James Gresham
McCleveland Harver
Elnora Howard
Arnie James
Ulysses Johnson
Fannie Luckette
Elizabeth Majors
Sylvester Marshall
Orange McNair
John Morris
Anne Newman
Emma Newman
James Norman
Bertha Parker
Issac Pollard
Richard Randall
Thomas Robinson
Lamar Scoby
Curtis Seaberry
Aaron Thomas
J. P. Watts
Robert Weddington
Melvin Wiggins
D. W. Wilburn
Andrew Wollwans

1934

Lannyus A. Armstrong
Estus L. Barron
Harvey Lee Beale
Kenneth Charles Brooks
Mary Kate Brown
Nathaniel Burger
Albert D. Clark
Malcolm Leon Coleman
Goldie Taylor Collins
Laura Powell Gibson
Henry Leroy Graves
Leroy Percy Johnson
Tecumeseh C. McLaurin
Willis Turner Sias
Bernice Allen Stimley
Lawrence Guice Towers
Cordelia Ella Watkins
Julius Pettibone Watts
Eugene Webster

1935

Florence D. Allen
Addie N. Burger
William Camphor
Charles Coleman
Milton Dean
Charles Fletcher
Meredith Johnson
Vernie T. Magee
Benjamin McLaurin
Annie Patton
Edgar Rails
Maggie Redmond
Calvin Rhodes

Mahala Smith
Pernella Smith
George W. Spears
Rufus Stennis
David E. Thomas
Maggie L. Turner
Annie White
Hilliard P. Young

1936

Hettie Smith Cain
Julia M. A. Dillon
Edward Duncan
Velma Palmer Elliot
Rollo Fletcher
Odessa Hayes Graves
Nola J. C. Hayden
Theodric B. Hendrix
Sargent P. Jackson
Curtis Kelly
Eva Jones McCune
Lewis S. Sinclair
Ruth C. Powell Sledge
Leola B. H. Turner
Ruby L. Wheatley

1937

Jason W. Allen
Bernice Bishop
Willie Calbert
Joseph Coleman
Ruby W. Coleman
Katie Collins
Joseph Davis

Edith Dickens

Bertha W. Edwards

Annie N. Gaston

Ruby Hammond

Laura H. Hearn

William Hunt

Marguerite B. Jeffries

Shirley Neal

George Russell

Ruby Jones Seymour

Alma S. Warren

Claude Watson

1938

Charles Carson

Bennie W. Cooper

C. F. Edwards

J. W. Grantham

Lillie Stutts Handy

Lela Hawkins Hardy

Joseph Henderson

John H. Hope

J. W. Keller

Inez Stutts Knowles

Robert Lee

James Miller

Lillian O. Palmer

Branch Ray

M. C. Sterling

Robert L. Stewart

Willie Mae L. Taylor

Cleopatra D. Thompson

William H. Travis

1939

Frank D. Boston

Sidney Brent

Lawrence Campbell

Hooker D. Davis

Arnie W Downs

Allie V. Dunn

James H. Gross

Mary L. Howard

Rufus F. James

James McKay

Lula K. O'Neal

John L. Page Sr.

Wallace C. Rials

Anna Ross

Nolan Tate

1940

Edward W. Barrett

Vancheal Booth

John Boston

Helen D. Coleman

Allen L. Coney

Inez G. Gray

Eugene Isaac

Millicent B. Jackson

Celeste J. Jacques

Thomas J. Jones

Lillian C. Lane

Mary H. Masters

Thomas Moman

Willy R. Patton

Tyree J. B. Pendleton

Elizabeth R. Pharr

Felton P. Posey

William D. Purnell

Henry R. Smith

Willa N. Smith

Alex C. Warren

1941

Syna M. Boston

Aurabelle M. Caggins

Luberta G. Caldwell

John W. Davis

Walter M. Downs

Ruth U. Hansen

Claude Higgins

Audell O'Neil Horton

Lois B. Ingram

Allene R. Leggette

Joseph D. Leggette

Dr. Albert Lott

Alphonse Marks

Willie Y. Miller

Odessai Rials

Horace D. Robinson

Elois B. Rogers

Annie B. Smith

Jessie J. Smith Jr.

Willie D. Smith

Etheline B. Stewart

Emmett J. Stringer

Leonard Walker

Dessye M. Warren

Amos Wright

Florence N. Wright

1942

Juanita A. Adams

Mildred D. Allen

Ada B. Brown

William Brown

Alma E. Carter

Annie Clemons

Eunice Conley

M. Alberta Delgado

Helen Diamond

Pinkie L. D. Ellis
Alma Coney Evans
John Luther Frisby
John Hannah
Eva H. Harris
Isom Herron
Juanita Herron
Vera Gadsberry Hunter
Zeddie Q. Hyler
Walter J. Jones
Ireland O'Brien Kee
Hattie M. Knox
James S. Logan
Mary B. Marks
Aretta B. Moore
Cyrus H. Nero
Dorothy H. Overstreet
Frank R. Robinson
George Robinson
Charles Rowlett
Henry J. Sanderson
Exermenia Searcy
Ernestine P. Strong
Issac L. Thomas
William Leroy Triplett
Charles L. Varnado
Grace Varnado
Myrtle W. Wyche
Rose B. Wynn

1943

Mildred J. Armstrong
Douglas L. Conner
Bessie Ruth Johnson
Clymathes B. King
Corrine B. Porter
Mattie B. Reed
Flora G. Stringer
Carmen P. Walker

Albert Woolfolk
Loretha Woolfolk

1944

Alma Elexia Brent-Edwards
Ora Lean Drake-Creasy
Mattye Bertille Richards
    Mingo
Jewell Hazel Moore-Hull
William J. Rice

1947

Margie Fairley Cunningham
Alma Sutton Duffy
Rena Dean Fortenberry
E. Everett Jackson
Kathryn Moore Jones
Maudie Rene Kirkland
    Jordan
Woodie Hawthorne Magee
Benjamin B. Montgomery
Madison S. Palmer Sr.
Birta M. Bickman Sanders
Lloyd Allison Smith
Helen Velora Sansing
    Stephens
Dewey Townsend
Lurene L. Jones Traynham
Velma F. Turner
Elmond Quinn Williams

1949

John Calvin Berry
Alonzo Crosby
Fred Douglas Cunningham

Margie LaVerne Price
    Funches
Joseph James Hardy
Ann Rose Walker Hookfin
Myrtle Leatrice Lenoir Jones
Needham Jones
Illinois B. Jackson Littleton
Ora Lee McGee
Willie Lee Mimms Powell
Cinderalla Scott Williams
    Smith

1951

Annie M. Anderson-Paulin
Ponjola Posey Andrews
Helen McEwen Barron
Mildred Pegues Beadle
Willie A. Brown
Frank Crump Jr.
James Charles Evers
Catherine B. Fairman
Esco Hemphill
Mary L. Collins Hendricks
Walter L. Hutchins
Carrie B. M. James
Annie Jefferson-Crudup
Leroy P. Jones
Willie Alma Jones-Black
Theresa Davis Lewis
Alexander E. Martin
Emma Ree H. Moore
Willie M. Nettles
Doris Aldridge Payton
Robert J. Peavie Sr.
Arthur B. Peyton
Charles Raines
Inez Jordan Raines
Bennie Rayford
Leon S. Sartin Jr.

Elizabeth J. Smith

Modestine Smith

Annie R. Johnson Stepney

James O. Taylor

Charlie M. Thames Jr.

Evelyn Evon Sansing Townsend

Beachman Williams Sr.

1952

Eula Lewis Anderson

Nathaniel Anderson Sr.

Bythella Bryant Andrews

Addie Stubbs Bolton

James E. Brown

ReJohnna Risby Brown

Zollie Cole Clayter

Timothy Crudup

Orelia Peterson Crump

Christine Frelix Doby

Ruby Ruffin Draughn

Wilma Emmons Fortenberry

Colyar Frierson

Bernice Moore Gamblin

Lee N. Garner

Elizabeth Wilson Hackman

Johnny Joseph Halsell

Earnestine L. Holloway

Annie Ball Holmes

James F. Hoskin

Moses L. Howard

Harold Hudson

Velma Caston Jackson

Waldo James

Samuel Knight

Dolly Caston Martin

Ola F. Morgan

Alpha L. Morris

Eunice Moore Northington

Theresa O'Neal Prater

Henry Purnell

Thomas C. Randle

James H. Ratliff Jr.

Myrtle Brown Shanks

Robertha Petty Simmons

Lawrence W. Sutton Jr.

Charles E. Thomas

Mattie McCann Thomas

Samuel H. Whisenton Jr.

Henry O. White Sr.

1953

Robert F. Alexander

Doris May Anderson

Pauline Pittman Beal

Willie Z. Brock

Napoleon M. Brown

Shelton Buckley

Joe T. Dockins

Minnie Dean Hall Dodson

Katie Grays Dorsett

Samuel Echols

Mattie Winters Elam

Bessie Parker Fowler

Allene Demby Gayles

Myrtle Foules Gibson

Artimissie Hutcherson Hayes

Mary Robinson Henderson

Ruby D. Eiland Holloway

Roy P. Huddleston

Irma P. Alexander James

Samuel Jenkins

Petro Langdon

Leon D. Lemons

Richard Lyles

Lionel A. Martin

Lorene Johnson Miller

Carrie Bryant Moses

LaPearl Younger Myricks

Catherine Barnes Norris

Vera Price Oatis

Jefferson R. Perry

Geraldine Frazier Peyton

Robert L. Prater

Vernon Purnell

Hilda Debro Rayford

Odessa Martin Reeves

Ella Watson Robinson

James B. Rowan

Jeffalone Brantley Rumph

Edna Martin Scott

Mamie Herron Shields

Mable Brown Sims

Eugene Spencer Jr.

Lutillie Stepney

Floyd Stewart

Adrian Swainer

Joseph T. Travillion Jr.

Luzene Tucker Triplett

Jack H. Watkins

Gladys Martin Wells

Charlie Woodruff

1954

Rebecca Green Anderson

Earl Britton

William Brown

Irma P. Burks Daily

Bennye Morris Hayes

Carrie M. Jackson

LaPlose T. Jackson

Clarence E. Magee

Edna Windham Mclain

Henry E. Middleton

Janie Coleman Middleton

Elijah Moore
Wyvette Polk
Judge V. Posey
Esther C. Martin Rigsby
John D. Rigsby
James L. Robinson
John A. Ward
Mary F. Jones Woodson

1955

Nevers Abrams
Luther Alexander
John W. Bennett Sr.
Henry L. Berry
Marvin E. Bridges
Augustine Tillman Buie
Army Daniel Jr.
Bobra L. Yarbrough Esters
Littleton P. Evans
Emma B. Phipps Gorman
Jeanette I. Evans Hampton
Herdicene Hawthorne Hardy
Eleanor Liddell Harris
Henderson Howard
Samuel S. Jackson Sr.
Richastine Parker James
Macy Mongomery Johnson
Fannie L. Knight
Wright L. Lassiter Jr.
Vernell Lewis
John A. Lindsey
Bernice Alexander Long
Willard Magee
Leo Marshall
Olivet T. Hardy Maston
Lucy Vaughn Myricks
Amos Newman Jr.
Bernice J. Anderson Ott

Lena E. Smith Pope
Theresa Neal Prater
Franklin Purnell
Jessie Mae Williams Rushing
Jay T. Smith Sr.
Richard H. Smith
Mary Varnado Stewart
Betty B. Thompson
Betty J. McGill Tillman
James L. Tucker
Edward Vanderson
Avery W. Washington
Davis Weathersby
Andrew V. Weddington
Princy L. Jenkins Williams
Exie O. Griggs Williamson

1956

Lamar A. Braxton Sr.
Joseph Brown Jr.
Juanita M. Brown
Bertha Floyd Byers
Levernis Eiland Crosby
Mary Prater Demby
Will Fitzgerald
Charles Flowers Sr.
Margaret Mack Harden
Benjamin F. Harper Jr.
Rosalie W. Hawkins
Johnette Tillman Holloway
June Roselyn Porter Hutchins
Mary A. Norris Jacobs
Audrey Wayne Jones
Cleo Knight
Jewel C. Lockhart
Christine Miller
Carrie Atlas Randle
David E. Roberson

Marva S. Russell
Charles J. Smith
Albert L. Sterling
James L. Stewart
Mamie S. Thompson
Barbara Kimbrough Wade
Lula P. Duck Wade
Georgia R. Walton
Ruby Nell West
Betty Calloway Whitaker
Mary Vanderbilt White
Horace W. Wicks
Althea Elois Woodley

1957

Commattee S. Anderson
Clementeen Bennett
Willie J. Brumfield
David L. Conner
Warren E. Cox
Marguerite Clark Davis
Powhatan L. Fluker
Ruby M. Gaylor
Roosevelt Grenell
Charles L. Harris Sr.
Josephine Dobbins Hosey
Howard E. Hudson
Mary E. Hudson
Bethew B. Jennings Jr.
Grady C. Jordan
Susie Burns Koonce
Mildred Williams Lee
Marshall Longmire
Purvis McCarty
LeVern McClelland
Hortense M. McCullough
Alene Otis Owens
Robert E. Pickett

Ida M. Raspberry
Dorothy Bolden Risby
Hollis Stevens
Lola Mae Strayhorn
Excell Terrell
Myrna Raspberry Turner
Bertha L. Williams

1958

R. V. Anderson
Martha Atlas
Walter Barnes
Bertha Brown
William Calloway Sr.
Cora Cater
Alpha Cox
Ernest Cubit
Lovell Davis
Thelma Giles
Berta Griffin
Elvenia Harrison
Elnora Jackson
Ollye James
Sidney James
Laverne Johnson
Mary Johnson
W. B. Jones
Marion Jordan
Bennie Knox
Ruth Lockhart
Jessie Lucas
Hosea Lyles
Margie Maxwell
Celess McEwen
Clynell Moses
Fred Prater
Mary Polk
Ethel Powe

Vernice Smith Rencher
Joseph Risby
Johnny Robinson
Ernestine Rucker
Franklin Shelton
Cleo Short
Clyde Smith
Doris Smith
Elma Smith
Eunice Smith
Daisy Tillman
Mamie Washington
Elnora Wiggins

1959

Eddie M. Alexander
Bernell S. Allen
Merlene Davis Allen
Rhenette White Blake
Sarah F. Glover Britton
Clara J. Coleman Butts
Theodore R. Cosey
Rosie L. Daniel
Nancy Winston Denham
Lonnie Eiland
Estelle D. Mayberry Fleming
Bobby L. Floyd
Norma Washington Graham
Willie Green
William Hammond
Dennis Jackson
Johnnie R. Jordan Keys
Marjorie A. Kinds
Eugene J. Liddell
Marilyn R. Johnson Lynn
Katie Gilliam McCullough
Ellawese Barnes McLendon
Joanna D. Franklin Monroe

Dorothy L. Williams Moore
Irene Braxton Moore
John T. Newkirk
Annie R. Williamson
    Richardson
Madeline Hudson Robinson
Mary G. King Stanton
Margaret Wilson Therrell
Dorothy J. Beene Townsend
Annette M. Watkins Whiting
Leroy Whiting
Eloise D. Ervin Williams

1960

Arthur James Anderson
Martha D. Bell
Verdean Allen Buford
Kenneth V. Coleman
Caroline Stutts Collins
Limea E. Daniels
Mary S. Davis
Creevy Harnes
Chester Harrington
Arnold Harris
Marvin E. Harris Jr.
Peter Jackson
Thelma Jackson
Jessie Mildred James
Oliver Johnson Sr.
Lizer Ann Gammage
    Marshall
Eugene McCray Jr.
Doris E. McGowan
Loretta Palmer
Hortense Ransom
Joseph Russell
Juanita Wilson Smith
Donald Sowell

Earline Strickland
Murlene Terry Taylor
Myrtle E. Gilmer Terrell
Carl Warfield Weathers
Christine B. Williams

1961

Barbara Darris Bacon
Lucinda Crawford Belin
Charles E. Brown
Osborne S. Burks
Deloris P. Cagins
Bessie L. Cole Carroll
Christler C. Chaffee Jr.
Alyce Griffin Clarke
Della Larkin Cooper
Frank Dobbins
Dessie L. Washington
    Easterling
Edna Mae Bryson Ellis
Larscie Ellis
Anita E. Parrott George
Shirley Crawford Harris
Helen R. Jefferson Hood
Lula S. Benson James
Roger L. James
Erlexia C. Lewis Johnson
Emma L. Smith Jordan
Walter F. Logan Jr.
Everette L. Allen Luvert
Lucile Boykins McCarty
Willie E. McGowan Sr.
Ella L. Moore
Dorothy P. Newman
Carrie Dunbar Parrott
Ernest C. Qualls
Angeline Smith Roberson
Claudette Johnson Rogers
Elizabeth R. Samuel

James A. Shelby Sr.
Christine L. Brown
    Simmons
Dora H. Prater Simpson
Dorothy B. Singleton
Johnny Singleton
Mary L. Smith
Robert L. Smith
Georgia Marsalis Stepney
Roy Thigpen
Marjorie E. Newell Thomas
Macelle Richardson Turner
Samuel L. Washington
Helene G. Combest Watson
Fannie L. Wheaton Williams

1962

Johnny Earl Anderson
James H. Barnes
Lawrence Barnes Jr.
Lessie J. Barnes
June D. Barron
Alma T. Bates
Clara T. Beamon
Lillie M. Bell
Izeal Bennett
Audrey N. Berry
Vernon E. Bogan
Roland Bowser
Catherine J. Brent
Alice Hilliard Buford
Vera Bullock
Lovell C. Campbell
Grace Carter
Eddie Chambers
Larry E. Claiborne
Calmeter T. Clark
Donald R. Clark
Genola A. Clark

James Calvin Clark
William M. Clark Jr.
Wilbert Cobb
Melvin Thomas Coleman
Johnny L. Crisler
Bernadine Haley Davenport
Leon Davenport
Vallie W. Davidson
Carolyn J. Davis
Wesley H. Davis
Arnetta Graham Faulkner
Walter E. Gardner
Lanie Mae Wheeler Green
Lena W. Green
Marzine Green Jr.
Margaret B. Hall
Catherine T. Harvey
Vera B. Hayden
Hattie M. Higdon
Catherine T. Hillsman
Ruby Holden
Letha B. Howard
Lillie Cole Huff
David D. Jackson
Howard H. Jackson
Fred L. Jeffries
Ethel H. Jennings
Oliver Johnson Sr.
Allen Jones Jr.
Gerald Jones
Mildred B. Jones
Sheral P. Jones
Vera H. Keahey
Barbara M. Little
Steve Luse
Shirley F. Manard
Grady Marshall
Lessie Brantley Maxwell
Mamie C. Mazique
Vera M. McCall
Fannie J. McCormick

Willie L. McGee

Zana C. McKelphin

    McKinnie

Bernice B. McNeil

Fate W. Mickel

Joyce C. Newbill

Ethel Chlorenda Wallace

    Odom

James Uriel Paige

Peacola B. Parker

William Parker

Bennie J. Parrott Jr.

Celia Dean Gordon Pearson

Florence Terry Pullen

Bertha W. Reed

Eula P. Ross

Bobbie T. Sanders

Rosie Barnes Seals

Vergie B. Shelton

Willie Neal Simpson

Grace Smith

James Smith Jr.

James Spurgeon

Emma Banks Stamps

Julia W. Thigpen

Charles J. D. Tillman

Lafayette Townes

Elnois R. Tucker

Queen C. VanNorman

Janie R. Walker

Comoleta Jamison Watts

Benjamin F. White

Mary Russell Wiley

Clementine Williams

Deloris T. Williams

Doris Thigpen Williams

Georgia L. Williams

Malvin A. Williams Sr.

Shirley Mae Riley Williams

Jessie Annette T. Wilson

Annie A. Woods

Ruthie L. Woods

Inez Campbell Wright

Ruby Yarbrough

Lemoyne Young

Lonnie M. Young

1963

Mattie P. Allen

Doris Arbuthnot

Gertrude Ashley

Mordine Bailey

Thomas Bailey

James E. Barner

Wilma L. Bates

Charles O. Beasley

Etta D. Bell

Ann A. Bennett

Chester Bennett

Alyce G. Bibbs

Marcella C. Birtha

James Bridges

Alice G. Brown

Artis S. Butler

Kathy A. Buxton

Vertye W. Caples

Willie T. Carter

Charles Christian

Delphine W. Colman

Wilma Copeland

Johnnie Crosby

Edna Crowell

Eva R. Daniels

Thomas Davis

Juanita Denson

Thomas Dillon

Joseph Dunbar

Mary C. Ellis

Yvonne Ellis

Charles E. Fells

Frances B. Frazier

James C. Gales

Johnnie C. Gales

Rea J. Grady

Vivian W. Graham

Johnny C. Greer

Jonathan Grennell

Renza M. Grennell

Minnie W. Hamberlin

Ann Hardy

Kermit Harness

Mary H. Harrington

Jewel F. Harrison

John D. Harrison

Joe A. Haynes

Mildred K. Haynes

Annie R. Herron

James W. Hill

Savannah B. Hill

Mary M. Holder

Myrtis Holmes

Orbazean Hoskin

Willie J. Hoskin

Willie N. Hunter

Nellie W. Jackson

Ora M. Jackson

Thelma Jackson

Joyce J. Johnson

Pyndora B. Jones

Samantha Jones

Annie V. Kelley

Willie D. Kelly

Georgia A. Kemp

Flora M. Keys

Emanuel Lang

Artis Lewis

Joseph E. Lloyd

Mary W. Lloyd

Mary A. Martin

Doris J. McCann

Vernadette L. McCaskill

Barbara A. McCoy
Audrey S. McGee
Daisye R. McGee
Mildred McGhee
Samantha McGill
Ronald E. McLaughlin
Ruthie Nelson
Rozella S. Newson
Robert R. Norvel
Raynor C. Paige
Samuel L. Perry
Langston B. Pickett
Nina R. Poole
Elsie S. Qualls
Clara K. Raine
Harriet Reese
Rosie Reese
Percy Rhines
Veronica L. Richardson
Ella W. Riley
Jimmie L. Roberson
John M. Robertson
Dorothy W. Robinson
LaQuetta S. Ruff
Frankie A. Rushing
Laura J. Saulsberry
Charles R. Scott
Emma L. Sims
Roosevelt Smith
M. H. Stapleton
George Sutton
Thelma N. Tate
Martha B. Thomas
Willie T. Thompson
Carol S. Tillman
Charles Trice
Dorothy T. Walker
Leroy Walters
Helen M. Warner
George W. Watkins
Margaret Watts

Frances A. White
John A. Wicks
Shirley R. Wicks
Doris F. Williams
Marilyn D. Williams

1964

Willie M. Bacon
Leola C. Beasley
Betty S. Bowser
Willie O. Brown
Luada L. Buckner
Sarah M. Coleman
Jewel Crawford
Hargie D. Crenshaw
Mildred B. Day
Rosa I. Demby
Lola M. Ducksworth
Eva L. Miller Fountain
Emiel Hamberlin
Mattie T. Hampton
Kertrina M. Haynes
Donell Harrell
Delores M. Hemphill
Josie B. Hightower
Elsie S. Holmes
Hurtice S. Howard
David Hunter
Mary D. Jackson
Wiley F. Jones
Eloise A. Lamar
Mary G. LeBlanc
Emanuel L. Johnson
Charles F. McClelland
Rosie T. McDonald
Bobbie Preston McGee
Bettie L. Minor
Edna J. Murry
Evelyn H. Smith

Robert E. Smith
John Turner Jr.
Washington Wells
Christine J. Williams
Harper B. Wilson

1965

Lizzie E. Anderson
David C. Ashley Sr.
Etta R. Ashley
Joseph Bartee Sr.
Jeanette J. Bell
Annie G. Bennett
Maudine Boston
Helen B. Bowman
Dorothy S. Chesser
Betty W. Coleman
Isabell Coleman
Mosby Dixon
Abram H. Dunbar Jr.
Brenda P. Earhart
Selma V. Fluker
James H. Gaddis
Maggie L. Gaddis
Vergia A. Goldsberry
Annie Harper
Eloise Baldwin Harris
Wonso W. Hayes
Dorothy K. Haynes
Linden S. Haynes
Worth Haynes
Travis E. Hill
Barbara K. Hooper
Lou T. Hudson
Benjamin F. Johnson III
Shirley P. Leggett
Alice S. Lewis
Carnell Lewis
Margaret D. Little

Gertrude S. Magby	Juanita M. Norwood	Dorothy R. Thompson
Andrew Mae G. Martin	Earlene F. O'Neil	Priscilla W. Thompson
Willie L. McCoy Jr.	Clara M. Pinkney	Lillian Brooks Townsend
Vernice S. McKnight	Douglas Posey Jr.	Ola Mae T. Tucker
Elouise A. McLaughlin	Earnest L. Ray	Sarah H. Tucker
Dessie W. McLendon	Benard Robinson	Gladys C. Vaughn
Grady McMillon Jr.	Ethel J. Jackson Robinson	Percy Walker
Barbara T. McMorris	Buford Satcher	Annie H. Walton
Lizzie S. Miles	Minnie S. Sims	Marietta G. Wheeler
Vincent P. Miles	Dorothy P. Smith	Edna M. H. White
Geraldine T. Montgomery	Myrtle H. Smith	Rufus L. White
Frances G. Morris	Nathaniel Smith	David Williams Jr.
Shirleye H. Myers	Eleanor E. Stewart	Julius Williams
Nancy M. Norvel	Carolyn W. Strothers	Bernice S. Young
Charles Norwood	Matthew W. Thomas Jr.	

---

43. EXCERPT FROM "A DESIRE TO EDUCATE" BY BEATRICE SMITH YOUNG

My parents did not get a college degree, but they did what they could to make sure their eleven children did.

Bud, my father, was the breadwinner for the family and he instilled in us the importance of an education. We didn't have transportation to and from school; therefore, we walked regardless of the weather.

So determined to do his best for the youngest children, he walked to Alcorn Practice School for eight years. I remember him saying, "Why pay to go to college when education is free." Betcha he was a wise old man. After five of the oldest children left home, my daddy provided for us to attend Alcorn Agricultural College, now Alcorn State University. He paid for three of us to attend, $32 per semester.

My father made the statement, "I'm going to give you an education, but what you do afterward is left up to you."

I must admit that out of the eleven children, the seven sisters graduated from Alcorn; one brother graduated from Mississippi Valley State University; two of us went through the college door, but didn't finish; and, one did not go at all.

So, all the praises go to my father—without a public job, but was determined and dedicated to the cause of his children's success.

The sons were military men and the daughters were educators and a social worker.

My father was a biblical scholar. He knew the Bible so well that he could tell you where to find any scripture in the Bible. He loved to talk about Jesus. He told us there were three things in life he wanted instilled in us so that we would go a long way: 1) attend church, 2) get an education, and 3) respect others. These were the things he required us to do, which have been fulfilled. So, Bud, thank you for everything you did for us.

I remember when Mr. Floyd was the manager of the dairy at Alcorn and had problems with the cattle. He would contact my father to come and see about the cattle. Whatever was wrong, my father had medical advice to make them well.

44. "ALCORN SPIRIT" SONG

Chorus
Gim'me that old Alcorn spirit
Gim'me that old Alcorn spirit
Gim'me that old Alcorn spirit
So I can get revived, energized,
And rekindle it in my heart.

Verse
She provided me an education,
ASU—on the reservation—
Gim'me that old Alcorn spirit
So I can get revived, energized,
And rekindle it in my heart.

Verse
I will tell you that I'm grateful
'cause she helped me become successful—
Gim'me that old Alcorn spirit
So I can get revived, energized,
And rekindle it in my heart

Verse
Now it's my turn to give back
To the best school in the SWAC
Gim'me that old Alcorn spirit
So I can get revived, energized,
And rekindle it in my heart.

Written by Jessica Hayes Williams
Class of 1976

45. Alcorn Quilt Centerpiece

Dr. J. Janice Coleman, an artist in unique creations and innovations, is an associate professor of English at Alcorn State University. She demonstrates excellent creative ability, and one of her greatest examples is the creation and development of an Alcorn quilt. Having received her bachelor of science in English from Alcorn in 1984, a master's degree in popular culture from Bowling Green State University, and a doctorate degree in English from the University of Mississippi, Dr. Coleman possesses what it takes to be successful in her endeavors. For the past twenty-five years, she developed a patchwork art exhibit entitled "Quilts and Other Quadrilaterals." The creative exhibit included not only quilts, but also pillows, tote bags, tablecloths, cotton sacks, and pin cushions. Her hometown, Mound Bayou, Mississippi, welcomed her back on several occasions to showcase one of the prides of their community. She taught a self-designed patchwork writing course at the Mississippi Governor's School. She was also selected for the 2010–2011 Mississippi Humanities Council Teacher Award by the Mississippi Institution for Higher Learning.

The Alcorn Quilt, which measures 8 feet by 6½ feet and is therefore queen-size, would be just another purple and gold quilt were it not for the centerpiece, which depicts four features unique to the university: the year of the university's inception, an image of Oakland Memorial Chapel, an image of the campus's giant trees, and an image of a "balmy Southern breeze." In the upper left-hand corner of the centerpiece is the year 1871, the year in which the Mississippi legislature established Alcorn University and named it in honor of Governor James Lusk Alcorn. As a start-up institution, the university would retain the name Alcorn University until 1878, when the state legislature reorganized and named it Alcorn Agricultural and Mechanical College. Nearly 100 years later, because of an expanding curriculum and concomitant programs, the university once again underwent a name change. Since 1974, the institution has been Alcorn State University, or, as the centerpiece of this quilt reflects, ASU.

In the upper right-hand corner of the quilt is an image of Oakland Memorial Chapel, Alcorn State's iconic landmark. As such, it has been the site of many momentous occasions in the university's history. For example, in 1888, when Beulah Turner Robinson became the first woman to receive a degree from the university, the graduation ceremony was held in the chapel. In more recent years, a memorial service for Alcorn State's fifteenth and longest-serving president, Dr. Walter Washington, was held in the chapel, as was the state viewing of the body of the university's sixteenth president, Dr. Clinton Bristow Jr. The quilt's image of the chapel highlights three important features of the building: the clock tower atop the chapel, the six ivory columns that line the front of the building, and the black staircase, which was salvaged from Windsor Ruins. Towering above the chapel is a giant tree, one of many that shade the campus.

In the lower corner are images of two campus attractions that Estelle Charlotte Bomar immortalized in the "Alcorn Ode." In the left-hand corner are giant trees. The first tree is of the bright green of oak leaves in late spring and early summer, and the other is of the ever-green's darker hue. Together, these trees represent the spectrum of green among the trees that shade the campus.

In the right-hand corner is an image of the abstract "balmy Southern breeze" presented in concrete form. This image features a male student with an Afro and a female student with French braids as they enjoy an afternoon under the shade of the giant trees. It is a casual day on the campus, as their choice of clothing indicates. Both are wearing purple ASU T-shirts. With his shirt, the young man is wearing jeans and sneakers trimmed in red and blue, colors that, if combined, make purple. The young woman's T-shirt matches her purple skirt, which has a gold ribbon drawstring at the waist. With her legs crossed at the ankles, the young woman shows off her low-heeled black leather shoes. As they sit on the ground, the young man and woman witness a common scene on the ASU campus—squirrels playing with the acorns that they have gathered for lunch. The balm of the breeze in this image is most mani-fest in the bright yellow sun, which is surrounded by soft blue and white clouds, while the breeze itself is manifested in the leaves that are falling gently from the bright green trees and the young woman's book bag, which is hanging from a tree and swaying gently in the wind.

46. ALCORN ALUMNI DAY AGENDA

Sponsored by the Alcorn State University National Alumni Association

Purpose: To expose and introduce current Alcorn students to the National Alumni Associa-tion and create an alumni presence that will eventually foster a lifelong affiliation with the association.

When: March 30, 2005

Time: Pre-registration Required

10:00 a.m.–2:00 p.m.

Participants: Mississippi alumni chapters and out of state alumni chapters

Mississippi alumni chapters will be asked to send a minimum of three representatives to dialogue and meet with students.

Out of state alumni chapters will be asked to submit information about their chapter to be disseminated to the students.

Activity: Alcornites can assist the new graduate or current enrolled student with securing employment, housing, banking and finding a place of worship if the student moves to the alumnus area of the country.

Refreshments: Hot dogs, potato chips, cookies, drinks (soda and water)

Outcome: Alcorn students will be made aware of the Alcorn alumni presence throughout the country and the benefits of developing an affiliation with the local alumni chapter.

Greater interest and participation in the Alcorn State Pre-Alumni Association.

Greater chance of new graduates becoming involved with the National Alumni Association at an earlier stage in their life, ideally right after graduation.

Contact Persons: Marilyn Shelton, Coordinator; Charles Davis and Janice Gibson 1000 ASU Dr. #809 Alcorn State, Miss. 39096-7500.

47. A DEDICATION TO TIM AND STEVE MCNAIR

Who would have thought
Some years ago
Those little baby boys born
To Lucille McNair would be heroes?

Such humble beginnings Tim and Steve share
But to give less than their best—they did not dare.
They have shown us all that determination and hard work have paved the way
To a brighter day.

Monk, Mack, Steve or Shine
Whichever name you choose will be fine.
This young man just hated to lose,
Losing was the thing that gave him the blues.

Tim, Kid, Sam II or Ike
Just call him whichever you like.
Always there with that big wide grin,
He too just wanted to win.

But if they didn't, it could not be said
That they did not give it all they had.

Remember God who has gotten you there
Of all his blessings always be aware.
Put your trust in Him and to Him be true
And He will always take care of you.

So best wishes guys in all you do
For we are all very proud of you.

When you get to come back on the yard on game day

You will probably be coming in a different way
But if you will
Don't forget, to look for the gang on the hill.

Good luck Tim and Steve.

Kermit and Helen Milloy
April 22, 1995

48. PROFESSIONAL ATHLETES

Name	Year	Team
Football		
Jack Spinks	1952	Pittsburgh Steelers
Frank Purnell	1956	Cleveland Browns
Williams Bailey	1963	New York Giants
Smith Reed	1965	New York Giants
Samuel Shivers	1966	Minnesota Vikings
Donnie Wallace	1966	Minnesota Vikings
Eddie Johnson	1966	Minnesota Vikings
Prince Borton	1967	Washington Redskins
Robert Brown	1967	St. Louis Cardinals
Raymond Brown	1967	St. Louis Cardinals
Joe Robinson	1967	Minnesota Vikings
St. Elmo Cain	1967	New Orleans Saints
Leroy Hardy	1967	Houston Oilers
Terry Lewis	1967	Los Angeles Rams
Craig Walker	1967	Montreal Beavers
Willie Banks	1968	New York Giants
James Williams	1968	Cincinnati Bengals
Joe Owens	1969	New Orleans Saints
Lawrence Watkins	1969	Detroit Lions
Dock Mosley	1969	Pittsburgh Steelers
Joe Leasy	1969	Boston Patriots
Robert Bell	1969	Ottawa Lions
Rayford Jenkins	1970	Kansas City Chiefs
David Hadley	1970	Kansas City Chiefs
Willie Peake	1970	San Francisco 49ers

Lawrence Estes	1970	New Orleans Saints
David Washington	1970	Denver Broncos
Marvin Weeks	1970	Cincinnati Bengals
Leroy Byars	1971	Miami Dolphins
Willie Young	1971	Miami Dolphins
Cleophus Johnson	1971	Denver Broncos
Floyd Rice	1971	Houston Oilers
Willie Alexander	1971	Houston Oilers
Richard Sowells	1971	New York Giants
Eddie Hackett	1971	Minnesota Vikings
Franklin Roberts	1972	Minnesota Vikings
Leon Gorror	1972	Buffalo Bills
Robert Penchion	1972	Buffalo Bills
Harry Gooden	1972	San Diego Chargers
Charles Davis	1973	New England Patriots
Clifton Davis	1973	New York Giants
Willie McGee	1973	Los Angeles Rams
Alex Price	1973	New Orleans Saints
Billy Howard	1974	Detroit Lions
Jimmy Davis	1974	Detroit Lions
Leonard Fairley	1974	Houston Oilers
Larry Cameron	1974	Denver Broncos
Bobby Huell	1974	Pittsburgh Steelers
Izell Gunner	1974	San Diego Chargers
Boyd Brown	1974	Denver Broncos
Francis Reynolds	1975	Los Angeles Rams
Willie Porter	1975	Dallas Cowboys
Adrian Capitol	1975	San Diego Chargers
Ernes Guynes	1975	Philadelphia Eagles
Jerry Dismuke	1975	New Orleans Saints
Barry Brady	1975	Chicago Bears
Lawrence Pillars	1976	New York Jets
Jimmy Giles	1977	Houston Oilers
Henry Bradley	1978	San Diego Chargers
Larry Willis	1979	Kansas City Chiefs
Roynell Young	1980	Philadelphia Eagles
Otis Wonsley	1980	New York Giants
Issiac Holt	1985	Minnesota Vikings

Wayne Dillard	1986	St. Louis Cardinals
Milton Mack	1987	New Orleans Saints
Elliot Smith	1989	San Diego Chargers
Michael Andrews	1989	Buffalo Bills
Jack Philips	1989	Kansas City Chiefs
Garry Lewis Jr.	1990	Los Angeles Raiders
Dwayne White	1990	New York Jets
Torrance Small	1992	New Orleans Saints
Cedric Tillman	1992	Denver Broncos
John Thierry	1994	Chicago Bears
Steve McNair	1995	Houston Oilers
Marcus Hinton	1995	Oakland Raiders
Bryant Mix	1996	Houston Oilers
Donald Driver	1999	Green Bay Packers
Chad Slaughter	2000	New York Jets
Louis Green	2004	Denver Broncos
Nate Hughes	2008	Jacksonville Jaguars
Charlie Spiller	2008	Tampa Bay Buccaneers
Emmanuel Arceneaux	2009	BC Lions (CFL)
Lee Robinson	2010	Denver Broncos
Tim Buckley	2010	Atlanta Falcons
Baseball		
Stanley Barker	1981	Detroit Tigers
Alfornia Jones	1981	Chicago White Sox
Keiver Campbell	1990	Toronto Blue Jays
Corey Wimberly	2005	Colorado Rockies
B. J. Hubbert	2006	New York Mets
Marcus Davis	2007	Pittsburgh Pirates
Angel Rosa	2013	Anaheim Angels
Earl Burl III	2015	Toronto Blue Jays
Basketball		
Willie Norwood	1969	Detroit Pistons
Julius Keyes	1969	Denver Rockets
Larry Smith	1980	Golden State Warriors
Albert Irving	1982	Golden State Warriors
Michael Phelps	1985	Seattle Supersonics
Alex Owumi	2008	London Lions

49. History of the A-Club

In the year of 1990, when Davis Weathersby completed his coaching and teaching career, he contacted former Alcorn State University athletes with the idea of organizing an Alcorn State University letterman club, and the name would be the A-Club.

The purpose of the A-Club is to promote the welfare of athletics at the university. From 1991 to 1993, athletes met and discussed plans to organize the A-Club. It was decided in these meetings to contact other universities that had established programs and get their by-laws and constitution to use as a guide.

After gathering all the information needed to form the constitution, the group organized the A-Club Association at the 1994 Mid-Winter Conference in Biloxi, Mississippi. The following officers were elected: Davis Weathersby, president; Lonnie Moore, vice president; Waldo James, secretary; Peter Boston, special assistant and the director of Alumni Affairs; and Charles Davis, secretary-treasurer. The president appointed the following committees: Constitution, Fund-Raising, Hall of Fame, Program, Publicity, Courtesy, History, and Economic Development.

Charles McClelland served as chairman of the Alcorn State University inaugural Sports Hall of Fame Committee. He welcomed the honorees and their guests. Hundreds of Alcornites across the state and the nation converged in Vicksburg, Mississippi, to honor twenty-two of their fellow alumni in the inaugural Alcorn State University A-Club Athletics Hall of Fame Induction Ceremony. It was a meeting of near epic proportions, with legends of the gridiron, hardwood, diamond, and track gathered together.

All of the officers of the A-Club Alumni Association and the Board of Directors are separately charged with the primary duty of promoting the best interests of Alcorn State University, the A-Club alumni, and the Alcorn State University National Alumni Association.

Those eligible for membership shall be all former students of Alcorn State University who have earned their varsity letter in a sport classified by the athletic department. There are three classes of membership:

1. Active paid members;

2. Inactive nonpaying members; and

3. Honorary alumni, coaches and friends (they are not eligible to vote or hold office).

50. 2015 PURPLE AND GOLD DAY AGENDA

Alcorn State University National Alumni Association
www.asunationalalumni.com

Purple & Gold Day '15

Mississippi State Capitol Building
Jackson, Mississippi

Agenda

Tuesday, February 10, 2015

- **9:00 a.m. to 10:00 a.m.**
  Coffee and Conversation Special Briefings – Room 201-H
  House Ways & Means Committee Meeting Room (2nd Floor House Side)
  Alcorn State University Legislative Liaison will lead an overview of the 2015 Legislative
  Priorities Agenda along with greetings and insights into the 2015 Legislative Session from key
  committee chairmen, Alcornites in the Mississippi Legislature and other state legislators.

- **10:00 a.m. to 10:30 a.m. – House Chamber Public Gallery (4th Floor House Side)***
  ASU Administration, Alumni Leadership & 2014 SWAC & SBN National Champion ASU
  Football Team will be honored with a special presentation on the Floor of the Mississippi
  House of Representatives.

- **10:30 a.m. to 11:00 a.m. – Senate Chamber Public Gallery (4th Floor Senate Side)***
  ASU Administration, Alumni Leadership & 2014 SWAC & SBN National Champion ASU
  Football Team will be honored with a special presentation on the Floor of the MS Senate.

- **11:00 a.m. to 1:00 p.m.**
  *Lunch with Legislators & Legislative Staff – Capitol Rotunda (1st Floor) ***
  A wonderful "Mississippi River Bluffs" buffet lunch offering an opportunity to interact with
  legislative leaders and other state officials.

- **11:00 a.m. to 2:00 p.m.**
  Locate My Legislator – House Floor & Senate Floor Receptionist Desk (3rd Floor)
  Alumni and friends are encouraged to seek out and find their respective State
  Representative and State Senator from their home (city/county) district to share the
  importance of supporting the 2015 Legislative Priorities Agenda.

THE BRAVES SPIRIT HAS NEVER BEEN STRONGER THAN IT IS TODAY!

Alcorn State University National Alumni Association – 1000 ASU Drive #809 – Lorman, MS 39096-7500
Phone: 601-877-6323 • Fax: 601-877-6326 • Email: alumniaffairs@alcorn.edu
www.asunationalalumni.com   *subject to change

51. Sports Hall of Fame Inductees

1996

Charles Boston...Football, Baseball
Peter Boston ....Football, Baseball, Track
Marino H. Casem ....Coach—Football
Dwight D. Fisher... Coach—Football and Basketball
James Samuel Ford ....Football
William Foster.. Coach and Player—Baseball
Mildrette Netter Graves ....Track
Willie Harper ....Football
Waldo James...Basketball
Sadie E. Magee ....Basketball
Alphonse Marks.. Football, Basketball
Levern McClelland .... Basketball, Track
Lonnie Moore ....Basketball
Carrie Beatrice Bryant Moses...Basketball
Richard Polk...Football, Baseball
E. E. Simmons ....Coach—Basketball, Track
Richard Smith .... Basketball, Track
Johnny R. Spinks.. Football
Claude Watson .... Football
Davis Weathersby .... Football, Track
Mary Vanderbilt White..Basketball
Davey L. Whitney .... Coach—Basketball

1997

James Brown...Football
Louis Crews...................................... Coach—Football, Baseball, Women's Basketball
Samuel L. Crump .... Football, Track, Baseball
Sarah "Sis" Green Faulks ....Basketball
Lee N. Garner.. Basketball, Track
Lillie R. Beasley Garner...Basketball
Leon Griffith .... Basketball, Track
George Holloway Jr. .... Basketball, Track
Ernestine Pittman James ....Basketball
Orsmond Jordan...Basketball

Levern Kennedy...Basketball
Clayton Love .... Football, Basketball
Elijah Moore... Football, Track, Baseball
Bessie L. Henry Polk...Basketball
William Price ....Basketball
Vernon T. Purnell .... Basketball, Track
John Spriggs ....Football
Charles Thomas... Football, Track
Robert Weddington .... Baseball
Oscar Wright..Football

1998

Kenneth C. Beal Sr. ....Football
Shelton Buckley ....Basketball
James "Bo" Clark ....Football, Baseball
John H. Clay...Football, Basketball, Baseball, Track
Felix H. Dunn.. Football, Track, Baseball
Joseph Rusell Frye...Football, Track, Basketball
George A. Green Sr. .... Football, Track
Joseph J. Hardy.. Football, Basketball
Evan Tyree Hawkins ....Football
Gene Henderson..Football
Willie Lucas... Basketball, Track
Willie "Rat" McGowan ....Football, Baseball
Alpha Lockhart Morris.. Basketball, Track
Calvin Rhodes.. Basketball, Baseball
Cleopatra Davenport Thompson..Basketball
Q. Leon Toler.. Baseball
Henry L. Tucker .... Football, Track
Lucious Turner II..Football, Basketball, Track
Benjamin R. Williams ....Football, Basketball, Track
Ira Williams...Basketball

1999

Eddie Alexander ....Football
David L. Conner .... Football, Track, Baseball
Lonnie C. Crosby.. Football

Medgar W. Evers .... Football
Sidney James .... Baseball
Scott Jones Jr. .... Football
Nebraska Mays.. Football, Track
Mary L. Dennis Polk ....Basketball
Roland V. Pope .... Basketball, Football, Track, Baseball, Tennis
Frank Purnell .... Football, Track
Charles Raines Sr. .... Football
Inez Jordan Raines...Basketball
Leonia Beale Rhodes..Basketball
Monroe Stewart Jr. .... Football, Track
Leroy Taylor .... Football
Dave Washington Jr. .... Football, Basketball
Horace D. Williams .... Football
Charles Wilson .... Football, Track, Baseball

2000

Doris V. Hyde Bird...Basketball
Calvin E. Davis Sr. ....Football, Basketball, Baseball, Track
Nathaniel Eiland ....Football, Baseball
Charlie Floyd.. Football, Track
Johnny Gilmore .... Football, Track
Carl E. Jones ....Tennis, Football
William I. Long Sr. ....Track, Baseball, Basketball
Willie Norwood ....Basketball
Robert E. Pickett..Basketball, Track, Baseball

2001

Willie J. Alexander.. Football
Arthur J. Fielder Jr. ....Football, Basketball, Baseball, Tennis, Track and Field
Willie C. Jones.. Football, Baseball, Track and Field
Oscar Martin.. Football
Leal McMullen... Football
Luther E. Morris.. Football
Aubrey W. Owens .... Baseball
Elex D. Price Sr. .... Football
Henry R. Smith ....Basketball

Walter J. Thompson .... Baseball
Craig Walker .... Football
Willie C. Young Sr. .... Football

2002

Percy C. Bailey .... Baseball
Leroy Byars .... Football
Jessie L. Conerly .... Basketball
John W. Cooley .... Basketball
Jerry M. Dismuke .... Football
Joe Owens Sr. .... Football
Willie E. Peake .... Football
Larry Smith .... Basketball
Melville C. Tillis .... Football, Track
Charles Watkins .... Basketball
William G. Wooley .... Football

2003

William Brown .... Football
Teddy M. Davis .... Football
Lawrence Estes .... Football
Mason Denham .... Football, Track, Baseball
John Robertson .... Football, Track
Willie Simpson .... Football, Track

2004

Ruthie B. Harris Atkins .... Basketball
Mordine Bailey .... Baseball
Thomas Davis III .... Basketball
Joe Frelix .... Football
Margie Price Funches .... Basketball
Joe A. Haynes .... Football
Earl Johnson .... Basketball
Charles F. McClelland Sr. .... Basketball
Thomas J. Morgan .... Football
George V. Morris Sr. .... Basketball

Melvin Spears Jr. .... Football
Phillip West.. Baseball

2005

Boyd Brown Jr. .... Football
Robert E. Brown.. Football
David Hadley .... Football
Henry Harper.. Football
Cardell S. Jones.. Football
Terry Lewis .... Football
Fred L. McNair.. Football
Steve L. McNair.. Football
Willie J. Outlaw .... Football
Lonnie Walker...Basketball
Dwayne A. White.. Football
James H. Williams.. Football

2006

Johnny E. Anderson .... Football, Track
Newtie J. Boyd.. Football
Barry S. Brady .... Football
Wellington Cox..Track
Lonnie C. Eiland.. Football, Track
Leroy Hardy.. Football
Marcus Hinton .... Football
Johnette T. Holloway ....Basketball
Timothy McNair.. Football
Alvin Moore .... Football
Dellie C. Robinson...Basketball
Donald Ray Ross.. Football

2007

Odell Agnew..Basketball
Hayward Ashford.. Football
Carl T. Chalmers .... Football
Theophilus Danzy..Coach—Football

Grady Marshall Jr. .... Tennis
Joseph L. Martin .... Basketball
Willie McCoy .... Track, Football
Richard Myles Sr. .... Football
Robert E. Penchion .... Football
Richard Pickens .... Football
Willie Ray .... Football
Lawrence Watkins .... Football

2008

Arthur James Anderson .... Football
Marvin Arrington .... Football, Track and Field
Don Bell .... Football, Track and Field, Golf
Larry D. Brown .... Track and Field
Adrian Baxter Capitol .... Football, Track and Field
Grant A. Dungee .... Track Coach
Jimmy Giles .... Football, Baseball
Polly J. Joiner-Rogers .... Basketball
Hiawatha Clark Knight .... Basketball Coach
Willie MaGee Jr. .... Football, Track and Field
Lawrence Pillars .... Football
Floyd E. Rice .... Football
Jerry Sims .... Track
Kenneth Tillage .... Football
Albert Watts Sr. .... Football, Basketball, Baseball

2010

Charles Beckwith .... Baseball, Football
Albert D. Clark Sr. .... Baseball
LaMarcus Collins .... Track
Leonard Fairley .... Football
Tony Hampton .... Football, Track
Bobbie Hill .... Baseball
Cleophus Johnson .... Football
Malachi McGruder .... Track
James O. Nelson .... Football, Track
Dennis E. Thomas .... Football

Larry Warren...Football
Ernest P. Young..Football

2011

Thomas Bailey...Football, Basketball, Track
Willie Brock..Football
Murray Creshon ....Football, Track
Terry Fluker...Baseball
Augusta Lee Jr...Football
Quitman Lewis...Football
Houston Markham Jr..Football
Frankie Pilate ....Football
Marvin Weeks ....Football
Roynell Young ....Football

2012

Cedric Bush..Football
Leslie Frazier ....Football
Teresa Hooker ....Basketball
James "Scat" Jackson ....Football
Cecil Martin ....Football
Juanita Magee Martin ....Basketball
Ronald J. Stevenson ....Baseball
Smith Reed ....Football
Rufus White...Basketball
Levi Wyatt...Basketball

2013

George Cole...Football
Edward Davis ....Baseball
Elbert Foules Jr..Football
James Horton ....Basketball
Gertrude Payton ....Basketball, Track
Carlton Reese ....Football
Michael Reese ....Football

Kalvin Robinson ....Football
Charles Ruth...Track
Louis White ....Basketball, Football, Track

2014

Henry Bradley...Football
Robert L. Brown Sr. ....Football
Fred B. "Tiger" Carter Jr. ....Football
Lit Parker Evans...Football
Lionel "Jo-Jo" Fantroy...Football
James C. Gales..Football
Richard Horton...Basketball
Moses Leon Howard ....Football
Rayford Earl Jenkins ....Football
Kattie G. McCullough ....Basketball
Jacqueline Bush Thompson.. Volleyball
Clarence Toliver..Football
Eunice Mosley Warren...Basketball
Tony Woolfolk...Football

2015

Nathaniel Archibald ....Basketball
Rober C. Bell ....Football
Harry G. Brown ....Baseball
Tracy M. Cook ....Football
Eddie Hackett..Football
Percy Harris..Football
Ivy Davis Jones..Track
Richard A. Sowells ....Football
William Tate Sr. ....Football
Andrew Tatum..Basketball
Johnny Thomas ....Football
Alpha Sherman Young ....Track
Harry Brown Sr. ....Baseball
Ocie Brown Sr. ....Football
Samuel Sing..Basketball

52. MISSISSIPPI'S BEST KEPT SECRET

Reprinted from **"Opinions"** section of the *Prentiss Headlight*, *Prentiss, Miss.* Wednesday, May 8, 2002

By: Patsy Speights
Prentiss Headlight Editor

"Mississippi's best kept secret," according to my friend Charlie Mitchell at the Vicksburg Post, is a 1700 acre campus set in rolling hills just off Highway 61 between Natchez and Vicksburg, sorta. It is the campus of Alcorn State University. Few people happen by, but for those who do, they are in for a great surprise, or there are those of us who have had reason to go, who were also delightfully surprised.

Our board of directors for the Mississippi Press Association set a goal some years back to visit all the state's universities in our efforts to attract Mississippi graduates for our field. Where most of the state's campuses are crowded with more buildings than earth, Alcorn is beautifully designed with space for the buildings, parking lots, plus trees, shrubs and flower beds.

We were told that the Presbyterians began the institution in 1830 as a school for boys and called it Oakland College which makes it the oldest campus in Mississippi. In 1871 the state bought property and named it Alcorn which was the second state institution of higher learning.

This year the enrollment was 3100 and in the field of mass communications, they had a newspaper, a radio station, a TV station and a public relations emphasis. They graduate about 25 each year in mass communications.

Dr. Clinton Bristow, Jr., is the 16th president of Alcorn and he calls Alcorn the "Academic Resort" of higher education.

Alcorn was the nation's first state supported institution for the higher education of African Americans. It has seven schools offering programs leading to an associate, baccalaureate, master's and specialist degrees. It is accredited by the Southern Association of Colleges and Schools. There are 174 full time faculty members and 19 part-time with more than half holding doctoral degrees. The student to faculty ratio is 16-1. They play football in the Southern Athletic Conference and other sports in the NCAA Division 1-A.

But that's not what makes Alcorn the best kept secret in the state. The secret is the beautiful campus. One enters the campus via a landscaped driveway leading to a guard house where visitors are greeted with a hearty good morning and directions if needed. The grass is manicured on every side, but buildings are stately and well kept, the stadium is big and inviting.

Inside the buildings we visited the floors are shiny, the furnishings are inviting and everything has a touch of purple and gold.

There are parking lots on the front, at the back and to the side of most buildings. The campus is so spread out that students often drive to class.

Our host served us lunch in the new honors co-ed dormitory complete with full cafeteria and dining hall.

The old football stadium is now the track field.

Oakland Chapel built in the early 1800's is still in use and breath taking.

Just as there is a front gate, there is a back gate where students and visitors check-in to campus. "Town" is just a few feet away consisting of a few stores.

Leaving Alcorn, one is drawn to the ruins of Windsor. The columns almost surrounded by a pine tree farm. The grass is mowed and the stately columns still reach for the sky. I never see sights like Windsor that I don't wonder how people built such beautiful structures with so little to work with and how they have out lasted the whims of nature and man.

There are many wonderful places to see in our state, perhaps we should all start thinking of them for vacations.

LIST OF SOURCES

"A" Club 2010 Sports Hall of Fame Induction Publication
Against Great Odds: The History of Alcorn State University, 1994
The Alcorn Quilt Centerpiece by Dr. J. Janice Coleman
Alcorn State University Athletics Website
Alcorn State University Catalogs
Alcorn State University Commencement Programs
Alcorn State University Fact Books
Alcorn State University Football Media Guides
Alcorn State University Founders Day Convocation Programs
Alcorn State University Inauguration Programs
Alcorn State University Mid-Winter Conference Programs
Alcorn State University National Alumni Association Mid-Winter Conference President's
    Messages
Alcorn State University National Alumni Association Reports
Alcorn State University National Alumni Association Reunion Programs
Alcorn State University National Alumni Association Website
Alcorn State University Website
Alcorn State University Yearbooks
Alcorn State University, Office of Alumni Affairs
Alcorn State University, Office of Student Engagement
Alcorn State University, Office of the President
Alcorn, The University Magazine
ASU Foundation, Inc.
ASU Mini Facts Newsletters
Black Issues in Higher Education
Bureau of Building, Grounds and Real Property Management, Annual Capital Facilities
    Study, 1988
Centennial History of Alcorn A&M College, 1971, by Melerson Guy Dunham
Department of Defense/Office of Naval Research
Department of Homeland Security
Diverse Issues in Higher Education
Excellence at Alcorn: A Collection of Feature Articles, Lillian M. Fears, 2006
Frederick D. Patterson Research Institute "Just the Facts" Publication, 2001

International Federation of Library Association and Institution (IFLA)

The Jackson Family

The Johnson Family

The Jones Family

Mississippi Board of Nursing's 3rd Quarterly, 2001

Mississippi Institutions of Higher Learning Website

National College Basketball Hall of Fame (NCBHOF) Press Release

National Council for Accreditation of Teacher Education (NCATE) Documents

National Science Foundation

Philadelphia Inquiry

Pushing Forward, 1938 by Milan Davis

Printiss Highlight, 2002

Reading First Teacher Education Network (RFTEN)

Redemption: The Last Battle of the Civil War by Nicholas LaMann, 2006 (Shared by Latoya Hart, director of Institutional Assessment at Alcorn State University)

School of AREAS: Celebrating 125 Years of Providing Access and Enhancing Opportunities Publication, 2015

Simply Sharing publications by Dr. Jerry Domatob

The Smith Family

Southern Association of Colleges and Schools (SACS) Commission on Colleges Documents

Sweet Potato Publication

U.S. News and World Report

United States Department of Agriculture

United States Department of Education

Vicksburg Post

About the Author

Dr. Josephine McCann Posey, a former dean of the School of Education and Psychology, interim vice president for Academic Affairs, and special assistant to the president at Alcorn State University, is the first female to hold the first two positions in the history of the university. She holds a Bachelor of Science degree from Alcorn State University and Master of Education, Education Specialist, and Doctor of Education degrees from Mississippi State University. She finished high school at the age of sixteen and signed her first teaching contract at the age of nineteen. She worked in the public school system for nine years inclusive of Yazoo City, Covington County, and Washington County, and full-time at the university level until retirement inclusive of Mississippi Valley State University, Mississippi State University, and Alcorn State University. She also served as professor and department chairperson at Alcorn State University.

Posey is affiliated with many professional organizations. She is past president of the Zeta Delta Omega Chapter of Alpha Kappa Alpha Sorority, Inc.; past president of the Natchez Chapter of Links, Inc.; and past president of the Campus Chapter of Phi Delta Kappa. She served on the State Advisory Committee for implementing kindergarten in Mississippi and was a state evaluator and trainer for the Mississippi Teacher Assessment Instrument, state evaluator for the Mississippi Administrator Assessment Instrument, as well as the Guidance Assessment Instrument. She served on the Comprehensive Certification Study Committee appointed by the state superintendent of education, Richard Thompson, during his first tenure. She has participated in many performance-based and accreditation site visits at the local, state, and national levels. She also served as president of the Mississippi Association of Colleges for Teacher Education (MACTE).

Posey has published, conducted workshops, served on forums and rendered many scholarly presentations at the local, state and national levels. She authored the history of Alcorn State University published in the spring of 1994 entitled *Against Great Odds: The History of Alcorn State University* and a pictorial history entitled *Alcorn State University and the National Alumni Association* sponsored by the Alcorn State University National Alumni Association in 2000. She has also written articles for newspapers and other publications.

Josephine McCann Posey.

Posey has received numerous honors, including leadership, service, and research awards from Phi Delta Kappa, Outstanding Woman of America, Distinguished Leadership Award, Outstanding Personality of America, Outstanding University Faculty recognized by the Mississippi State Legislature, Alpha Kappa Alpha Basileus (President) of the Year Southeastern Region, and Faculty Alumnus of the Year Alcorn State University National Alumni Association, to name a few. She was selected as a Fulbright Scholar during the summer of 1996, where she studied in China for six weeks. She is often requested to sing, speak, or both, by social, civic, and religious groups. Posey was one of several women recognized as a "Classic Woman" during the annual Capital City Classic held in Jackson, Mississippi, during fall 2008.

Posey is the oldest of four siblings, all Alcorn graduates, born to the late Calvin McCann and her surviving mother, Aline Moffett McCann, of Collins, Mississippi. She has two sisters, Helen (Kermit) Milloy, retired assistant superintendent of education in Covington County, and Connie (Charles) Fairley, retired Medicaid assistant area supervisor, Laurel, Mississippi, and a brother, John (Allene) McCann, federal grain inspector service supervisor, United States Department of Agriculture (USDA), New Orleans. In addition to Posey and her siblings being alumni of Alcorn, her son, Carlos, and daughter-in-law, Remona, as well as nieces, nephews, aunts, uncles, cousins, and other in-law family members, also make up the great Alcorn State University family. She has four loving grandchildren.

Her parents, along with the wisdom of her grandparents, were her inspiration to always be the best that she could be and to put God at the head of her life in all endeavors, and he would always be her safety net. Her grandparents are the late Morrell and Girdia Mae Moffett, and the late Willie and Annie McCann.

She is married to Curtis Leon Posey, a retired physical education instructor in the Vicksburg-Warren School District. She is the daughter-in-law of the late Willie E. and Ruby Posey. The family holds membership at Old Hopewell Baptist Church in Collins, Mississippi.

INDEX

Page numbers in **bold** refer to illustrations.

academic degree programs, 84–85, 200
academic schools and major support divisions, 190–93
accreditation, 5, 16, 18, 28, 51–52, 71, 79–80, 106, 107, 124
Acholonu, Alex D. W., 107
A-Club, 99, 233
Adams, Willie, 58
admissions requirements, 83–84
adult programs, 4
Ag-Academic Camp, 73
Against Great Odds, 4, 21, 60, 64, 99, 101, 108, 113
Agricultural Enhancement Camp, 73
agricultural programs, 3–4, 11, 24, 26, 31, 65, 73–74
Agyepong, Kwabena, 52
Alcorn (university magazine), **59**, 60
Alcorn, James L., 3, 9, **9**, 10
Alcorn Agricultural and Mechanical College, 4, 10, 11, 21
Alcorn Concert Choir, **87**
Alcornite of the Year recipients, 93, 101–2, 215
Alcorn Jazz Festival, 70, **72**
"Alcorn Ode," 44, 96
Alcorn Quilt, 96, **97**, 227–28
"Alcorn Spirit," 96, 226
Alcorn State University National Alumni Association, 21, 59, 61, 73–74, 91–92, 103, 206, 207–10

Alcorn Student Recruitment Program, 71
Alcorn University, 4, 9
Alipoe, Dovi, 37
alumni, 5–6, 16, 20–21, 47, 61, 63–64, 73–74, 91–104
Alumni Bells, 44, **45**
Alumni Day, 96–97, 228–29
Alumni House Bed and Breakfast, 93, **94**
America Reads Mississippi (ARM), 89
Ames, Adelbert, 10
Anderson, Ella, 35
Anderson, LaShunda, 106
Anderson, Shawn, 90
Arnold, Jessie, 28
Arrington, Wandra, 44
Association for Black Educators, 15
ASU Foundation, Inc., 21, 61, 81, 152
ASU Mini Facts newsletter, 27
athletes (professional), 230–32
Athletic Academic Success Program (AASP), 71
athletics, 6, 19–20, 31, 58–60, 69, 80, 88, 97
Award of Excellence recipients, 183
awards, 38, 60, 64–65, 72–76, 79, 92–93, 96, 99, 101–2, 105–8
Ayers, Jake, Sr., 34
Ayers desegregation settlement, 34, 107

Banks, Ivan, 6
Baptist Student Union, 19

Barbour, Haley, 62
Barnes, Emanuel, 97, **110**
Barnes, Johnny B., family, 96
Bartee, Joseph, **111**
Barthwell Group, 48
baseball, 17, 59, 61, 98–99
basketball, 59–60, 78–79
Batty, Lakesha, 59
Beaute' Noire, **88**
Bell, William H., 10, 16–18, **18**
Bequette, Barry, 74
Biotech Application in Vegetable Production Project, 29
Biotechnology Research Center, 29, **30**
black universities, 3, 5, 14, 23, 26, 55
Board of Trustees. *See* Mississippi Institutions of Higher Learning (IHL) Board of Trustees
Bounds, Hank, 51, 68, 189
Bowles, Preston S., 10, 18, **18**
Bowles Industrial Hall, 16, 81
Boyd, John Dewey, 10, 19, **20**
Boyd, Newtie, 53
Boyd, Noland, 80
brass band, 11
Braves Kids Club, 71
Bristow, Clinton, Jr., 10, 25–32, **25, 26, 27, 28,** 33, 34–35, 39–40, 41, 195–96
Bristow, Joyce Moore, 25
Brooks, Jerry, 106
Brown, Lola, 89
Brown, M. Christopher, II, 10, 55–66, **55, 61,** 68, 100, 194
Brown, Michael, 106
budget, 57, 68, 88, 204
Buie, Kimberly, 79
buildings, 6, 16, 19, 21, 26, 98–99, 126–28
Bunch, Cecile, 23
Burrus, John H., 9, 11–12, **12,** 15
Bush, George H. W., **109**
Butler, Albert, 103
Butler, Malinda, 27, 71

Callaway, Thomas J., 10, 12–13, **13**
Campus Police Department, 52
Capitol City Classic, 102
career plan, 197

Carpenter, Santa, 59
Carr, Robert, Jr., 71
Carson, LaShundia, 27
Casem, Marino, 99
Catchings, Tracy, 106
cattle gap, 5, 113
Cayton, Madge Revels, 47
Celebrity Basketball Camp, 59
Center of Excellence in Research Symposium, 73
Central Michigan University, 42
Chamberlain, Jeremiah, 3
Child Development Laboratory Center, 73
Children's Defense Fund, 64–65
Claiborne County, 5, 62
Clarke, Alyce G., 103, 107, **110**
coaches, 6, 16–17, 97, 129–30
Cochran, Thad, 75
Cole-Gary, Dorothy, 107
Coleman, Bernadine, 88
Coleman, J. Janice, 96
commencement, 24, **24,** 52–53, 62–64, **64,** 70, 73, **75, 90,** 94–95, **95,** 107, **109,** 182, 186–87; speakers, 184–85
Commission on Colleges of SACS, 27
Community and Junior College Board, 85
"Communiversity" Outreach Initiatives and Extension Programs, 35, **35**
conservation research, 30
Cooperative Extension Program, 77–78
core values, 4, 48, 118
Cornell University, 19
Council for Accreditation of Educator Preparation (CAEP), 71
Customer Service Task Force, 73

Dancing with the Stars, 99
Davis, Charles, 91
Davis, Jefferson, 47
Department of Agriculture, 40
Department of Blacksmithing, 11
Department of Carpentry, 11
Department of Health, Physical Education and Recreation, 98
Department of Industrial Education, 13, 14
Department of Mass Communications, 106
Development and Alumni Affairs, 91

dining hall, 19
diversity, 32, 42, 105
Division of Finance and Administrative Services, 57
Division of Marketing and Communication, 60
Dodgen, Anthony, 78
Domatob, Jerry, 54
Donald, Samuel, **109**
dormitories, 4, 14, 19, 26, 47, 57
Douglass, Frederick, 10
Dr. Clinton Bristow Jr. Dining Facility, **31**
Driver, Donald, 99
Ducksworth, Keiera, 36
Duncan, Jan, 27
Dungee, Darlene, 28
Dunham, Melerson Guy, 23
Dupre, Carolyn, 57
Dyn-O-Mite Marching Band, **87**, 88

Edney, Lillian, 51
Edney, Norris A., Sr., 10, 50–54, **50**, 55, 65–66, 67, 194, 195
Edwards, Juanita, 23
Edwards, Tonya, 60
1871 Club, 100, **101**
Enactus, 35–36, **39**
enrollment, 11, 14, 16, 19, 26, 34, 47, 51–53, 56–57, 70, 72, 82–83, 198–99
Entrepreneur Academy, 71
Eunice Powell Home Economics Building, 19
Evans, Akosua Barthwell, 48
Evers, Medgar Wylie, 61–62, **62**
Evers, Myrlie, 61–62, 73, **75**
Experiment Station, 21, 29, 78

faculty, 5–6, 12–15, 17–20, 24, 27–28, 35–39, 42–44, 48, 51, 53, 66, 88–89
Faculty Convocation, 48, 57
farmers, 29, 31–34, 56, 72, 77, 96–97, 107
financial aid, 23, 83, 85
First Year Experience Program (First and Second Year Experience Program), 58
fitness center, 53
food services, 88
football, 17, 46, 58, 78, 86, 97, 99

Foster, William "Bill," 99, **100**
fuel cell research, 29
Fuller, Cora, 71
funding, 15, 20, 23, 34, 42, 57, 65, 74, 76, 88–89, 101, 113

Galtney, Alfred, 89
Gary, Doris, 27
General College, 53
Gershwin, George, 105
Gibbs, Karl, 103
Gibson, Janice, 91, 103
Gilchrist, Jan Spivey, 47
Gill, John, 6
Global Programs, 37
goals, 4, 15, 48, 51, 53–54, 89, 91–92, 117
Golden Classes, 94–95, 216–25
Gospel Choir, 70
Goss, Benjamin, 47
Gossin, A. J., 5
graduation, 15, 24, 27, 31, 63–64, 89–90, 95. *See also* commencement
grants, 35, 38, 42–44, 56–57, 71, 74–75, 85, 88, 98
Gray, William "Bill" H., III, 62–63
Green, Montrell, 94
Griffin, Samuel, **87**

Hall of Honor inductees, 93, 211–14
Harness, Jessie, 78
Hayden, Donna, 39
Health and Disability Services, 73, **74**, 90
Heard, Jadtrl, 63, **64**
Hendricks, Espy, 28, 80
Hendricks, John I., 27–28
Henry, Lenell, 58
Heritage Convocation, 61
Higher Education Appreciation Day Working for Academic Excellence (HEADWAE) Award recipients, 38, 154–55
Highway 61, 5, 17, 18, **31**, 62
Himes, Estelle Charlotte Bomar, 96
Himes, J. S., 96
Hogan, Devina, 63
Holloway, Gregory, Sr., 103
Holloway, James "Chicken," 96

Home Management House, 19
Honors Convocation, 82, **83**
Honors Program, 79
Hopson, Jay, 58–59, **59**
Hoskin, Myra, 90
Howard, Andrew, 9, 12
Hunt, Dorothy, 88
Hunt, George, 59
Hurricane Katrina, 35

Idleburg, Dorothy, 52
Idusuyi, Dickson, 39
Igbokwe, Patrick, 29
Igwebuike, John, 79–80
image, 5–6, 20, 34, 103–4
inaccessibility of main campus location, 5, 17
inaugural programs, 10, 131–48
Intellectual Renewal Grant, 38, 155–57
internships, 31, 39, 44, 56

Jackson, Jesse, **111**
Jackson, Laplose, 83, 106
Jackson, Willie Fred, 106
Jackson family, 95
Jack Spinks–Marino Casem Stadium, 99, **99**
James L. Bolden Campus Union, 24, 53
J. D. Boyd Library, 16, 28–29, **85**, 203
Jenkins, Cameron, 63, **64**
Johnson, Brandy, 106
Johnson family, 95
Jones, John, 62
Jones, Lillie, 23
Jones, Wiley, 106–7
Jones, Yolanda, 39
Jones family, 95

Kariuki, Cheryl, 6
Keys, Patricia, 79

Lady Braves basketball, **32**, 59, 78–79
Laing, Roberta, 108
land-grant institution and mission, 3–4, 11, 18, 19–20, 24, 26, 28–32, 34–35, 51, 56, 61, 68, 74–76, 113
Lanier, William H., 10, 14, **15**
leadership of presidents (1994–2015), 194–96

leadership skills, 4, 11
Lee, Donzell, 52, 79–80
Lewis, Garry, 98
literary society, 11
literature, 18
Lorman, MS, 29, 56
Lott, Albert L., 21
Louis Stokes Mississippi Alliance for Minority Participants (LS-MAMP), 36
Lyles, Ivory, 74, 76
Lynch, John R., 3

Malik, Peter, 52, 80
Married to Medicine, 73
Martin, John Adams, 10, 15, **16**
Martin Elementary School, 15
Master of Business Administration (MBA) program, 26, 108
Maxwell, Melvin, 52
McAfee, Dalton, 76–77
McClelland, Charles, 103
McDaniel, Todd, 58
McDonald, James, 92
McGowan, Doris, 27, 61
McGowan, Willie "Rat," Sr., 61, **65**, 98–99, **100**
McLaurin, Anselm, 14
McNair, Fred, 98
McNair, Steve Latreal "Air," 44, 46, **46**, 98, 229–30
McNair, Tim, 98, 229–30
mechanical programs, 3–4, 11, 14, 24, 76
Medgar Wiley Evers Heritage Village Complex, 47
Middleton, Chuck, 103
Mid-South Partnership for Rural Community Colleges, 89
Mid-Winter Conferences, 61, 74, 92–93, 180–82
Miller, Hilton, 107
Milloy, Helen, 97
Milloy, Kermit, 97
Milloy family, 97–98
Minor, Chandra, 106
Minority Health International Research Training (ASU-MHIRT), 36

minutes, 5, 120–23
Miss Alcorn State University Queens, 24,
 152–53
mission statement, 4, 48–49, 119
Mississippi Association of Teachers in Col-
 ored Schools, 15
Mississippi Coalition of Partners in Preven-
 tion Seminar, 70
Mississippi Department of Education
 (MDE), 27
Mississippi Hall, 14
Mississippi Institutions of Higher Learning
 (IHL), 27, 48, 189, 204
Mississippi Institutions of Higher Learning
 (IHL) Board of Trustees, 4, 10, 12, 13–14,
 16–19, 22, 33, 68, 85, 103, 149–51
"Mississippi's Best Kept Secret," 243
Mississippi Senate Agriculture Committee, 70
Mississippi state legislature, 3–4, 10, 17, 23, 101
Model United Nations Student Club, 39
Morgan, Kimberly, 106
Morrill, Justin Smith, 76
Morrill Act of 1862, 4, 11, 76
Morrill Act of 1890, 11, 12, 56, 76
Morris, Alpha, 64
Morris, Jesse, 64
Morris, Jesse, Jr., 64
Moses, Dyann, 23
Moses, Napoleon, 28, 80
Moses, Willie, 24
Moss, Linda, 59
Multicultural Festival, 37, 37
Murphy, Lafayette, 5
Murphy, Manny, 59
Murphy, Zelmarine "Mama Brave," 102, 102
Murray, Renardo, 87

Nash, Woodrow, 47
Natchez, MS, 6, 26, 34, 54, 56, 57, 71, 105, 108
Natchez Festival of Music, 105
National Council for Accreditation of
 Teacher Education (NCATE), 27
National HBCU Choir, 70
National Teacher Examination (NTE), 27
National Vocational Education Act, 18
Natural Products Initiative, 30

newspaper, 12, 13
Newtie Boyd Center for Academic Support,
 53, 57–58, 85
Noble-Jones, Brittany, 106
Norwood, Percy, 92

Oakland College, 3, 44
Oakland Memorial Chapel, 44–46, 45, 105
Obama, Barack, 105
Office of Academic Affairs, 47, 81
Office of Admissions, 84
Office of Career Services, 82
Office of Institutional Research, 81
Office of Marketing and Communication, 81
Office of Pre-Professional Programs, 44
Office of Public Relations, 48
Office of the President, 81
Office of the Vice President, 20
Oredein, Olayinka, 57
Otis, Jesse R., 10, 18–19, 19
outreach programs, 34–35, 56, 74–75
Owens, Freddie, 92

Paden, Orlando, 103
Parker, Carolyn Williams, 94
Parnell, Jack, 109
patents, 40
Patterson, Roderick, 68
Patton, William, 30
Payne, Ralph, 23
Peoples, Dottie, 70
People to People Ambassador Program, 65
Philadelphia Inquiry, 99
physical education, 15, 17
physical plant, 18, 19
Pipes, William H., 10, 18, 19
Pizza Hut, 82, 84
Plump, John, 94
Porgy and Bess, 105
Posey, Josephine, 23, 27, 47, 52, 80
Prater family, 96
Presidential Award of Excellence, 65, 188
Presidential Encampment, 57
President's Home, 47–48
Price, Woodrow, 106
Pritchard Hall, 18

Product Development Center, 71
Purple and Gold Day, 102, 234

Quality Enhancement Plan (QEP), 52,
    158–59

Raegan, Barbara, 6
Rajanna, Bettaiya, 36, **65**
Rankin, Barney, 68
Rankin, Katina, 94
Rankin, Regina, 83
Rankins, Alfred, Jr., 10, 53, 65, 68–81, **67**, **73**,
    93, 103, 106, **112**, 194
Rankins, Juandalyn, 69, **112**
Reading First Teacher Education Network
    (RFTEN), 37
recruitment, 35, 57, 70, 85, 89, 91
retention, 26, 31, 58, 70
Revels, Hiram R., 3, 9, 10–11, **12**, 46, 105
Rey, Barret, 60
Reynolds, Wilson H., 9, 12, **13**
Riley, Luther, 60
Robinson, Levi, 28
Ronald E. McNair Post-Baccalaureate
    Achievement Program, 90
Ross, Elizabeth, 42
Ross, George E., 10, 41–49, **41**, **43**, 55, 195
Rowan, Levi J., 6, 10, 14, 15–17, **16**, **17**
Rowan, Mattie Foote, 96
Rowan Administration Building, 16
Rowan Hall, 73, **74**

SACS. *See* Southern Association of Colleges
    and Schools
Sanders, Blanche, 28
Sanders, Isiah S., 10, 16, **17**
Sandoval, Arturo, 70
Saturday Science Academy, 39
scholarships, 10, 44, 57, 61, 63, 72, 85, 91–92,
    96
School of Agriculture, Research, Extension
    and Applied Sciences (AREAS), 28, 30,
    71, 74, 76–78, 107
School of Business, 6, 107
School of Education and Psychology, 27, 71
School of Nursing, 6, 53, 54, 108
science, technology, engineering, and math-
    ematics (STEM) programs, 39, 72, 78

Scurria, Cynthia, 52
Sellers, Majorie, **110**
Shedrick, Karen, 54, 69–70, **69**
Shelton, Marilyn, 96
Sheriff, Walter, 91–92, **93**
Simmons, Robert, 103
Simmons, Willie, 103
Simply Sharing, 54, 160–79
Simpson, Alvin, 27
Sims, Jerry, 105
Sizemore, Robert, 107
Small Farm Outreach Project, 56
Smith, Jimmy, 23
Smith, Larry, 60
Smith, Robert, 28
Smith-Cook, Ladonna, 94
Smith family, 95
Snodgrass, A. D., 5
Sodexo, 86
South Central Athletic Conference, 17
Southern Agriculture Consortium for
    Underserved Communities (SACUC),
    29
Southern Association of Colleges and
    Schools (SACS), 16, 18–19, 21, 23, 52, 58,
    71, 79–80
Southwestern Athletic Conference (SWAC),
    44, 46, 51, 58–60, 78–79, 99, 108
Spann, Buford, 94
Spears, Melvin, Jr., 58
sports. *See* athletics
Sports Hall of Fame, 103, 235–42
Square, Brenda T., 100
Stallings, Shundera, 71
Stamps, Clara Ross, 60
Stamps, Delmar, 78
State Board of Health, 16–17
Stewart, Douglas, 52
Stewart, Troy, 36
strategic planning, 34, 38, 40, 42, 48
Stubbs, James, 92
Student Government Association presi-
    dents, 24, 153–54
student organizations, 39, 158
Students in Free Enterprise (SIFE) program,
    35
Student Support Services (SSS), 83
Sturgis, Thomas, 44

summer programs, 86, **86**
Swine Development Center, 29

Tenner, Katangela, 23
1098-T form, 71–72
tennis, 78
Thomas, Cedric, 68
Thomas, Isaac, 62
Thomas, Jenetria, **27**
Thomas, Johnny, 27, 31, 71
Thomas, Matthew, Jr., **93**
Thomas, Mattie McCann, 62
Thomas, Seth, mantle clock, 46, **47**
Thompson, Bennie, 42, **111**
Thompson, Cassandra, 98
Thompson, Valerie, 58
Tillery, Wade, 69
Tillman, Charles, 96, **97**
Triplett, Edward H., 10, 13–14, **15**
tuition, 89, 205
Tutors with a Mission, 89

United Nations Conference, 70, **70**
university calendar, 85, 201, 202
University College, 57–58
University of Mississippi, 3, 30
University Press of Mississippi, 23
US House of Representatives, 63

Vashon, George B., 107
Vaughn, Edward, 57
Vicksburg, MS, 6, 26, 34, 56, 91, 98, 108
Vicksburg Expansion Program, 6, 71, 108
Vicksburg Post, 58–59

vision statement, 4, 26, 48–49, 119
Voice, The, 76, **77**

Walker, Beulah, 94
Walker, Kaelon, 68–69
Walker, Lonnie, 79
Walker, Shirley, 78–79, **80**
Walker, William L., 4
Walls, John, 63, 92, **93**
Walters, Jacqueline, 73, 106
Walter Washington Administration and
    Classroom Building, 81
Ward, Marcus, 100

Washington, Booker T., 12
Washington, Samuel, 103
Washington, Walter, 6, 10, 20–21, **20**, 22, 57,
    67, 196
Waters, Brenda, 94
Waters, Kathleen, 22
Waters, Rudolph E., 10, 22–24, **22**, **110**, 196
Weir, LLJuna, 100
West, Phillip, 108
White, George, 105
White, Samuel L., 79
Whitney, Davey "The Whiz," 60
"Why We Love Alcorn: Top 100 Reasons,"
    6, 125
Williams, Connie Larkins, 63
Williams, Delores, 33, 37
Williams, Jessica Hayes, 96
Williams, Malvin A., Sr., 10, 33–40, **33**, 41, 195
Winters, Rev. Neddie, 105
women, admission of, 4, 13, 14
Woodson, Susan Cayton, 46, **46**
Wooten, Adrienne, 103
World Class Teacher Academy (WCTA), 71
World War II, 17
Writing Center, 38
Wyatt, Helen, 71

Young, Beatrice Smith, 225–26
Young Men's Christian Association
    (YMCA), 11

Zholondz, Vera, 38